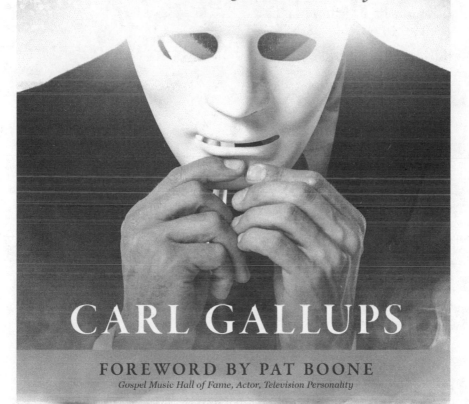

# MASQUERADE

PREPARE FOR THE
*Greatest Con Job in History*

## CARL GALLUPS

FOREWORD BY PAT BOONE
*Gospel Music Hall of Fame, Actor, Television Personality*

DEFENDER

CRANE, MO

# ACKNOWLEDGMENTS

To my research assistants, ministry associates, and sources of a continuous flow of information, new findings, and theologically stimulating conversations: Brandon Gallups, Mike Shoesmith, Zev Porat, Caspar McCloud, and Chris Gortney.

To the entire team at Defender Publishing. Thank you for your continual encouragement and your dedication to excellence in publishing. You are not only co-laborers with me in the kingdom ministry, but I also count you as very dear friends.

To my family. All of them! But especially my precious wife and my friend since early childhood—Pam. You are the reason I have been able to continue going forward, even when I was convinced that I wanted to give up. You are an unspeakable gift from the Lord in my life.

To the people of Hickory Hammock Baptist Church. Since 1987 you have encouraged me to use the gifts the Lord has given me. And, along the way, you unselfishly allowed me to walk through those open doors of Heaven-sent opportunity.

## OTHER BOOKS BY CARL GALLUPS
## AND DEFENDER PUBLISHING

*Gods of the Final Kingdom* (July 2019)

*The Rabbi, the Secret Message, and the Identity of Messiah* (February 2019)

*Gods of Ground Zero* (October 2018)

*Gods and Thrones* (October 2017)

# FOREWORD

It seems Carl Gallups is forever digging up treasures of scriptural truth that have often been buried within the back corners of the halls of modern theological difficulties and exegetical timidity. But truth is truth, and like diamonds or gold, it is not diminished by time.

This time he's pulled the mask off of Satan's deepest end-time ruses. You're guaranteed to be stunned by what you're getting ready to read. This work should prove to be a huge wake-up call for today's end-time church—at least the part of it that has "eyes to see." And I hope that includes you.

As always, Carl has accomplished this task by using contextual scriptural connections, biblical-language word studies, scholarly attestation of his findings, and the concise words of Jesus' own instructions, the ones in red letters. Most importantly, he's done it in a way that will draw you back into the very pages of Scripture itself.

Steel yourself for an amazing journey. Prepare to be challenged. And, as you come to the last pages, get ready to be profoundly heartened.

~Pat Boone

# A WORD FROM THE AUTHOR

This book is not for the faint of heart.

It peels back Satan's most diabolical masks and charades, ultimately exposing the most overwhelming con job in human history.

As with all of my books, when addressing enigmatic theological truths, I heavily reference my postulations with reliable scholarly sources. In so doing, I often make liberal use of the writings of the classical scholars. I reference these older scholars for the specific purpose of revealing that the long-veiled truths we will uncover have been expounded upon for centuries, some for almost two thousand years. Yet, a number of these vital biblical truths have disappeared from many of our pulpits and Bible studies. You might find yourself asking along the way, "Why have I never been told these things before?"

Sadly, an elusive deception has been gliding through the modern church like yeast in a batch of dough, tares planted among wheat, or a cunning serpent slithering through a weed-laden garden. As a result, the enemy's trick has gone largely unnoticed, until its diabolical effects have finally become appallingly apparent.

But, through God's Word—His love letter to His called-out ones—*we have been informed*. We have never been without access to the enemy's battle plans. We have not been abandoned in the midst of this present darkness. Far from it. The truth is right before our eyes, in black and white, for those who have "eyes to see."

By the time you've finished reading the last pages of this book, not only will you have a much clearer understanding of what the enemy is up to, but you will have also been encouraged and profoundly strengthened. There is even an addendum that offers biblical counsel and resources for healing for those caught in some of Satan's deadliest webs of deceit and despair.

Finally, just a quick note to those who have read my other books: *Gods and Thrones, Gods of Ground Zero,* and *Gods of the Final Kingdom*: You may notice some of the information from those books scattered throughout this one. Be assured that it's only enough to set a foundational context for certain topics, and I have done this for the benefit of those who haven't read my previous work.

If you've read those books, I can assure you that a brand-new expedition awaits you in this one, and you will find plenty of new revelations and surprises along the way. I pray the Lord uses what you're about to discover to bless you—especially in the context of our living for the kingdom of Jesus Christ in the midst of these prophetic days.

I am grateful you've chosen to take this journey with me.

It is not at all to be wondered, that the emissaries of Satan dissemble, and pretend themselves to be what they are not, for even Satan himself, who is the prince of darkness, in order to the deceiving and seducing of souls, transformeth himself into an angel of light.

~MATTHEW POOLE (1624–1679)[1]

# CONTENTS

# PART I

# MODUS OPERANDI

The great masquerade of evil has played havoc with all our ethical concepts. For evil to appear disguised as light, charity, historical necessity, or social justice is quite bewildering to anyone brought up on our traditional ethical concepts, while for the Christian who bases his life on the Bible, it merely confirms the fundamental wickedness of evil.

~Dietrich Bonhoeffer[2]

# FIRST KINGDOM

*I will raise my throne above the stars of God.*
*I will make myself like the Most High.*

~ISAIAH 14:13–14

The kingdoms of men rise and fall. They always have. They always will. Some ascend with great clamor, only to eventually collapse into a whimpering heap. Others rise more slowly, until they are ultimately revealed to the world as a force with which to be reckoned—a coveted standing among nations.

Still, down through the totality of the ages, most civilizations can only aspire to greatness. The world is just too big. The prevailing powers are simply too great...*and much too evil.*

Such are the ways of the kingdoms of men.

However, countless eons before fleshly mortality drew its very first breath, and as the sons of God shouted for joy on the day of the Garden's burst of primordial life, there was the *First Kingdom.*

That kingdom had always been. There was never a time when it did not exist. And that kingdom will always be glorious, beyond what the mortal mind can comprehend.

That kingdom is *His.* It is all powerful.

And in the end, it will *always* prevail, regardless of who vainly howls into the face of Heaven's throne, imagining that *they* will finally be the one to bring about its overthrow.

# WHEN WORLDS COLLIDE

CIRCA AD 30

NEAR THE SHORES OF LAKE GALILEE

# 2

They were merely taking a casual breakfast stroll through the grain fields just outside Capernaum on that Sabbath morning. That's when He first saw them approaching.[3]

It was early June, and the morning sun had just begun to ratchet up the temperature of the already-parched air. Jesus stopped to wipe the sweat out of His eyes with the back of His sleeve. As He did, His sight became a little clearer.

A cabal of Pharisees[4] had spotted them. The black-robed ones had been dispatched to spy on Jesus while He was in the region of Galilee. They had been assigned the task of delivering a full report to their overlords back in Jerusalem.[5]

This one from Nazareth had already begun to shake the powers of the unseen realm. The *dark god* had immediately taken notice of this mysteriously powerful man who was moving so comfortably among the people of earth.

Had the Nazarene actually tracked him here, to Galilee? *Who did He think He was?* Was the wilderness confrontation[6] just a few weeks back not enough for Him? Did He not know this domain of fallen earthlings belonged to the darkness alone? If it was war this "son of God" wanted, it was war He would have. But the lord of darkness was determined to never allow what he considered to be his rightfully occupied kingdom to slip from his hands. *Never.*

# THE FRENZY

Jesus had been in the region of Galilee for several weeks. He came here straight from Nazareth, His hometown.[7] From among the fishermen of Galilee, He had selected His first disciples. He found them in the midst of their meager lives, scattered along the beaches of Lake Kinneret.[8]

For the last several weeks, Jesus had been traveling from village to village along the Galilean shoreline and preaching in their synagogues. He healed their sick and delivered from bondage those who were tormented by the demonic realm.

News of His remarkable exploits spread like a wind-whipped prairie fire. Consequently, the people flooded the area. Day after day they came. Some arrived in small family groups, others in large caravans. They made their way from all over Galilee, Syria, the Roman cities of the Decapolis, and from Jerusalem, Judea, and the lands across the Jordan River.[9] The population of the region had already swelled by thousands. And yet, the people still came.

That is why the Pharisees were here. They had arrived some time back. Jesus was becoming a genuine threat to their own suffocating power over the people. They were here to keep a close eye on Him—even to stop Him—lest He upset their traditions beyond respectable recovery.

The boundaries of Jesus' present ministry encompassed the ancient lands of two of the original twelve tribes that first inhabited these lands, Zebulun and Naphtali. Joshua brought them here after Moses died in the wilderness. The profoundly prophetic nature of these domains was something with which the people were keenly familiar.

# THE GREAT LIGHT

For this reason, the multitudes were already quoting from the scroll of Isaiah concerning Jesus' presence among them. Could this really be the longed-for Messiah for whom they had been waiting? "After all," they reasoned, "no one could do the things He did unless He had been sent from Yahweh."

Their bold messianic speculations infuriated the religious elite. That renegade John the Baptizer started this debacle in the first place!

The Baptizer had sparked the frenzy by announcing to the masses of people at the Jordan River, "Behold! The lamb of God who takes away the sin of the world!" The religious elite of Judaism now took comfort in the fact that the desert troublemaker was finally out of commission. Herod Antipas[10] had imprisoned John only a few weeks back.[11]

But the people, especially those in the caravans, still insisted on crying out the words of the prophet. They shouted the promise of the prophecy as they moved from place to place, rejoicing and dancing as they worshipped, singing the words as they went:

> The land of Zebulun and land of Naphtali, the Way of the Sea, beyond the Jordan, Galilee of the Gentiles—the people living in darkness have seen a great light; on those living in the land of the shadow of death a light has dawned![12]

As they celebrated, roars of ecstasy went up from the crowd, echoing off the surrounding mountains and hills. With tambourines banging and shofars shrieking, their worship thundered out across the otherwise serene waters of Kinneret. The waves crashed upon the shore, as if answering their praise.

## THE ENTOURAGE

The human counterparts of Satan's kingdom were just now arriving at the grainfields to confront Jesus and His disciples. The procession of self-important, black-robed, religious elite waddled with wild-eyed enthusiasm towards Jesus and His men. They flailed their arms in rage as they approached.

The leader spoke up first: "Look at this!"

Jesus glanced around as if to say, "Look at what?"

"Your disciples are desecrating the Sabbath yet *again*!" They walked right up to Jesus, huffing as they came, standing at the edges of the field. Their faces were blood red.

"This is despicable! You must command your followers to *stop*—this very moment! *Cease* this lawless outrage!"[13] The leader's face further darkened as he strained out the angry words.

The disciples gathered closer around Jesus. They stood scrutinizing this screaming cohort of the orthodox elite. As ridiculous as they might have looked in their dramatic display, the Pharisees still weren't finished with their admonishment.

"Why on earth would you instruct your followers to do such things?" they asked, then exclaimed, "You should be ashamed to call yourself their 'teacher!' Back in Jerusalem even the elders are talking about how you continually break our Sabbath laws. They speak of how you teach others to do so as well! And now—this day, in front of our very own eyes—we have actually caught you in the act!"

They paused for an answer, searching Jesus' face for a response. But He gave them absolutely nothing. It was a reaction that unnerved them, especially in the awkward silence that followed.

Finally, losing patience, the group's leader insisted upon a reply.

"Well? ...*Answer us!* What have you to say for yourself?"

## HEAVEN'S REPLY

Jesus worked the grainy material back and forth in His hands with a rapid scrubbing motion. His body language indicated He might not have even heard the charges against Him—or perhaps the charges meant nothing to Him.

The action of His hand-scrubbing, separating the grain from the shuck, produced a small fistful of kernels. His eyes met those of His listeners as He discarded the chaff and popped the kernels into His mouth. As they watched, He smiled.

"Have you not read what David did?" Jesus asked as He chewed His meager breakfast and raised His questioning eyebrows.

They bristled at the challenge of His interrogation. Mumbling among themselves, they wondered: *Where is this conversation leading?*

Jesus waited for a response. The disciples returned to casually consuming their own morning meal as they, too, awaited an answer.

Seeing that the Pharisees had no immediate plan to reply, Jesus proceeded. "Surely you remember when David and his companions entered the house of Eli the high priest, and of the prophet Samuel?[14] There, the famished men asked to eat the showbread—something lawful only for priests."

The Pharisees glanced at each other. They didn't know exactly how to respond to this truth. If they attempted to address the charge too specifically, they risked condemning the celebrated King David, as well as the high priest, Eli—not to mention the revered prophet Samuel. This was something they couldn't chance. So, again they remained silent. And seethed.

"Or haven't you read in the Law," Jesus continued, "that the priests, performing their holy Sabbath duty in the temple, desecrate the Sabbath and yet they are deemed by that very same law to be innocent?"

Again, the Pharisees stood dumbfounded. They also knew this statement to be a legitimate fine point of the law. A faint smile formed on Jesus' lips. It was barely visible…but *they* saw it. And they hated Him for it.

Taking advantage of the moment of their frustrated introspection, Jesus brought an abrupt end to their smugness. He decided He would give them something they could discuss amongst themselves for the rest of the day.

He already knew what was in their hearts. They had not tracked Him down this morning merely to correct Him. They had shown up in the field with conspiratorial intentions. They were developing a plan to remove

Him as a threat. More specifically, they were determined to kill Him, if need be…but not yet. At this moment, they were still collecting their "evidence." He would give them a morsel of the evidence they sought.

## A NEW TEMPLE

"And…*if you care to hear it*…I'll tell you something else," Jesus continued. The men lifted their eyes toward Him, anxious to hear His next declaration.

"One greater than the temple is here among you—*right now*."[15] Several gasped as Jesus spoke what they perceived to be blasphemy.

"If you had only understood what these words mean, 'I desire mercy, *not sacrifice*,'[16] you would not have condemned the innocent ones who stand before you on this Sabbath day." As He spoke, Jesus jutted His jaw toward the disciples standing next to Him.

Then He continued. "In so doing, it is *you* that violates the Sabbath," He said. "For I tell you the truth, it is the Son of Man who is Lord of the Sabbath. It is not you or your manmade rules that are its overseers."

With that, Jesus turned and walked away. His body language declared that *He had now said all He was going to say.* Jesus and His men disappeared like apparitions among the grain-laden stalks.

As the ruminating Pharisees stormed off, headed to the village synagogue, they could faintly hear Jesus and His disciples chuckling deep within the camouflage of the field. When Jerusalem's dark spies stopped to listen, the laughter coming from the field sounded childlike—similar to the innocent bliss of those who are simply enjoying their time together.

Almost hissing as he spoke, the leader of the religious gaggle sputtered to the others, "This ha*sss* to stop. This man and His blasphemous teaching will be the ruin of us all! Who does He think He is? Who is He to instruct u*sss*?"

The leader's minions huffed in agreement. Surely, they thought, this blasphemer and His group would show up for a synagogue service sometime soon? After all, He had already been in the region's synagogues several times in the recent past. *That's it! That's where we can trap Him! In our synagogue! We can set Him up there—in front of the very people who profess to adore Him! We will crush His Sabbath blasphemies on the Sabbath itself!*

As the plotting ones walked along, they were accompanied by a demonic horde. Of course, Satan's "birds of the air" were unseen by them and anyone else who might have passed their way. The dark ones preferred to remain undetected in the shadows. They would simply *prod* their human subjects along, pulling the strings of their already-blackened hearts and minds, convincing them that their intentions were truly righteous.

The more the thoughts of Jesus' murder mulled around in the minds of the religious ones, the more the power of the plan invigorated them and the more self-assured they became…

…and the more the *dark god* had them in his grip.

# SYNAGOGUE SHENANIGANS

**3**

*They had a plan; rather, they had what
they thought to be a perfect trap.*

The grainfield affair had now been a week ago. But much had happened since then.[17]

Just this morning, the continuing spectacle of the Pharisees' incessant provocations moved into the Capernaum synagogue. Sabbath officially began at sundown on the evening before.

It was now early the next morning and the people of Capernaum were beginning to gather at the community's house of worship. Here they would recite prayers, read Scripture, and listen to teachings from an elder who would soon be chosen from among them by the synagogue president. The remainder of the day was to be spent in respite until sundown that evening.

The synagogue at Capernaum was much more than just the Sabbath meeting place. It was the epicenter of everyday village life. It was also used as a community center where public events were frequently held. During the week, the synagogue served as the local schoolhouse and, occasionally, it was used as the town's courtroom. The synagogue was attached to the lives of Capernaum's residents in the same way as the village well from which they drew their daily, life-sustaining water supply.

On this day, however, the synagogue would fill to the capacity of standing-room only. It had been rumored throughout the region that *today* Jesus and His disciples would be here. They had already been involved in several verbal fracases with the Pharisees during the course of the last several days. If Jesus showed up here today, it should prove to be a very interesting day indeed. No one wanted to miss it.

On the previous occasions of the Pharisees' confrontational meetings with Jesus, He had thoroughly confounded them. Yet, His demeanor had been remarkably calm, and His commanding presence seemed to never fail to unnerve His challengers.

And that's not to mention His *words*. His instructions dripped with heavenly authority and supernatural wisdom. Every time He opened His mouth to speak to the religious authorities, He set them on edge. They had yet to be able to catch Him in a trap—but it wasn't for their lack of trying.

## THE ORDER OF THE DAY

As the people flowed into the building making their way to their places, the elders were among them, directing the synagogue affairs and the internal movements. Benches, generally reserved for dignitaries, were aligned on three sides of the room. The common congregants usually sat on the floor on mats or carpets. But it soon became obvious that protocols would have to be set aside for this morning's service. It had been ages since this building had held so many occupants.

From among the elders emerged Simeon, the president of the synagogue. He was giving the final seating directions and preparing the people for the commencement of the liturgical portion of the services. That liturgy would be followed by the teachings of the village rabbi, or whomever Simeon might call upon for the task. The president then set about selecting those who would have the morning's honor of reading from the selections of the Law and the Prophets.

As these customary preparations were being sorted out, Jesus and His disciples entered as a group. When they walked through the doorway, it was as if the air had been sucked out of the room. People pointed and murmured. A few began to weep, reaching out to Him as He passed. The synagogue's president called for order. The elders and Pharisees bristled at the commotion, particularly at the deference the people showed this upstart teacher among them. *Who does He think He is?*

Jesus and His group found a spot and stood together against the wall.

Humble.

Unobtrusive.

Silent.

Respectful.

A man with a severely deformed hand was ushered by a synagogue elder to a place on the floor just a few steps away from where Jesus stood. The man appeared to be startled, wondering why he had never been given such preferential treatment in the past. But in his heart, he knew.

The elder, upon having seated the poor soul, looked up at Jesus with a faint and almost evil grin. His expression boasted that he knew something that Jesus did not, and he wanted Jesus to know that fact.

Jesus' eyes met the elder's until, embarrassed, the self-important man could hold the gaze no longer. Jesus looked down at the crippled man and smiled. The man faintly smiled back, then lowered his head.

The leaders among the Pharisees took their seats in their places of honor while the others stood along the wall opposite Jesus. Winks and nods were signaled among the elite. They had a plan; rather, they had what they actually thought to be a perfect trap. It had been arranged before they even entered the building.

The Shabbat service began in its usual manner. The *Shaliach Tzibbur*[18] began by leading the congregation in prayer. The prayers were enveloped with a chanting musical intonation. The congregants joined in at their appropriate places, with the women and children responding "*Amen!*" After the opening prayers, the synagogue president led the congregation in the ancient ritualistic recitation of the *Shema* "Hear, O Israel: The LORD our God, the Lord is one."[19]

Other prayers followed. The people knew the liturgy by heart. They and their families had been reciting its main elements for generations.

Next came the reading of multiple excerpts from the scrolls of the *Torah*, followed by additional readings from the *Nevi'im*.[20]

Each specially selected person stood to read the Hebrew Scripture passages in sections of only several verses, which were then interpreted into Aramaic summaries by the synagogue translator. This was a necessity, since not all those attending understood Hebrew. After the readings, with their corresponding paraphrases, it was time for the message.

Someone who had been chosen from among them would bring a "lesson." *Which man would be the one to preach on this Sabbath morning?* the people wondered.

That's when it happened…

# THE CHALLENGE 4

*"I will answer your question,
but first, you must answer mine."*

**M**ore winks and nods were exchanged among those draped in black robes.

The synagogue president cleared his throat, signaling the commencement of the next event. Malkiel, the chief Pharisee, suddenly spoke in a booming voice, startling the crowd when he did. The crippled man lowered his head in shame. He knew what would happen next.

"Tell us *teacher*..." Malkiel looked squarely at Jesus as He spoke from across the room. The congregation fell silent.

When he called Jesus "teacher," the speaking of that lofty title dripped with sarcasm. The religious elite hoped to drastically diminish Jesus' popularity among the masses, and they were determined to begin that process today. Amidst the growing tension, all those in the synagogue directed their gaze upon the miracle worker from Nazareth.

Malkiel moved closer to Jesus as He spoke, slipping through the seated crowd. "*Tell us teacher*, is it lawful to heal on the Sabbath?" His voice was cavernous, invoking a sense of authority.

## THE SNARE

As he approached, Malkiel pointed with his chin toward the crippled man on the floor, sitting at Jesus' feet. "What about this one?" Malkiel

17

challenged. In humiliation, the man once again looked away from Jesus. Hot tears began to trickle down his cheeks.

This was what they considered to be their perfect plan, a trap from which they were certain Jesus could not emerge unscathed. The Pharisees knew that even amongst themselves they couldn't agree on the proper answer to the question. Even the great rabbis of the past had struggled with the intricate workings of this Sabbath matter. Their many written commentaries on the topic reflected their factional frustration.[21]

Consequently, various teachings had been passed on to the synagogues and the several congregations had become divided over the legalistic issue. So, in whichever way Jesus answered the question, He was certain to divide the people. *Perfect!* How could this plan go wrong? This ploy *had* to work! They finally had Him in front of a crowd, and right in the middle of a synagogue worship service, of all places!

"I will answer your question," Jesus replied, "but first, you must answer mine."

Members of the Pharisee enclave glanced around the room at one another. Their expressions belied their exasperation: *Here we go again...*

The crowd gasped when Jesus offered the challenge. No one had ever spoken to the elders in this fashion before—especially not in a synagogue service. These men were powerful. They held deep ties with the Sanhedrin in Jerusalem and even with powerful government officials in Rome. Everyone knew it wasn't wise to cross them...everyone, apparently, except for Jesus. He seemed to have no fear of their black robes and phylacteries.[22]

Jesus motioned for the crippled man to rise. The timid man looked up at this preacher from Nazareth with a glimmer of hope in his eyes. Jesus took the man by his good hand and assisted him to his feet. Then Jesus gently put His hand upon the shoulder of the slightly built man and refocused His gaze at the gang of his inquisitors.

Malkiel had not yet responded to Jesus' challenge; he had only glowered at Him. Jesus opened His mouth to speak, directing his address toward the group of Pharisees, but also glancing around at the entire congregation as He spoke.

"If any *of you* has a sheep and it falls into a pit on the Sabbath, will you not take hold of it and lift it out?" Jesus paused for a few painfully long seconds, then continued. "Could it really be that you would value the life of a sheep—a mere animal—above a fellow human being, especially one who lives among you, and who suffers so much?"

Many of the congregants were agreeing with Jesus, their heads shaking in the affirmative and approving smiles forming on their faces. *Of course* they would help one of their sheep—even on the Sabbath!

Then they began to think: *Why hadn't we thought of this before?* This simple illustration settled the whole theological issue of their divisive interpretations! After all, those sheep represented their livelihood; their very existence depended upon them. But surely, in the greater scope of all things, a genuinely hurting man was much more valuable than a lowly sheep. *This Jesus fellow is brilliant! What a teacher!*

Malkiel stiffened. The rest of his entourage was silent. They could already imagine where this might be going. What they had thought to be a perfect trap was taking a very bad turn.

*And, what if?* What if Jesus actually *were* to heal that man right in front of everyone? They didn't want to consider the ramifications of such a spectacle. So, they remained mute, swallowing hard as they waited.

"It seems you are having trouble formulating an answer to My question," Jesus said. "Let Me make the issue sparkling clear. I will ask you again, in yet another way." He continued, "Which is the most lawful work to perform on the Sabbath: to conduct an act of mercy or to do evil? To save a life or to ignore it? And if that life *is* ignored, could it not turn out that the hurting one might perhaps be destroyed?"

The Pharisees still stood dumbfounded. Was Jesus going to perform a miracle in the midst of this congregation? Would He heal the man's hand in front of all these witnesses? Would He dare attempt an act of such outrageous insolence in their presence—on a Sabbath? In a synagogue? If so, there would be no end to the news that would spread throughout the region!

Had they been caught in their own trap? They had failed to consider that they might be providing Jesus the very stage He needed in order to gather even *more* followers. Several of the Pharisees leaned into each other's ears as they whispered their panicked concerns.

Jesus—knowing their thoughts—smiled at them. As He and the crippled man stood in front of the whole congregation, and as the Pharisees conferred, the people began to weigh the gravity of the moment as they, too, murmured amongst themselves. Would they witness a bona fide miracle right here in their midst? This would be something to talk about for generations to come! As their eyes grew wider in suspense, expressions of exasperation continued to bloom upon the faces of their leaders.

Without removing His gaze from the Pharisees, especially the one who had issued the challenge, Jesus called the man by name as He instructed him to show his hand to the congregation.

"Yosef, stretch out your hand."

Gasps went up from the crowd as Jesus turned His full attention to the crippled man.

"Come on," Jesus gently coaxed, "let everyone see what the Lord has done for you today." The expression on Jesus' face made known His genuine love for the man.

As Yosef began to push from within the folds of his sleeve what had once been a grotesque deformity, his hand emerged whole. The skin was healthy; his hand was firm and muscular. He was moving his fingers and making a hard-gripping fist! It was as if it had never been deformed! Yet, for many years, a long time before this little village had even heard of Jesus, Yosef had lived among them with a hideously shriveled, completely useless hand. *How could this be?* What was *this* they now beheld with their own eyes?

Yosef began to weep uncontrollably. He held his hand before his face, gazing at it, working it back and forth and extending his fingers in and out. He couldn't believe what he saw and felt. How could this be? *Who was this man?*

Yosef's life had been given back, forever transformed and restored. Several of his fellow citizens from Capernaum jumped from their seats and gathered around him. Some came to get a closer look and even to touch the miraculously healed hand. This was a day none of them would ever forget.

Who was this man that could command even the fundamental elements of life to rearrange a deformed hand into a whole one? Had Yahweh somehow come among them on this day through the presence of this Heaven-sent one?

The crowd exploded into squeals of delight, thunderous applause, and finally shouts of worship. A number of them shot to their feet, raised their hands in praise, and began to pray aloud, thanking God for sending Yeshua of Nazareth to them.

The ecstatic scene was more than the elite could bear. The smile never left Jesus' eyes. He was still staring at those who had challenged Him. The look on His face seemed to say: *You started this. Now, it's your move.*

Almost instantly, the Pharisees huddled together in a seething, black-robed wad. Malkiel led the heated discussion. Even the Herodians[23] joined them. They eventually shuffled outside the synagogue as a group, hatred simmering from every fiber of their being.

The whole affair appeared to have detonated right in their faces. They had to get serious now—deadly serious. They had to do something before this situation got completely out of hand and perhaps spread to every corner of the Roman Empire.

Jerusalem had sent them to confront this Jesus and put a stop to His madness. Instead, their plan had miserably failed. So, together, just outside the synagogue, they came up with yet another strategy.

They began their plot to assassinate the miracle worker from Nazareth.

# THE STRONG MAN'S HOUSE  5

*It is only by Beelzebub, the prince of demons,*
*that He drives out demons!*

Jesus finally withdrew from the synagogue. With His disciples in tow, they started down the beach road together.

The crowd followed, with no urging from Jesus or His disciples. Yosef made his way to the head of the throng. He was singing at the top of his voice, his song interrupted by moments of glorious weeping. *His life was new! He was whole!* Yesterday, he had been a lowly, often-ignored beggar from Capernaum. Today, he was a celebrity leading a procession of worshippers! And the man from Nazareth had merely spoken all of this into existence!

The people were overwhelmed by this miracle worker and master teacher who was in the midst of their humble community. Many vowed to follow Him wherever He went—an oath that most would overlook as time went on and the cost became too high. But for now, they reveled in the moment.

Trailed by a growing sea of people, Jesus moved a good way down the road from the synagogue. The thoroughfare bordered the glistening Lake Galilee. Jesus and His disciples started up the side of a small hill just across the road, to a point overlooking the lake. A select group of Pharisees followed. A portion of the crowd did as well. The rest of the multitude remained below. From this hillside vantage point, Jesus could be heard and seen by all.

The people brought their sick to Him by the dozens. With simply a word or a touch, Jesus healed each of them. One after another, shouts of delight rose from the crowd and reverberated through the hills, across the waters of Kinneret. The Pharisees were beside themselves, stewing in their collective resentment. *This man has the crowds bewitched!*

How could this phenomenon be contained without causing an awful uprising? Had Jesus already become too big? There had to be a way to disrupt His ministry. Perhaps they should infiltrate it? Maybe they could develop a traitor from within the midst of His own closest disciples? Maybe there would be someone very close to Him, one they could convince to deliver this Jesus into their hands—maybe even someone within His inner circle? They certainly had more planning to do; that was apparent. But for now, they had to deal with the matter at hand.

## EVEN THE DEMONS OBEY HIM

Just then, a band of people broke through the tightly huddled crowd and presented Jesus with yet another pitiful man, one who was deaf and mute. His friends said, "We don't know how this happened. One day he could both speak and hear; the next day—and until this day—he can do neither."

Jesus said, "This man's limitations are caused by a demonic infestation. Please understand: Not all infirmities originate from a spiritual assault, but this one did. He knows what he has done. And he knows what his deeds have cost him. In his healing, Heaven will be exalted." Jesus looked at the man through eyes of love. What the deaf and mute man saw in those eyes warmed him to the depth of his soul. He began to weep as he reached out to touch Jesus' hand.

With a startling and authoritative command, Jesus drove out the demon. Immediately, the man began to speak and to praise the Lord of

Heaven. He had actually felt the sudden change from within his own body! A powerful grip upon his very being was suddenly released.

A roar of jubilation went up from the crowd. A number of the people shouted, "Surely this one is the Son of David!"

The more the masses magnified Jesus, the more determined the Pharisees were to defame Him. "*Stop!* Stop your praise of this fellow! It is only by Beelzebub, the prince of demons, that He drives out demons! He's not to be trusted. He's working with the devil himself! It will be to your peril to continue to follow this evil man!"

Jesus rebuked them. "You are not even close to the truth of the matter," He said. "Think about what you are claiming." The Pharisees stood with a look of exasperated unbelief upon their countenances. Who *was* this one to teach and correct *them*—right in front of the crowds?

Jesus continued. "Every kingdom divided against itself will eventually be destroyed. And even a house divided against itself will not stand. Therefore, if Satan drives out Satan, then he is divided against himself."

Again they were dumbfounded by the Nazarene's challenge, and He continued: "Therefore, if I am driving out demons by Beelzebub, then tell me…by whom do *your own* people drive them out? What name do *they* invoke? What power do they possess? *Whose authority is it?*" The Pharisees simply stood there, some with clinched fists, others with eyes growing wilder with barely contained rage.

"I see you will not answer the question," Jesus said, as their faces reddened.

"So then, if it happens to be by the Spirit of God that I am driving out demons, then *you should know*—that is, if you have true spiritual discernment."

"We should know *what?*" Malkiel finally spoke.

Jesus replied, "You should know that the kingdom of God has come into your very presence, right here. *Today.* In the sight and hearing of all these witnesses." Jesus motioned with His arm sweeping the crowd, yet He never took His eyes off Malkiel.

# THE STRONG MAN'S HOUSE

"And consider this truth," Jesus went on. "How can anyone enter a strong man's house and carry off his possessions unless he first incapacitates that strong man? Only then can the strong man's house be plundered." The Pharisees were silent.

"It is for this purpose that I have come into the world," Jesus declared. "I have come to wreck the house of the evil one—and of those who serve him." Several of the Pharisees winced at the words. Was He accusing *them?*

Jesus continued, "I'm surprised! You are the rabbis of Israel, yet you don't even know these basic spiritual truths?"

At this, the gaggle of religious elites opened their mouths to rebuke Jesus. Their ever-darkening faces betrayed their thoughts and their next words. However, Jesus never gave them the chance to speak. Instead, He kept teaching. He turned His back on the Pharisees and faced the crowd.

"Whoever is not with me is against me, and whoever does not gather with me scatters," He said. "And so I tell you the truth, every type of slander can be pardoned before the Father, but blasphemy against the Holy Spirit will not be forgiven." Jesus paused to let that stunning declaration settle within His listeners' minds.

"Anyone who speaks a word against the Son of Man will be forgiven." Jesus then motioned behind Him, over His shoulder, in the direction of the Pharisees. "But anyone who speaks against the Holy Spirit will not be forgiven, either in this age or in the age to come."

Something was happening among the crowd; an awakening was taking place. The people were beginning to understand what Jesus was telling them. Awareness of the revelation could be seen upon their faces.

This man, *this Jesus*…He was different. Never had they heard such power, such authority—such freshness. He was uncompromising in His delivery and, at the same time, was possessed of an unction from on High. What He spoke made sense.

This message was focused on a personal relationship with the Creator of their souls. It wasn't about keeping man-made religious rules and rituals. This was a word of hope. It was a message of *life*—real life—the way it was meant to be lived.

But Jesus wasn't finished. He still had much more to reveal.

# RIPPING OFF THE MASK

# 6

*"What more could you have desired?*
*Yet you did not see."*

Jesus thundered out His next words, making certain that everyone who had gathered on that hillside would hear them. "Make a tree good, and its fruit will be good, or make a tree bad, and its fruit will be bad, for a tree is recognized by its fruit."

A bad tree calling its rotten fruit *good?* The minds of the people harkened back to the Garden of Eden. Jesus was pointing to the Genesis account! He was speaking of trees and fruit, and of good versus evil![24]

Could this Jesus from Nazareth be the long-awaited "Seed" that would crush the head of the enemy? Was He claiming to be the Messiah? Was *that* what He was doing? Was He trying to tell them something by using such speech?

## INVOKING THE GARDEN

Looking at the Pharisees, Jesus once again pierced the veil. He pulled off the mask of evil that lurked behind that shroud, the unseen malevolent spirits that enveloped the black-robed ones standing before Him.

"You brood of vipers!" Jesus exclaimed, pointing at the Pharisees. Now it was Jesus' face that was reddening.

The crowd froze. The one from Nazareth continued to reach back to the account of the Garden of Eden and the beginning of all evil.[25] The people murmured amongst themselves: *Leveling a charge like this, in the face of the religious elite, and in front of such a crowd, could not bode well for Jesus.*

But Jesus wasn't finished. He knew the murderous thoughts in the hearts of the evil men who were presently cutting Him to pieces with their dagger-eyes. He knew they had been plotting His death.[26]

Jesus hammered them again. "Your masquerade is exposed! How can you who are evil say anything good? For the mouth speaks what is truly in the heart. A good man brings good things out of the good stored up in him, and an evil man brings evil things out of the evil stored up in him. But I tell you, everyone will have to give account on the Day of Judgment for every empty word they have spoken!"

## GOING HOME

Jesus turned from Malkiel and his cohorts and began the descent from the hillside. Upon reaching the road, He started back toward Capernaum, the inner circle of His disciples at His side. The crowds followed. So did the Pharisees. They would, in one way or another, spy upon Jesus the rest of His earthly life and ministry. They were resolute in their plan to destroy Him.

As they entered the village, the residents who had been unable to make the trek into the surrounding countryside swamped Him with their presence. Jesus took His time as He made His way through the crowd praying, touching, healing.

He had come home—at least to the home of His ministry head-quarters, Peter's house.[27]

They finally made it to the front door and went inside. At Jesus' urging, those who could comfortably fit were allowed to enter, directed by His disciples.

The others hung inside from the windows, like children at a sporting event peering over the barricades. Some in the crowd even went up to the roof and looked down through openings in the slats. The others filled the property and the dusty street in front of the house. A respectful hush finally swept over those outside in order that they might hear everything Jesus was teaching on the inside.

## A SIGN

Malkiel stepped forward, understanding that they might lose this crowd completely if cooler heads among them did not prevail. He was one of only several of the Pharisee clan inside the house.

Stepping through the midst of the indoor crowd and coming face to face with Jesus, he whispered, "Teacher, could you just show us a sign, *perhaps?*" His arms were opened wide, and he had a childlike countenance. He was almost begging Jesus to succumb to his simple request, one that Malkiel implied could settle the whole matter right then and there.

"Maybe there's something you could do, proving you are a man sent directly from God. Perhaps then, the doubters among us could be placated. Perhaps a sign? Just *one? Please?* For the sake of peace?"

Jesus answered: "A wicked and adulterous generation asks for a sign, my friend. Sign after sign has been done before your group on this very day, as well as throughout the weeks before. What more could you have desired? Yet you did not *see* any of them. Apparently, you did not wish to *see.*" Jesus simply stood looking into the man's eyes—and into his soul.

"So, therefore, no sign will be given to you except the sign of the prophet Jonah," Jesus continued. "For as Jonah was three days and three nights in the belly of a huge fish, so the Son of Man will be three days and three nights in the heart of the earth."

*What was the meaning of this strange teaching?* Malkiel wondered. Yet again, the embarrassed Pharisee was at a loss for words.

Jesus turned from Malkiel and directed His words to the gathered crowd. "Hear and understand this truth! When an impure spirit comes out of a person, it goes through arid places seeking rest and does not find it. Then it says, 'I will return to the house I left.' When it arrives, it finds the house unoccupied, swept clean and put in order. Then it goes and takes with it seven other spirits more wicked than itself, and they go in and live there. And the final condition of that person is worse than the first. That is how it will be with this wicked generation."

Jesus explained, "When miracles from my Father's throne are done before your eyes, in that moment your soul has been given the opportunity to be swept clean. However, if those miracles are rejected, if my Father's grace is spurned, then, your condition will be worse than before. Rejection of what heaven offers only emboldens the kingdom of darkness."[28]

A few moments earlier, while Jesus had still been talking to those inside the house, His mother and brothers had arrived and were now standing just outside. They had come to try to convince Jesus to leave this place. They feared for His safety, *and not without cause.*

They had received word of Jesus' vibrant challenges against the religious ruling class. They had even heard the rumors about a plot to assassinate Him. Not only had they become fearful that harm might come to Jesus as a result of His unprecedented straightforwardness, but some among the family feared He might have actually become unstable.[29]

Someone in the crowd spoke up. "Your mother and brothers are outside. They want You to come outside so that they might have a private moment in Your presence."[30]

Jesus responded, "Who is My mother, and who are My brothers?"

Knowing the intention of His own unbelieving brothers,[31] He pointed to His disciples and said, "Here are My mother and My brothers. For whoever does the will of My Father in Heaven is My true brother and sister, and My true mother."

Jesus knew the evil one, through the influence of the wicked ruling elite, had finally persuaded even members of His own family to question His motives. Jesus had known this moment would come. Satan had gone right for His heart.

But Jesus also knew this battle was just beginning. The worst was yet to come. It would culminate at a Roman flogging post and a cruel crucifixion beam. But the worst pain of all would be the utter rejection and the jeering crowd that would watch Him die…and celebrate as He gasped for one final breath.

But today, there was still work to be done.

There was another message the people needed to hear, the most important one of the day. It would be a message specifically for them, and it would also be a communication for the generation right around the corner, during the days of the early church. Likewise, His teaching would ring true for every generation from that day forward.

But, most importantly, it was for the generation that would be living in the very last days.

Jesus' message would also be for us.

# THE KEEPERS 7

*They needed to understand exactly
what they were up against.*

It was late afternoon. Jesus and His disciples had just left Peter's house, headed to the seashore.

The sun wasn't far from beginning its illusory descent. That fiery primordial planet would soon melt into the mountains. Those ancient stony sentinels had encircled and guarded the lake for thousands of years. Today, these very same mountains would, once again, be witnesses to the booming voice of their Creator.

It had been another scorching day. But, mercifully, the breeze was just now beginning to bring its eventide refreshment. Drawing in a deep breath of the Galilean air, Jesus closed His eyes and lifted His face heavenward, savoring the falling coolness that wafted across His brow.

There was still a little more time before the last light of Sabbath would erode into a heavy dusk. It was enough time to teach an important lesson to the seaside congregation, a crowd that continued to blossom in size along the shores of Kinneret.

The flow of longing souls—so desperately poor in spirit—persisted in searching Him out and following Him almost everywhere He went. They came hungering for the righteous words that He would impart to them and for the stunning miracles He might continue to work in their midst—not to mention the fact that the authority of Heaven's throne itself seemed to be attached to every word He uttered.

The gathering masses had not, in their relatively simple existence, enjoyed the presence of anyone among them as much as they had with this one. Today had been the most memorable Sabbath day of their lifetime. They certainly had *never* witnessed anything like what they had just seen this morning in their own synagogue.

Now the crowds were here, mingling on the beach and brimming with enthusiasm. They came to the shoreline, still pouring out of the middling lakeside villages, the outlying regions, and their settlements, because *this* was where *He* was. This was where they wanted to be right now, more than anywhere else.[32]

## THE LITTLE ONES

The men came first, leading the crowds and families. The women and children followed. *Ah yes!* The children…the laughter and infectious emanations of the purity of childhood that flowed from those little ones. It was lovely to hear and to behold. Wherever they clustered, they stirred up a dust cloud of innocent havoc.

*Bless their hearts,* Jesus thought. The children squealed and frolicked in the midst of the crowd, chasing each other like a bouncing litter of carefree puppies. Those precious little ones had no awareness of the evil that lurked among them.

It was just as well that they didn't yet know the depth of their depraved world and even the true state of their own fallen existence. They would, soon enough, discover all of that on their own. But woe unto the one through whom that evil knowledge flowed! His demise would be horrible—and eternal. And, in the relative scope of all eternity, that end would be coming soon. That's why Jesus was here. It was His divine mission.

For now, though, Jesus sat in a boat enjoying the serenity of the moment. Seagulls circled overhead, gossiping among themselves midflight, hoping to find one last morsel to eat at the closing of the day.

Only a few moments earlier, the vessel had been jostled from the shore and anchored with just enough distance separating Jesus from the growing crowd. The boat sat swashing in rhythm with the subtle lake breeze, cradling its Heaven-sent cargo.

Several of Jesus' closest disciples were with Him in the boat. Peter was busy preparing the bow of the vessel as a makeshift speaking platform. The others were adjusting the anchoring in such a way so that it would remain sturdy as Jesus stood and preached to the throng on the beach.

The rest of the disciples stayed onshore, attempting to put in place some type of order among the people and ministering to their personal needs. They offered bits of food and ladles of water. It had been a long, hot day. But the people had simply refused to leave Jesus' irresistible presence.

Jesus positioned Himself on the bow of the Galilean fishing vessel and looked out over the multitude, shielding His eyes from the slowly descending ball of fire that reflected its celestial glory upon the lake's surface. *Yes.* Satan's human emissaries were still there. He spotted them immediately. They had been skulking amid the people all day long.

## HERESY HUNTERS

Here they were again—*the Pharisees.* Like exasperating gnats that buzzed around one's face without mercy, they hovered together and again tucked themselves amongst the crowd. Jesus' eyes pierced their souls...*beyond their souls*...into another dimension. It was a dimension of profane and suffocating darkness, unseen by the crowd, yet enveloping them nonetheless.[33]

Of course, the Pharisees were clothed in their unmistakable garb.[34] The striking adornment draped upon their bodies set them apart from everyone else. From head to toe, they were wrapped in a flowing outer garment, layered with another important addition—the *tallit.*[35]

Often embellished with phylacteries strapped to their heads and wrists and long, flowing tassels on the hems of their garments, these men served as a constant reminder to the people that God's laws were supreme. The daily practice of the regulations, as they had been interpreted by the Sanhedrin, were to be honored above everything else in life. This, they proclaimed, was the only hope the people would ever have of being made "right" with their Creator.

There was scarcely a village within the Judean countryside that didn't have its gaggle of Pharisees among them, or at least those who would visit regularly. As they moved among the people, their ecclesiastical uniforms commanded attention, invoking a sense of awe and respect.

They were the *keepers* of the Law—the administrators of righteousness and the hunters of heresy and blasphemy. And now a new "teacher" was among the people. Jesus' every word would be dissected and scrutinized by these ecclesiastical surgeons of orthodoxy. Their findings would be discussed at length and eventually reported to their elders.

But for now, *the keepers* had positioned themselves amongst the people who stood upon the otherwise serene seashore. They had chosen their perches so they could not only hear every word that Jesus would utter, but just as importantly, so they might also observe the reactions of the crowd as He spoke. They needed to understand exactly what they were up against.

The black-robed ones looked like human-shaped birds of prey roosting in a rotted branch of a dying tree, peering down upon the people below as though they were mere carrion. But by now, they had convinced themselves that they were on a divine mission. After all, the sanctity of the Law was at stake...and so were *their* reputations.

But, for the time being, the Pharisees' attention was steeled upon the one standing in the bow of the boat. The Teacher was going to speak again to the still-gathering throngs.

Jesus raised a hand. A respectful hush washed over the crowd.

His voice thundered into the early evening atmosphere: *"Hear these words! Take them to heart! Ponder them in your soul! Do you have the ears to hear?"* Nothing but the occasional yelp of a seagull could be heard. The people were awestruck yet again. What would the Teacher say next?

"A certain farmer went out to sow his seed. And as he was scattering the seed, some fell along the path, and *the birds of the air came* and ate it up…"

Jesus emphasized the words "birds of the air," then paused. He closed His eyes. When He opened them again, He looked directly at the Pharisees.

Actually, Jesus wasn't looking *at* them—not in the way one might otherwise perceive a look. He was looking *through* them, and beyond—down through the ages. His multidimensional vision pierced several realms of reality. At the same time, He was also peering into the vile, unseen realm that enveloped the perching Pharisee-birds.[36] He saw the unclean spirits standing at their sides, invisible to those who only thought they could "see."[37]

Then Jesus turned His gaze back upon the crowds and readied Himself to continue His message.

As the black-robed ones glared at Jesus, understanding that somehow He was speaking about them, they thought: *There's that smile again! The same one we saw in the grainfields a week ago and in the synagogue earlier this morning!*

The Pharisees held their collective breath…

# PART II

# THE HOLY PLACE

[Jesus said to them] "And this gospel of the kingdom will be preached in the whole world as a testimony to all nations, and then the end will come."

~Matthew 24:14

# SOMETHING WICKED COMES 8

*He has embedded his hooks almost everywhere.*

Think of what you've just witnessed.

In the theater of your imagination, you've stood with Jesus in the grainfields, in the synagogue, and among the crowds along the shore of Lake Galilee. Did you *see* what happened there on those days and in those places—within the spiritual realm?

The greatest challenge to life in this fallen world is that Satan's tactics are often adroitly veiled within the otherwise mundane substance of daily living. He has embedded his hooks almost everywhere...even within our church life.

Satan frequently operates behind the veil, cloaked in darkness, yet presenting his various tactical scenarios as though they have come straight from an angel of light. He uses religious leaders, political figures, and the politically correct norms of our times. He also invokes suffocating pressure from peers and societal expectations, and he even infiltrates church services.

And, just like in Jesus' earthly life, don't be surprised if Satan also manipulates some of our own family members in his attempts to thwart the kingdom work in our lives. And these are just the beginnings of the serpent's onslaughts. This is a huge part of the message we are supposed to see in the words of Matthew 12–13.

We are upon this earth to live as ambassadors for the glorious, restored kingdom that is soon to come. However, for now, the fallen creation is Satan's domain. It is filled with his illusions and deceit.[38] A part of our mission involves pulling off his deceptive masks and exposing the darkness.

- "Have nothing to do with the fruitless deeds of darkness, but rather expose them" (Ephesians 5:11).
- "We are therefore Christ's ambassadors, as though God were making his appeal through us. We implore you on Christ's behalf: Be reconciled to God" (2 Corinthians 5:20).
- "Finally, be strong in the Lord and in his mighty power. Put on the full armor of God, so that you can take your stand against the devil's schemes. For our struggle is not against flesh and blood, but against the rulers, against the authorities, against the powers of this dark world and against the spiritual forces of evil in the heavenly realms" (Ephesians 6:10–12).

Even the earliest church was not immune to the diabolical offensive launched by the unseen realm. In fact, the attack started almost the moment the church was first conceived. Jesus regularly warned His followers that it would happen.

He also cautioned that the phenomenon would grow worse as the earth draws closer to His return. A massive demonic inundation, unlike anything humanity has ever witnessed, would be unleashed across the globe in the very last days. A number of prophecy watchers believe we are at least in the beginning stages of those days right now.

But here's the diabolical thing about those days: The flood of that demonically driven permeation will be camouflaged in such a way that most of the visible church will miss it entirely. Have a look at some of those most prominent warnings.

- "For such men are *false* apostles, *deceitful* workers, *masquerading* as apostles of Christ. And no wonder, for **Satan himself masquerades as an angel of light**. It is not surprising, then, if **his** servants **masquerade** as servants of righteousness" (2 Corinthians 11:13–14, Berean Study Bible; emphasis added).

- "For there shall arise false Christs, and false prophets, and shall shew **great signs and wonders; insomuch that, if it were possible, they shall deceive the very elect**" (Matthew 24:24; emphasis added).

- "**The Spirit clearly says that in later times some will abandon the faith and** *follow deceiving spirits* **and things taught by demons.** Such teachings **come through hypocritical liars**, whose **consciences have been seared** as with a hot iron" (1 Timothy 4:1–2; emphasis added).

- "**Because of rebellion,** the LORD's people and the daily sacrifice were given over to it. **It prospered in everything it did, and truth was thrown to the ground**" (Daniel 8:12; emphasis added).

- "**A fierce-looking king, a master of intrigue, will arise**.... He will **cause astounding devastation** and will succeed in whatever he does. *He will destroy those who are mighty, the holy people.* He will **cause deceit to prosper**, and he will consider himself superior. When they feel secure, **he will destroy many and take his stand against the Prince of princes**" (Daniel 8:23–25; emphasis added).

- "**The coming of the lawless one will be in accordance with how Satan works.** He will use all sorts of **displays of power** through signs and wonders **that serve the lie**, and **all the ways that wickedness deceives** those who are perishing. They perish because they refused to love the truth and so be saved. For this reason **God sends them a powerful delusion** so that they will believe the lie and so that all will be condemned who have not believed the truth but have delighted in wickedness" (2 Thessalonians 2:9–12; emphasis added).

- "They are *demonic spirits* that perform signs, and **they go out to the kings of the whole world**, to gather them for the battle on the great day of God Almighty" (Revelation 16:14; emphasis added).

- **"Let no one deceive you in any way.** For that day will not come, unless the rebellion comes first, and **the man of lawlessness is revealed**, the son of destruction, who opposes and **exalts himself against every so-called god or object of worship, so that he takes his seat** *in the temple of God*, proclaiming himself to be God" (2 Thessalonians 2:3–4, ESV; emphasis added).

## THE COMING NIGHT

As you can see, the Bible doesn't sanitize the truth. The very last days will become the darkest times the planet will ever endure. Especially note the emphasized sections of the following passages.

- "As long as it is day, we must do the works of him who sent me. **Night is coming, when no one can work**" (John 9:4; emphasis added).
- **"Then you will be handed over to** *be persecuted and put to death*, **and you will be** *hated by all nations because of me*. At that time **many will turn away from the faith** and **will betray and hate** each other, and many **false prophets will appear** and **deceive many people**. Because of the **increase of wickedness**, the love of most will grow cold" (Matthew 24:9–12; emphasis added).
- "[Jesus said] For then there will be **great distress, unequaled from the beginning of the world** until now—and never to be equaled again" (Matthew 24:21; emphasis added).
- **"If those days had not been cut short,** *no one would survive*, but for the sake of the elect those days will be shortened" (Matthew 24:22; emphasis added).
- "For in those days there will be *tribulation unmatched* **from the beginning of God's creation until now**, and never to be seen again" (Mark 13:19, Berean Study Bible; emphasis added).

- **"Men's hearts failing them for fear,** and for looking after those things which are coming on the earth: for **the powers of heaven shall be shaken"** (Luke 21:26, KJV; emphasis added).
- "There will be a time of distress *such as has not happened* from the beginning of nations until then" (Daniel 12:1; emphasis added).
- **"But mark this: There** *will be terrible times in the last days.* People will be lovers of themselves, lovers of money, boastful, proud, abusive, disobedient to their parents, ungrateful, unholy, without love, unforgiving, slanderous, without self-control, brutal, not lovers of the good, treacherous, rash, conceited, **lovers of pleasure rather than lovers of God**—having *a form of godliness but denying its power.* Have nothing to do with such people" (2 Timothy 3:1–5; emphasis added).

The last days will be marked by a demonic web of charades, deceit, masks, demonic-driven signs and wonders, outright lies, and shadowy obfuscations—all of which result in persecution, death, and destruction—and at unprecedented levels. Only a direct intervention from Heaven's throne will finally stem the tide of horror.

The global alliances of governments, kings, and religious systems will eventually take on a diabolical life of their own. Revelation 13 attests that the developing unholy coalition of our own days will morph into something that can only be described as an overwhelming and all-powerful "beast."

And, as 2 Thessalonians 2:4 foresees, the head of that *beast* will ultimately set himself up in "God's temple"…

…and claim to be *God.*

# IN THE MIDST OF
# GOD'S TEMPLE

9

*He takes his seat in the temple of God,*
*proclaiming himself to be God.*
~2 Thessalonians 2:4, esv

Now we'll start to build a fundamental portion of our contextual theological platform. The key word here is "contextual." Doing this correctly takes a little effort. However, it should prove to be enlightening.

But first, take this little test.

What if you were *not* familiar with the rest of the New Testament and I were to quote the following verse. How might you interpret its meaning, absent of any contextual understanding?

[Jesus said] Whoever eats my flesh and drinks my blood has eternal life, and I will raise them up at the last day. (John 6:54)

If you had no other perspective from which to draw, you would probably be tempted to ask, "Did Jesus really tell us that in order to follow Him and have eternal life, we must become cannibals?"

Of course we know this isn't what Jesus meant, because we understand there is a much fuller framework supporting His statement. We know there are several other Scriptures—from both the Old and New Testaments—that shed enormous light on the interpretation of this isolated verse.

Let's try it again. *Test number two.*

What if I were to quote the next verse without examining everything else the Apostle Paul wrote in his other books of the New Testament?

He will oppose and will exalt himself over everything that is
called God or is worshiped, so that *he sets himself up in God's
temple*, proclaiming himself to be God. (2 Thessalonians 2:4;
emphasis added)

If that's all you knew about how Paul used the phrase "God's temple,"[39] what would you think he meant here—especially in light of the
fact that from AD 70, just three years after the apostle's death, until
today, there has not been another actual temple in Jerusalem? Also consider that when he wrote this sentence, Paul was referring to the very last
days before the return of the Lord…*maybe even our own days.*

## GETTING IT RIGHT

At first, the most sensible explanation of this verse might appear to be
that in the very last days, there will be a rebuilt temple in Jerusalem on
the Temple Mount. As you probably know, this is a popular view among
a number of evangelical Christians in our own time. That assessment
also proposes that it will be in that rebuilt temple where the "man of
lawlessness" of 2 Thessalonians 2 will finally enthrone himself and claim
to be God.

However, that interpretation concerning this particular verse has
only become popular in relatively recent times. It certainly was *not* the
prevailing view of the first 1,900 years of Christian scholarship. And, as
you will soon see, that's for a very good reason.

Please understand that, eventually, a third temple may in fact be
rebuilt on the Temple Mount in Jerusalem. It may turn out that the
Antichrist will somehow leverage that temple's presence to his own
advantage. But Paul's statement in 2 Thessalonians is flatly *not* referring
to that potentiality. As you'll discover in a few pages, Paul says so himself.
That's not just "my interpretation" of the matter. It's in the very words
Paul purposely employs.

The declaration of 2 Thessalonians 2:4 holds a direct link to Jesus' kingdom parables. Other related passages confirm this truth, and the majority of the earliest scholars agree as well.

Paul's revelation to the church at Thessalonica builds upon the truths Jesus revealed in Matthew 13 and then unveils the foundation from which Satan will begin to supplant the truth of God's Word. From that unfolding stage, Satan will eventually bewitch the entire planet into worshipping *his man,* the man of lawlessness.

I assure you that, as we move forward, I'm not going to get into the mechanics of a particular scheme of eschatology. There will be no date-setting, Rapture-timing, or end-of-days predictions in these pages. I will not bring forth charts, graphs, timelines, or maps. That's simply not what this book is about. I can also promise that there's much more to our excursion than this first theological mystery that we'll clear up over the next several chapters. So, please hang in there!

However, the passage we're examining appears to be so crystal clear in its surface text declaration—and thus so embroiled in theological controversy—that it must surely be a monumental clue about Satan's ultimate end-time agenda. Therefore, we must get this interpretation correct. And the farther we move forward in our journey, the more you'll understand why settling this issue from the beginning is so important.

# THE JEWISH VIEW | 10

*Only a miniscule number of Jewish people on the
planet expect the arrival of a Jewish Messiah.*

et's begin by taking a look at the current geopolitical and religious
affairs of the Middle East. This will set a modern contextual foundation for everything else we're about to uncarth.

Only a minority of the current Jewish population believes that a
restored temple must be built on the Temple Mount in order for their
messiah to finally arrive.[40] That shocks a lot of evangelical Christians,
especially in the United States, since they're often told "*the Jews* really do
want a third temple." While *some* Jews sincerely desire a third temple,
the plain truth is that most do not. This is no small consideration.

Very recently, the *Times of Israel* reported this in an article titled "Dr.
Theodor Herzl & Building the 3rd Temple": "There seems to be **only a
small minority** of the Jewish people who ponder and **contemplate the
need for the actual physical rebuilding of the Temple.**"[41] (Emphasis
added).

## MESSIANIC EXPECTATION

Equally surprising is that only a miniscule number of the Jewish people
on the planet, much less of those living in Israel, *expect* the arrival of a

Jewish Messiah. This is especially true in relation to how that arrival might be connected to a rebuilt temple. *The Guardian* reported that "**since the foundation of the state of Israel,** the idea of **Jews returning to the Temple Mount prior to the arrival of the messiah** has been the **obsession of a tiny minority**"[42] (Emphasis added).


# JEWISH ORTHODOXY

Yet another surprising revelation for many evangelicals is that fewer than 25 percent of all Jews living in Israel identify themselves as ultra-orthodox or religious Zionists.[43] This is an important consideration, especially when we understand that it would be from this minority of the total population that the *temple fervor* would originate. However, when we further explore the objectives of that same small group, we discover that a majority of even that 25 percent simply would not be willing to risk a literal World War III in order to begin the construction of a new temple.

A *New York Times* reporter recently stated:

> **Many archaeologists agree that the religious body of evidence, corroborated by other historical accounts and artifacts** that have been recovered from the site or nearby, **supports the narrative that the Dome of the Rock was built on or close to the place where the Jewish temples once stood.**
>
> **Nonetheless, the Waqf** [the Islamic controlling authorities of the Temple Mount] **has never permitted invasive archaeological work that could possibly yield proof.** "That's where you get to *the Catch-22*," said Jodi Magness, a professor of religious studies at the University of North Carolina at Chapel. "**The logical thing would be to dig,**" Professor Magness said. "If you did that, *you'd probably cause World War III to break out.*
>
> *It's not even in the realm of possibility.*[44] (Emphasis and brackets added)

# LOCATION, LOCATION, LOCATION

In fact, the fear of a major global war over the issue of a rebuilt third temple is so great that now there is even a brand-new movement among the orthodox minority who still insist they want a new temple. They claim they can build it in a location other than what is known as the Temple Mount and maintain that they have *new evidence* of another site that might have been the "real" location of the original.[45]

Do you see the problem? With more than 75 percent of Israel's current population flatly opposed to a rebuilt temple (or not caring about it one way or the other) and another sizable group of the remaining minority not quite sure *where* the temple should be built in the first place, the stark reality appears to be that this monumental undertaking would be next to impossible to accomplish anytime soon. The current political and geopolitical ramifications of such a project are too complex and controversial—and extremely dangerous.

However, before we come to any firm conclusions, let's first hear from a respected messianic rabbi who was born and raised in Israel. He and his family are entrenched in the orthodox rabbinical community, as well as in the current Israeli government under Prime Minister Benjamin Netanyahu. He presently lives in and ministers from Tel Aviv.

# A RABBI IN TEL AVIV

*To be sure, there are a few orthodox Jews who sincerely
want a new temple on the Temple Mount, but they
are in a great minority of all the Jews in Israel.*

Messianic Rabbi Zev Porat, founder of Messiah of Israel Ministries headquartered in Tel Aviv,[46] lives in the midst of the current temple controversy. He was born into a traditional orthodox rabbinical family and was raised to follow in the footsteps of his father, grandfather, and great-grandfather, all orthodox rabbis and influential leaders.

Rabbi Porat graduated from a renowned rabbinical training school, which qualified him to serve among the Sanhedrin rabbis. Hebrew is his first language, and he also speaks fluent English as well as some Mandarin Chinese.

In the midst of his rabbinical training, through a lengthy process, Zev became a believer in Jesus Christ (*Yeshua Ha Mashiach*), and he now beckons Jews and Gentiles all over the world to turn to Yeshua in genuine salvation.[47]

In regard to the third-temple question, Rabbi Porat had this shocking analysis to share with me:

I can tell you, Carl, only a very tiny part of the Israeli population wants a third temple, or even gives any thought to it at all. The majority simply do not desire to see it happen. I have known and understood this truth since I was a child.

You can poll thousands of Israelis and you will soon discover the reality of this fact. They mostly just want to live in peace with the Muslim citizens of Israel that live among them. They don't want another huge war if it can be avoided. The building of a third temple, they know, would spark just such a war. The bulk of the Israeli population is simply not religiously fanatic enough to risk such a thing.

Not only that, but I have a very influential contact who is deeply connected to the Israeli rabbinic movement, as well as to the Israeli government. He is also a ranking Israeli military official. We have had several conversations about the "third temple" phenomenon.

This individual assures me that the Temple Institute[48] in Jerusalem already has *many billions* of dollars collected for the purpose of building a third temple! He told me that they could have already built ten temples on the Temple Mount by now if they wanted to. My source also assured me that the Israeli authorities, both political and rabbinical, have no plans to build such a temple.

It appears the reality is that the rebuilding of the temple is pretty much a money-making project designed to extract funds from evangelicals in America and around the world. It is largely the evangelical Christians who think that the Jews desire this rebuilt temple. My source told me "I can promise you—most of the people who could actually make it happen don't want another temple."

I can also tell you firsthand that the vast majority of the citizens of Israel don't even know where the Temple Institute is located! Very few people from Israel ever visit it! All they know is that it is "somewhere in Jerusalem." The majority of the people who visit the Temple Institute Museum are Christians, and the largest part of those Christians are from nations with large evangelical populations. Only about half of the Institute's visitors every year are actual Israeli citizens. And probably only a minority of them are actually Jewish. That would mean that less than thirty-five thousand people out of the over nine million who live in Israel—*and only eight million are Jews*—ever visit the Institute.[49]

As you know, Carl, I am a native to Israel. Hebrew is my first language. I was born into a deeply rabbinic family, and in the most orthodox community in Israel—*B'nai Brak*. I trained to be an orthodox rabbi and graduated from a very prestigious yeshiva.[50] My family enjoys many prominent connections inside the orthodox rabbinic movement, as well as within the Israeli government. I know what I am talking about in this matter.

To be sure, there are a few orthodox Jews who sincerely want a new temple on the Temple Mount, but they are in a great minority of all the Jews in Israel. They have no real power to even come close to getting it done.

Whether or not people like what I'm saying, this is simply the plain truth of the real situation here. The largest frustration is that it seems like this fact is a big secret, just about everywhere. That is, except in Israel.[51]

The *Jerusalem Center for Public Affairs*[52] confirms the bulk of what Rabbi Zev Porat asserts:

**An even wider consensus is embodied in the almost comprehensive *Halakhic*[53] ruling that it is forbidden at present to build the Third Temple.... This opinion is common to** [the various groups of] **rabbis** who now permit entry to the Temple Mount and those who prohibit it. **The rabbis *categorically forbid* building the Temple,** whether the proposal entails building it in place of the mosques or within the mount compound but without harming them.

[The conclusion of the article] Taking all this into account, **the claim that the state and its institutions have formulated a plot to destroy the Temple Mount mosques, and establish the Third Temple in their stead, is absurd and invalid....**

At the same time, **the State of Israel does just about everything,** in both its statements and its actions, **to make clear that
*it has no intentions of building the Third Temple.***[54] (Emphasis
and brackets added)

The *Times of Israel* also records the historical truth that is still pervasive among the majority of Israeli Jews of today:

Following the Second Temple's destruction in 70 C.E., **most rabbis adopted the position that Jewish law prohibits reconstruct-
ing the Holy Temple** prior to the age of messianic redemption,
or that *the law is too ambiguous and that the messiah must come
first.*

**Many Israelis** view the goal [of a third temple] **as a danger
to the status quo** that has kept this site holy to Muslims and
Jews *from turning into a tinderbox.*

**Though observant Jews pray thrice daily in the Amidah
prayer**[55] **for the Temple to be rebuilt, few do anything about
it.** *That's as it should be,* says Michael Melchior, an Orthodox
rabbi and former Knesset member who is considered a religious
moderate.

"We pray for holiness, but we also need to be careful of others' desire for holiness," Melchior said. **"The moment you want
to translate that into building a Temple, you upset the sensitive
balance** we've created here, by which we exist here." *He called
Temple construction advocates "irresponsible."*[56] (Emphasis and
brackets added)

The Messianic Jewish publication, *Jewish Voice,* a ministry that also
appears to be largely in favor of a rebuilt temple, further reiterates:

**Many religious Jews do not support** [the idea of a third temple]
because they have adopted a Diaspora mentality and a spiritu-

alized way of thinking, which *sets aside hope in a literal ful-fillment* of the biblical prophecies regarding a future Temple. *For them, the present political situation on the Temple Mount with Muslims controlling the site is acceptable.*[57] (Emphasis and brackets added)

As late as December 2019, the *Jerusalem Post* was also reporting the truth of the matter:

> **"The ultimate goal** is to be able to offer sacrifices in the Temple," [Rabbi Eliyahu] Weber says simply. "*We are not really dealing with that right now* because there are many stages to this."
>
> There is religious controversy regarding Jewish prayer on the Temple Mount, *let alone when it comes to work aimed at rebuilding the Temple.* The influential Torah scholar Maimonides taught that the Temple would be built *by Messiah.* Other schol-ars believe that the Temple will *descend from the heavens* in the messianic era, while *the modern right-wing flank*[58] *has called for Jews to build the Temple now* and usher in the Messiah.
>
> Weber continued, "We are dealing more with restoring prayer to the site in an orderly fashion. I would love for it to be tomorrow, but offering sacrifices sounds to be a bit more distant."[59] (Emphasis added)

As it turns out, the *Jerusalem Post* is yet another legitimate source that confirms what Rabbi Porat told me: It's only the relatively modern and very small right-wing flank among the Israeli Jews who desire to build a temple on the Temple Mount. However, even that tiny group recognizes that their desire is only just that, a dream that most likely will not be fulfilled. And, according to Rabbi Weber, of the three most prominent views among the orthodox Jews today concerning a third temple, two of those views don't even teach that the Jews *must* build a new temple on the Temple Mount.

## PREVAILING SCHOLARSHIP

But there's more. From the birth of the church and through at least the next nineteen hundred years of the Church Age, the most respected Christian scholars did not interpret 2 Thessalonians 2:4 to indicate a literal rebuilt temple on the Temple Mount. This is regardless of whether other passages indicate that such a last-days temple project will truly take place.[60]

In fact, a number of classical scholars also believed that what Paul identified happened to perfectly line up with what Jesus taught in His kingdom parables of Matthew 13.

First, let's have a quick look at an honest, representative sample of the historic interpretation concerning Paul's pointed declaration. Then, we can more clearly see the direct connections to the kingdom teachings that Jesus laid before the crowds on that day.

After we've explored these connections, you'll see a number of shocking correlations to the prophetic times in which we currently live. That's when the Word of God and your daily life in this increasingly deranged world will finally make much more sense.

# SCHOLASTIC HONESTY | 12

*The historical facts are so undeniable
that they are simply too difficult to ignore.*

ollowing is a brief summary of more than two dozen classically represented positions regarding 2 Thessalonians 2:4.[61] I think you'll find
this study to be fascinating, and maybe even surprising.

The first twelve commentary entries are found on a single page
on one of the most highly respected online biblical study sources. The
remainder of the quotes have been gleaned from several other esteemed
exegetical sources, several of which also include multiple commentaries
on one page.[62]

Commentary entries, whatever their view, are listed in order, without my having filtered any of them. I want to be certain that what I
present is absent of any bias toward a specific interpretation so that we
might maintain the highest academic integrity in our study.

## THE EARLY SCHOLARS

Let's have a look at a sampling of the first twelve scholars. If you would
like to read those that aren't quoted in the text of this chapter, they've
been included in the endnotes, so you can read them there.[63]

Of the first dozen sources, eight believed the "temple of God" was
none other than the last-days church, not a rebuilt temple on the Temple

Mount. In a few pages, you'll discover why this was the interpretation of the majority.

The *Pulpit Commentary* represents those in the majority:

> **It appears more correct to refer the expression metaphorically to the Christian Church. It is** *a favorite metaphor of Paul* **to** compare believers in particular, **or the Church in** general, to the temple of God (comp. 1 Corinthians 3:17; 1 Corinthians 6:19; Ephesians 2:20–22).[64] (Emphasis added)

Only three of the twelve listed on the same page said the best interpretation allows for a literal temple on the Temple Mount in the last days.

The remaining commentary, *Vincent's Word Studies*, states *both* positions as possibilities, declining to take a definitive stand on the matter:

> According to some, a figure of the Christian Church. Others, the temple of Jerusalem.[65]

## THE NEXT GROUP

Of the remaining group of twenty-four scholars, the majority also fall within the same percentage divisions as the first group we examined.[66]

*Whedon's Commentary on the Bible* is a representative from the majority group:

> Temple of God—*Not the Jewish temple*, which is *never* **called so** in the New Testament, but *unquestionably the Christian Church*. See 2 Corinthians 6:16; Ephesians 2:21.[67] (Emphasis added)

However, the *Benson Commentary* reminds us of another important contextual fact:

After the death of Christ the temple at Jerusalem *is never called* by the apostles *the temple of God*; and that when they mention the house or temple of God, they mean the Christian Church in general, or every particular believer; *which indeed is very evident* from many passages in their epistles: see 1 Timothy 3:15; 1 Corinthians 6:19; 2 Corinthians 6:16; Ephesians 2:19-22; 1 Peter 2:5.[68] (Emphasis added)

The *International Standard Bible Encyclopedia*, the globally recognized standard biblical encyclopedia, illustrates that particular category's interpretation of Paul's meaning:

Here we would only indicate what seems to us *the most plausible view* of the Pauline doctrine. It had been revealed to the apostle by the Spirit that *the church* was to be exposed to a more tremendous assault than any it had yet witnessed.[69] (Emphasis added)

Another multivolume classical work, *The International Critical Commentary,* is informative about the interpretation problem of Paul's declaration:

The difficulty with the reference to the temple in Jerusalem is that the *evidence adduced for this interpretation is not convincing.*… The [temple] elsewhere used in the writings of Paul is used metaphorically. *The Christians are the temple of God,* or *the body is the temple* of the Spirit.[70] (Emphasis and brackets added)

Most of the earliest church scholars (often called the early church fathers) also believed that the "temple of God" meant either the last-days church exclusively or the church *and* the potentially rebuilt Jewish temple. Only a minority interpreted this verse to solely mean a literal Jewish temple. I have referenced every one of those views in the endnotes.[71]

## HISTORY SPEAKS

The historical facts are so undeniable that they are simply too difficult to ignore. The vast majority of the scholars for the first 1,900 years, starting from the time of the circulation of the New Testament documents among the early church, understood Paul's "temple of God" as the last-days church.[72]

The Apostle Peter was by Jesus' side for three years of public ministry. He preached the first sermon at Pentecost and became the lead pastor of the very first church. Peter also had this to say regarding *the new temple of God*:

> *And you also, as living stones*, be built up *and become spiritual temples* and **holy Priests** to **offer** *spiritual sacrifices* acceptable before God by Yeshua the Messiah. (1 Peter 2:5; emphasis added)

Also, please remember that both Paul and Peter had the best theology teacher in history! They learned from Him, personally.[73] I don't think they would have gotten this wrong. Neither do I believe they would have misled their congregations with fuzzy language and veiled interpretations, particularly concerning a matter of this magnitude.

*Coffman's Commentaries on the Bible*, a massive work written throughout the mid to late 1900s, succinctly summarizes the historical majority view:

> **There** *can be no way that this is a reference to the Jewish temple*. **Paul,** who wrote the Corinthians that "Ye are the temple of God," **would never have made** that den of thieves and robbers in Jerusalem—the "temple of God" historically.
>     **First, it means the** *church of Jesus Christ*;
>     [Second,] **in context it means** *the apostate church* of Jesus Christ, a *deduction that is mandatory* from the fact of the apostasy being Paul's subject in this paragraph.

**Therefore, whenever and wherever the "man of sin" appears** *it will be in the church apostate.*[74] (Emphasis and brackets added)

However, a handful of the classical commentators still struggled with this verse, to the end that they eventually left their readers with the idea that it is pretty much impossible to understand what Paul meant by "temple of God." Yet, even several who held that position also concluded that Paul's original audience knew *exactly* what he meant.[75]

I wholeheartedly agree with that assessment: Paul's audience *did* know what he intended.

In the next two brief chapters, you'll see precisely *what* they knew…

…and *how* they knew it.

# DON'T YOU REMEMBER?

*Don't you remember that when I was*
*with you I used to tell you these things?*
~2 THESSALONIANS 2:5

**13**

Professor Johann Peter Lange (1802–1884) is yet another classical scholar who attests that "God's temple" of 2 Thessalonians is none other than the *last-days church*.

However, the reason I am including Lange's view separately from what we have already seen is that within the entirety of his lengthy commentary, we're also informed that this was the *unquestionable majority interpretation* among early scholars, even those dating all the way back to the very earliest. This, as I hinted in the last chapter, is a hugely important consideration.

Observe a pertinent portion of *Lange's Commentary on the Holy Scriptures: Critical, Doctrinal, and Homiletical*:

> **The interpretation** *of the ancient Church*. The *Fathers are essentially agreed* in expecting, immediately before the still future appearing of Christ, the appearance of the personal Antichrist.
>
> The "sitting in the temple" *most explain*...of [the Antichrist's] *usurping the presidency or lordship in the* [institutional] *Church*, and giving himself out as Christ and God.
>
> **The Coming, of which the Apostle speaks, does not concern Jerusalem merely, but likewise the Thessalonians, because it regards the whole world;**

*...nor, according to Daniel* to whom Paul goes back, is the Man of Sin the Jewish people, or a party in it, or even a member of it, *but a tyrant ruling all the nations of the world.*[76] (Emphasis and brackets added)

Lange discusses a multitude of historical details concerning this topic and produced probably one of the most exegetically thorough of any study of its genre. The greater context of this massive commentary is that the early Thessalonian church *fully understood* what Paul meant when he first penned those words.[77]

However, for a more succinct expression of this vital truth, have a look at *Ellicott's Commentary for English Readers*:

**We need to put ourselves in the position of the young Church of Thessalonica,** *which was expected* **by Paul to make out the significant hints of his Letter with no other help than the recollection of his oral teaching and the observation of events.... *Antichrist pretends to be actually Jesus....* Such pretensions would, of course, be meaningless and ridiculous to all except believers in Jesus Christ** *and His Church.* (See Matthew 24:4–5; Matthew 24:10–12; Matthew 24:23; Matthew 24:26).[78] (Emphasis added)

## JESUS ALSO CLAIMED IT

Don't forget yet another vital truth, one that Jesus Himself laid out to the religious elite of Galilee while in the grainfields on that Sabbath morning. Jesus claimed to be "one *greater than* the temple":

But I say unto you that *in this place* [standing right before you] is one [a specific person] *greater than* the temple. (Matthew 12:6; emphasis and brackets added)

That pronouncement must have stunned His audience.

*Ellicott's Commentary for English Readers* connects the important dots of Jesus' declaration.

> The body of *the Son of Man was the truest, highest temple of God.* The range of the words is, however, wider than this their first and highest application. **We are taught to think of** *the bodies of other sons of men* **as being also, in their measure,** *temples of God* (1Corinthians 6:19).[79] (Emphasis added)

*Matthew Poole's Commentary* states:

> Greater than the temple. [Jesus said] "The temple was **but a** *type of me.*"[80] (Emphasis and brackets added)

And what did the Apostle Paul himself say about the "body of Christ" as being the true temple?

> For we were all baptized *by one Spirit so as to form one body*— whether Jews or Gentiles *Now you* [the Church] *are the body of Christ,* and each one of you is a part of it. (1 Corinthians 12:13, 27; emphasis and brackets added)

During the progression of Jesus' ministry, He also declared that He would raise *the temple* after three days. He meant, of course, that *the temple* was His own body (John 2:19–22). This claim would have had a monumental impact on the early church's understanding of the true *temple of God.* Note the emphasized portions that follow:

- "Jesus answered them, '**Destroy this temple, and I will raise it again in three days.**' The Jews replied, 'It has taken forty-six years to build this temple, and you are going to raise it in three days?' *But the temple he had spoken of was his body.* **After he** was raised from the dead, his disciples recalled what he had said." (John 2:19–22; emphasis added)

- "Finally two came forward and declared, 'This fellow said, "I am able to destroy the temple of God and rebuild it in three days."'" (Matthew 26:60–61, see also Mark 14:58; emphasis added)

- "You who are going to destroy the temple and build it in three days, save yourself! Come down from the cross, if you are the Son of God!" (Matthew 27:40, see also Mark 15:38; emphasis added)

Professor of Old Testament, Dr. Dean R. Ulrich,[81] in his 2015 scholarly work titled *Jesus and the Six Objectives of Daniel 9:24*, addresses Jesus' pointed assertion about the true "new temple:"

The first two chapters of **John associate Jesus with the tabernacle and temple.** The glory of God returned to take up residence *not in the Most Holy Place of Herod's temple but in a new Most Holy Place—Jesus' body.*

As Immanuel, which means God with us (Matthew 1:23), *Jesus is Daniel's anointed Most Holy Place and Ezekiel's new temple.*

*The parallels between Ezekiel 40–48 and Jesus* continue in John. In John 4, Jesus meets a Samaritan woman at a well.… **The river of God's grace that runs from Jesus into the woman** *makes her a temple* of the Holy Spirit.

The glory of God now dwells in her, and **she, in Christ, becomes Ezekiel's new temple and Daniel's [Most Holy Place].** *All who believe in Jesus*, not just the Samaritan woman, drink of his river and *become temples of the Spirit of Jesus* (John 7:37–39; 1 Corinthians 3:16; Ephesians 2:22; 1 Peter 2:5).

**With the benefit of Jesus' teaching in Luke 24, the apostles could say that what the prophets had announced was being**

**realized in Jesus.** *Jesus is the new temple, the Holy of Holies,* Immanuel, and the glory of God.[82] (Emphasis added)

Jesus' emphatic statement concerning the "genuine new temple" as being His body is most likely why, throughout *all* of Paul's writings to the churches, the apostle uses the phrase "the temple of God" as a direct connection to *the church*. How could Paul and the early church have thought otherwise (1 Corinthians 12:27)? The evident answer is: *They didn't.*

## WHY THEY KNEW

But here is the most obvious reason we know the church at Thessalonica understood exactly what Paul meant with the phrase "the temple of God." It is because Paul tells his audience, "You should have known":

- 2 Thessalonians 2:5: **"Don't you remember that when I was with you** *I used to tell you these things?"*
- 2 Thessalonians 2:15: So then, brothers and sisters, stand firm and **hold fast to the** *teachings we passed on to you*, whether by *word of mouth or by letter"* (Emphasis added).

The greater point is this: While there may eventually be an actual Jewish-led rebuilt temple constructed on the Temple Mount in the last days, we can't contextually develop that position solely from Paul's declaration in 2 Thessalonians 2:4.

Paul is not talking of an apostasy that's coming to the Jewish temple, or even among the unbelieving Jews exclusively. He is talking about something much grander. He's speaking of a coming apostasy that will settle squarely into the midst of the visible and institutional church of the very last days, wreaking devastating effects upon the entire planet. This will literally bring about the "great falling away" (2 Thessalonians 2:1–3).

So, how was it that Paul expected the Thessalonian church to know exactly what he meant by "temple of God"—with no misunderstanding on their part? What exactly were those oral "teachings" he had given them? And what did those "letters" actually say?

Hint: We possess several of the letters to which Paul was referring! And those written teachings certainly would have squared with his spoken teachings regarding the same subject.

# TWO WORDS

## 14

*Paul is not in the habit of varying
his expressions without a meaning.*
~Donald Spence Jones[03]

The fact is, the only other time in all of Paul's biblical writings wherein he used the words "God's temple" or "temple of God," he unambiguously spoke of the church. He never used this phrase to speak of the literal temple on the Temple Mount. *Never.*

That is probably why the second letter to the Thessalonians comes to us without a further defining context within the passage itself. The church at Thessalonica already *knew* what Paul was asserting: They had read his letters and heard his teaching on the matter. And, every one of Paul's letters was eventually circulated to *all* the early churches.

Consider what Paul told the Corinthian church regarding the proper understanding of the phrase in question.

> *Don't you know* that *you yourselves* are *God's temple* [the exact words of 2 Thessalonians 2:4] and that God's Spirit lives *in you?*
> If anyone destroys *God's temple*, God will destroy him; for *God's temple* is sacred, and *you are that temple.* (1 Corinthians 3:16–17; emphasis and brackets added)

Three times in those verses, Paul uses the specific phrase "God's temple." He even reminds the Corinthian church that they, too, were supposed to already know this. There are three additional declarations Paul had also preached to the churches at Corinth and Ephesus.

Here's the first:

> What agreement is there between **the** *temple of God* and idols? *For we* [the church] *are the* **temple** *of the living God.* (2 Corinthians 6:16; emphasis and brackets added)

Second, it is interesting to note that the only *building of a new temple* in the last days mentioned anywhere in the New Testament, other than what Jesus said about His own body, was declared by Paul. Consider what he said about that new temple:

> Consequently, you are no longer foreigners and aliens, but **fellow citizens with God's people and members of God's household** [the church], built on the foundation of the apostles and prophets, with Christ Jesus himself as the chief cornerstone. *In him the whole building is joined together* and rises **to become a** *holy temple* **in the Lord.** And in him *you too* [the church] *are being built together to become a dwelling in which God lives* by his Spirit. (Ephesians 2:19–22; emphasis and brackets added)

Paul's third declaration follows. Notice how he emphasizes that, again, his listeners should have already known this truth:

> *Do you not know* that *your body is a temple* of the Holy Spirit, who is in you, whom you have received from God? You are not your own; you were bought at a price. Therefore honor God with your body. (1 Corinthians 6:19–20; emphasis added)

Here's an additional bombshell. Only two words in the New Testament Greek are translated into English as "temple": *heiron* and *naos*. They possess shades of similarity, but they speak of two distinct things.

## THE TEMPLE EDIFICE: *HEIRON*

The Greek *heiron* is most often used when speaking of the literal temple structure—specifically, the edifice that stood on the Temple Mount in Paul's day.[84]

The apostle only uses this word in *one verse* in all of the thirteen New Testament books he penned.[85] And when he does, he properly equates it to the *actual temple structure* located on the Temple Mount.[86] The context of Paul's use of the word is clear:

> Don't you know that those who work in **the temple** [*heiron*] get their food from **the temple** [*heiron*], and those who serve at the altar share in what is offered on the altar? (1 Corinthians 9:13–14; emphasis and brackets added)

## THE HOLY PLACE: *NAOS*

Now, here's the clincher: In *every other* instance where Paul mentions a "temple" in his letters to the churches, he uses a word that comes from the Greek *naos,* which has two very different but completely acceptable usages.

It often speaks of the most inner sanctum of the temple on the Temple Mount—*the holy place*. It doesn't indicate the entire temple edifice, only its specific inner portion. That's the most prevalent way the word is used in all the other New Testament documents.

However, the Apostle Paul never uses the word *naos* in that particular context. Instead, he always uses it in its accepted metaphorical sense. In so doing, he compares the holy place of the temple to the *New Testament church*. Sometimes Paul also states that the "temple of God" is that "holy place" within the heart of each born-again believer.

Have a look at how *Thayer's Greek Lexicon* elucidates this matter:

*Naos*—Also used **metaphorically**, of a *company of Christians, a Christian church*, as *dwelt in by the Spirit of God*: 1 Corinthians 3:16; 2 Corinthians 6:16; Ephesians 2:21; for the same reason, of *the bodies of Christians*, 1 Corinthians 6:19. *Of the body of Christ*.[87] (Emphasis added)

To put it bluntly, the Apostle Paul himself "spiritualized" the concept of the literal "temple of God" to make the point that the church has now become the genuine and new "temple"—the body of the risen Jesus Christ.[88]

## THE BOTTOM LINE

When Jesus died and arose from the dead, He replaced the temple with His own body. Jesus' *body* is now represented as *the church*—not the structure of a church building or a particular denomination. And it is definitely not a rebuilt Jewish temple. Rather, the body of Christ is now the body of born-again believers, put into effect by the Holy Spirit of God. *We are the new temple of God*.[89]

Additionally, the sacrifices offered in the Jewish temple would eventually cease after its destruction in AD 70. They would especially terminate from amongst the Jews who had become believers in Jesus as Lord and Messiah even before the temple was destroyed. Paul had already proclaimed to the first-century church that the new and proper sacrifice was to be a living one—consisting of their own minds, souls, and bodies—offered to Jesus Christ during the course of daily living.

Therefore, I urge you, brothers and sisters, in view of God's mercy, to offer your bodies as a living sacrifice, holy and pleasing to God—this is your true and proper worship. (Romans 12:1)

Paul, in 2 Thessalonians 2:4, was speaking of the very last of the final days of the end times when he gave that prophecy to the early church. And he was the chief prophet to the early church until John gave the Revelation around AD 95.

Also, don't forget that Paul had been caught up to paradise a full thirty years (2 Corinthians 12) before John experienced something very similar (Revelation 4). Yet, neither Paul nor John gave a definitive statement, in exegetical context, that in the last days a literal third temple edifice would be rebuilt on the Temple Mount after the destruction of the second temple.[90]

That fact is vital, because Paul was martyred just a few years before the second temple was destroyed. John prophesied more than thirty years *after* it was destroyed. So, a third and rebuilt temple in the last days would have been a monumental revelation, clearly and pointedly given to the end-time church! Yet, neither Paul, nor John, nor Jesus Himself[91] spoke of a literal third temple in any direct manner whatsoever.

## THE ENEMY'S BATTLE PLAN

Now, back to Capernaum.

On that day, on the shores of Galilee, a blitzkrieg of demonic powers was unleashed upon the kingdom work of Heaven's throne. It was aimed most squarely at *the Word that had become flesh,* who now stood among them. He was the One who would bring about the birth of the church. And the church would serve, until the end of time, as the representation of His own body.

Jesus' very presence and rapidly swelling popularity among the masses announced Satan's destruction. And, that ancient serpent[92] knew it. The evil one, who had been expelled from Heaven's divine council[93] would pull out all the stops to try to slow his own inevitable demise.

But through those thought-provoking kingdom parables, Jesus outed the serpent's most despicable strategies of subterfuge. Satan's greatest ruse would be to firmly establish his diabolical presence within our very midst.

*Matthew Poole's Commentary*:

*The true church* hath the Holy Spirit that forms it into *a spiritual temple*, Ephesians 2:21, 22; *the false church* hath the spirit of the devil, forming it *into the synagogue* [Grk-"assembly"] *of Satan*, Revelation 2:9.[94] (Emphasis and brackets added)

This essential kingdom truth was given that day only for the benefit of those who had "eyes to see and ears to hear."

And so it is with us.

# PART III

# THE SUBVERSION

We have now reached one of the most important chapters in Matthew, chapter 13. It demands, therefore, our closest attention, and this more so because the revelation which our Lord gives here, the unfolding of the mysteries of the kingdom of the heavens, has been and still is grossly misunderstood and falsely interpreted.

We have often said if this one chapter would be rightly understood by the professing church, the consequences would be the most far-reaching.

~Arno Gaebelein (1861–1945)[95]

# SUBTLE INFILTRATION

*The kingdom work is the "temple of God"*
*that Satan intends to corrupt by his*
*enthroned presence, especially in the last days.*

**15**

Later that Sabbath afternoon, as the throngs congregated on the beaches of Lake Galilee, Jesus unfurled a total of seven truths about His kingdom.

The first four of those messages were given specifically to the crowds. The last three were given to His disciples after they returned to their headquarters/home in Capernaum.[96]

Jesus spoke the kingdom truths in the form of parables, which were earthly stories that contained hidden nuggets of vital spiritual realities. But those divine treasures were only available to those who were willing to search them out and "hear" them by the Holy Spirit, the way they were meant to be understood.

## THE SEVEN

The first four of Jesus' public parables were the most ominous. They warned the listeners of a coming demonic infiltration. In them, Jesus revealed that the diabolic intrusion of which He spoke would invest itself right in the middle of His most obvious kingdom work: *the soon-coming, visible church*. That incursion, He disclosed, would often come about within the subtle activities of everyday life, similar to what they had already seen on that very day.

The last three of the seven parables were reserved for Jesus' inner circle. Two focused on encouraging His closest disciples through straightforward illustrations: The work of the kingdom, no matter how hellish it might become along the way, was worth everything the disciples would have to invest in order to be a part of it.[97]

The last parable of the final four was an emphatic instruction: "Keep throwing the net! Keep making disciples! Don't give up! And do this in spite of the daily satanic onslaught that will come against you."[98]

A popular interpretation of the first four of those parables states that they are speaking about the supernatural growth of the church. That explanation, however, is contextually inaccurate, as you will soon see for yourself.

## THE KINGDOM OF HEAVEN

But before we go any further, we need to settle what Jesus meant when He used the term "kingdom of heaven." Dr. John McArthur offers a concise explanation:

> *There is no significant difference* between "the kingdom of God" and the kingdom of heaven.... Matthew 19:23–24 confirms the equality of the phrases by using them interchangeably.
>
> **In the broadest sense, the kingdom** *includes everyone who professes* **to acknowledge God.** Jesus' parable of the sower represents the kingdom as including **both genuine and superficial believers** (Matt. 13:3–23), and in His following parable (vv. 24–30) as **including both wheat (true believers) and tares (false believers). That is the outer kingdom, the one we can see but cannot accurately evaluate** ourselves, because we cannot know people's hearts.
>
> **The other kingdom is the inner,** the kingdom that includes

*only true believers*. God rules over both…and **will one day finally separate the superficial** from the real. **Meanwhile He allows the** *pretenders* **to identify themselves** *outwardly* **with His kingdom.**[99] (Emphasis added)

In other words, the work of the "kingdom of heaven" would eventually be fleshed out as the body of Christ on earth—*the church*. That body is made up of the outwardly visible and "institutional" church, comprised of everyone who "professes" Jesus as Lord, as well as the inner church, those who are truly born again by the Holy Spirit. Therefore, only the inner church is the genuine kingdom work.

In Jesus' first recorded sermon, He warned His listeners about the concept of the "two churches":

Not everyone who says to me, "Lord, Lord," will enter the *kingdom of heaven*, but *only the one who does the will of my Father* who is in heaven. (Matthew 7:21; emphasis added)

He also laid out a concise definition of the "will of the Father":

For **my Father's will** is that *everyone who looks to the Son and believes in him* shall have eternal life, and I will raise them up at the last day. (John 6:40; emphasis added)

## THE PARABLES

These collective teachings about the kingdom form one of the most vital chapters in the Gospel of Matthew. And, because Satan knows the parables expose some of his most important deceptive methods of operation, he attempts to befuddle their true meaning. As a result, they're also some of the most frequently misinterpreted of all Jesus' parables.

The following significant portions of the first two parables are highlighted. Remember, Jesus was talking to the leaders, along with perhaps some of the earliest members of the soon-to-be church.

## THE PARABLE OF THE SOWER

**A farmer went out to sow his seed.** As he was scattering the seed, **some fell along the path**, and *the birds came* and ate it **up. Some fell on rocky places, where it did not have much soil.** It sprang up quickly, because the soil was shallow. But when the sun came up, the plants were scorched, and they withered because they had no root. Other seed **fell among thorns, which grew up and choked** the plants. Still other seed fell on good soil, where it produced a crop—a hundred, sixty or thirty times what was sown. (Matthew 13:3–8; emphasis added)

## THE PARABLE OF THE WEEDS

*The kingdom of heaven is like* a man who sowed good seed in his field. But **while everyone was sleeping,** *his enemy came* and **sowed weeds among the wheat, and went away.** When the wheat sprouted and formed heads, then the weeds also appeared.

**The owner's servants came to him** and said, "Sir, didn't you sow good seed in your field? **Where then did the weeds come from?"** *"An enemy did this,"* he replied. The servants asked him, "Do you want us to go and pull them up?"

"No," he answered, "because while you are pulling the weeds, you may uproot the wheat with them. Let both grow together until the harvest. At that time I will tell the harvesters: First **collect the weeds and tie them in bundles to be burned;**

then gather the wheat and bring it into my barn." (Matthew 13:14–30; emphasis added)

Jesus' opening salvo alarmed His listeners. Even His closest disciples were shaken by His words. This talk of an enemy coming right into the midst of the kingdom work of God was unnerving and needed some explanation.

So, Jesus gave His listeners some crucial insight.

# KINGDOM CLUES

## 16

*Satan not only uses the demonic realm to do his work, but he also manipulates and persuades a number of unredeemed humans to engage with him.*

Jesus' teachings in those first two parables were so startling to His own disciples that Matthew actually recorded the interpretation of the key elements. Those revelations help us understand exactly where Jesus was going with His teaching on the subject at hand.

Regarding the parable of the sower, Jesus revealed the following startling interpretation key. It concerned His statement about the "birds of the air":

> When anyone hears the message about the kingdom and does not understand it, *the evil one comes* and snatches away what was sown in their heart. (Matthew 13:19; emphasis added)

Thus, the "birds of the air" represent not only Satan himself, but also his diabolical messengers that do his bidding. That otherwise unseen realm would serve as Satan's agents. They would attempt to destroy the power and outreach of the gospel of Jesus Christ.

> And this gospel of the kingdom will be preached in the whole world as a testimony to all nations, and then the end will come. (Matthew 24:14)

We are the first generation in history to be directly involved in the fulfillment of that prophecy, a prophecy spoken from the mouth of Jesus

Christ Himself. We're also the first generation to have the technologies of instantaneous global communications and information systems that assist us in its actualization.

As a matter of fact, we see the truth of the sower parable every day. In the midst of the gospel message being sown to the nations, the demonic influence is right there, gobbling up as much of the gospel seed as possible. Jesus' explanation of the parable of the weeds also gives us insight into this same truth, but from a slightly different angle:

> The field is the world, and the good seed stands for the people of the kingdom. *The weeds are the people of the evil one*, and *the enemy* **who sows them** *is the devil.* The harvest *is the end of the age,* and the harvesters are angels.
>
> As the weeds are pulled up and burned in the fire, so it will be *at the end of the age.* (Matthew 13:38–40; emphasis added)

Here we are told that Satan not only uses the demonic realm to do his work, but he also manipulates and persuades a number of unredeemed humans to engage with him. In other words, Satan has his own "people" planted within the kingdom work.

*Barnes' Notes on the Bible* sheds appropriate contextual light on the parable:

> This seed was, by various means, to be carried over all the world. It was to be confined to no particular nation or people. **The good seed was the children of the kingdom; that is, of the kingdom of God, or Christians.** For these the Saviour toiled and died. They are the fruit of his labors. **Yet** *amid them* **were** *wicked people*; and **all hypocrites and unbelievers** *in the church* **are the work of Satan.**[100] (Emphasis added)

Through yet another important clue, we realize that Jesus is tying all the kingdom parables to *the very last days,* at the end of the age.

The parables speak of Satan's camouflaged infiltration into the kingdom work of the church. Furthermore, *each generation,* starting from the very first day Jesus spoke those words, would be able to relate to them—until the day He would finally return to reclaim the fallen creation.[101]

We see the same clue in the last parable Jesus spoke that day, the parable of the net.

> This is how it will be *at the end of the age.* The angels will come and *separate the wicked from the righteous* and throw them into the blazing furnace, where there will be weeping and gnashing of teeth. (Matthew 13:49–50; emphasis added)

It's now getting very difficult to miss the meaning of Jesus' kingdom parables.

Jesus is warning His followers that the enemy plans to infiltrate and cripple the church from within. The evil one's attack will come through the various denominational institutions and sectarian ministry endeavors that claim to represent the church's visible presence in the world.

Satan's ultimate plan is to water down the Word of God. Rob it of its potential power. Defame its reputation. Discredit its leaders. And destroy its credibility. He will lampoon it. Deride it. And he will eventually cause the nations to laugh at it, until the world begins to believe Satan's lie that God's Word is no longer relevant. In all of this, Satan's *man of lawlessness* will eventually claim to be the true "God." He will exalt himself above the Word of God.

We are watching the beginnings of it happen today. It's in the world's headlines, yet skillfully disguised. Hidden in plain sight.

Now, let's have a look at the remaining two parables from the group of the first four. They are the parables of the mustard seed and of the yeast.

While there is still light, we will continue peering into the evil one's secret end-time battle plan…and into his closet full of disguises.

# THE VILE PERVERSION

*As long as it is day, we must do the works of him who sent me. Night is coming, when no one can work.*
-JOHN 9:4

17

Jesus warned His disciples that the kingdom work would eventually be taken up into the hands of unredeemed men. When that happened, there would be a particular ripeness for Satan's entry into it.

Here's what Jesus proclaimed in that teaching:

> The kingdom of heaven is like a mustard seed, which a man took and planted in his field. **Though it is the smallest of all seeds, yet when it grows, it is the largest** of garden plants and becomes a tree, so *that the birds* **come and perch in its branches.** (Matthew 13:31–32; emphasis added)

The Gospel of Luke records that Jesus used the phrase "the birds of the air" in this parable.

> It is like a mustard seed, which a man took and planted in his garden. It grew and became a tree, and *the birds of the air* perched in its branches. (Luke 13:19; emphasis added)

Through Jesus' explanation of His first teaching—the parable of the sower—we already know the "birds of the air" represent the evil one and his demonically empowered emissaries. This is why Satan is elsewhere called "the prince of the power of the air" (Ephesians 2:2).

93

Observe the commentary from *Cambridge Bible for Schools and Colleges* for an understanding of the domain of the "power of the air":

On the whole we gather, as the revelation of this passage, that as earth is the present abode of embodied spirits, mankind, so the airy envelope of earth is the haunt, for purposes of action on man. **Observe our Lord's use of "the birds of the sky"** (Luke 8:5) *as the figure for the Tempter in the parable of the Sower.*[102] (Emphasis added)

Without a clear explanation by the speaker that the context of that unique imagery has suddenly changed, a different meaning simply cannot be forced upon the metaphor. And Jesus made no such explanation. The "birds of the air" of the mustard "tree" must therefore suggest the same thing as the "birds of the air" that were the nemesis of the sower. Jesus had succinctly defined the parabolic imagery only minutes before. How can so much of today's church miss this obvious truth?

The *Wiersbe Bible Commentary* says:

**The Jews knew** their scriptures and **recognized the images** that Jesus used. **A mustard tree produces a shrub, not a great tree.** The Kingdom *would be infected with false teaching.* And the **small seed would grow into an organization** [a tree] **that would be a home for Satan.** The *birds represent the evil one* (Matthew 13:19).[103] (Emphasis and brackets added)

Also note what the *Forerunner Commentary* says:

Matthew identifies the *birds of the air as "the wicked one"* (Matthew 13:4, 19). Mark connects them *with "Satan"* (Mark 4:4, 15), and *Luke links them to "the devil".* (Luke 8:5, 12)....

In the parable, Jesus predicts the birds of the air would lodge in the branches. *These "birds," demons* led by "the prince of the power of the air" (Ephesians 2:2), **have** *continually tried to* *infiltrate the church.* Upon the unsuspecting early church, **Satan** **moved quickly to implant his agents in it to teach** *false doctrine* while *appearing to be true Christians.* [104] (Emphasis added)

Several other respected commentaries view this passage the same way.

*Coffman's Commentary on the Bible:*

> *None of the commentaries,* **as far as determined,** *make anything* *of the birds* **lodging in the branches,** other than an illustration of the kingdom's ultimate magnitude; however, **in the parable of** **the sower,** *Christ used the birds to represent the devil,* **and upon** **that it would seem wise to seek a meaning here.**
>
> **Coupled with John's prophecy of the apostate church,** that it should become "a hold of every unclean and hateful bird" (Revelation 18:2), **this parable makes it very likely that the ulti-** **mate corruption of the kingdom of heaven is intended;** that is, as manifested **in the so-called Christendom** of modern and medieval times.
>
> A glance in any direction during **the current century will** **afford many glimpses of foul birds that have built their nests** **in the kingdom!** Yet, just as the birds could not, in fact, cor- rupt the mustard tree, **neither can evil men succeed** in thwart- ing God's purpose, *however closely they may be allied with the* *visible church* and its activities. [105] (Emphasis added)

The commentary of F. W. Grant in *The Numerical Bible:*

> **The tree of the parable is a garden shrub** *out-doing itself.* It grows into a tree, and the birds...lodge in its branches.... *As* *growth it is dubious,* and the mention of the *birds of heaven* *cannot but remind us that the birds of heaven carried away the*

*good seed in the first parable*, and that the **Lord's interpretation** is, "Then cometh the *wicked one*." Great Babylon; the figure of a **professing Christian body in guilty connection with the kings of the earth**, becomes "a cage of every unclean and hateful bird" (Rev. 18:2).

*If we remember that…the previous parable* has shown us a mixed condition in fact, the result of the enemy's work, *then the anomalous tree becomes perfectly intelligible*. The state of the **whole has been affected** *by this mixture of diverse elements*. There has **resulted from it what we know as Christendom today.** *Christianity has been* more or less **assimilated to the principles of the world;** the **world, in consequence becomes more favorable** *to the adulterated Christianity*.[106] (Emphasis added)

*Arno Gaebelein's Annotated Bible:*

Here we have the **outward development** of the kingdom of the heavens as it grows and expands, *in an unnatural way*, **and becomes the** *roosting place of the birds of heaven….*

**At once the parable becomes illuminated with light. Looked upon in this light, in full harmony with all the Lord teaches in this chapter, all is easily understood. The little mustard seed,** which was *not destined to be a tree* but only a shrub, easily taken out of the garden where it had been planted, **develops** *against its nature* **into a tree.**

That which came from Him, the Son of Man, the Sower, develops, **committed into the hands of men, into an unnatural thing**—one might say, a monstrosity—for such a mustard tree is. **This unnatural thing, this monstrosity, is professing Christendom as a system of the world, professing Christ, without possessing Him and His Spirit.**

**What a fall it will be when at last that tree, the monstrous tree, falls** and is destroyed forever root and all![107] (Emphasis added)

The commentary entries of Arno Gaebelein and F. W. Grant sound ominously familiar, especially as they are related to the Book of Revelation:

"Fallen! Fallen is Babylon the Great!" **She has become a dwelling for demons** and a haunt for **every impure spirit**, a *haunt for every unclean bird*, a haunt *for every unclean and detestable animal.* For all the nations have drunk the maddening wine of her adulteries....

Then I heard another voice from heaven say: "**Come out of her, my people,**" so that you will not share in her sins, so that you will not receive any of her plagues. (Revelation 18:2–4)

The bulk of classical scholarship affirms that the "Babylon" of Revelation at least includes that part of the "visible church" that had fallen into utter apostasy in the last days. It would be made up of those merely claiming to be Christians, or pretending to be Christians, or somehow deluded into thinking they were Christians when, in fact, they had not been genuinely born again. It would also include that fake form of genuine Christianity's unholy alliance with governmental powers—a beast that would eventually spread on a global scale.[108]

Paul, writing to the church at Corinth some thirty years previously, had also warned of this very thing. He cautioned them that, by blending their lives, doctrines, and church practices with the things of the world, they were transporting demonic influence squarely into their midst.

**You cannot drink the cup of the Lord and the cup of demons too**; you cannot have a part in both the Lord's Table and the table of demons. (1 Corinthians 10:21; emphasis added)[109]

Do not be **yoked together with unbelievers**. For what do righteousness and wickedness have in common? Or **what fellowship can light have with darkness? What harmony is there between**

**Christ and Belial** [Satan and his demons]? Or what does a believer have in common with an unbeliever?

**What agreement is there between the** *temple of God* **and idols? For** *we are the temple of the living God.* As God has said: "I will live with them and walk among them, and I will be their God, and they will be my people." Therefore, "*Come out from them and be separate,*" says the Lord.[110] (2 Corinthians 6:14–17; emphasis and brackets added)

John's warning in Revelation, "Come out of her, my people," is practically identical to Paul's warnings to the church at Corinth, and the context is the same as well. Here again, in 2 Corinthians, Paul identifies *the church* as "the temple of God."

Then, right on the heels of the parable of the mustard seed comes yet another warning from Jesus' sermon. It would be the last lesson for those gathered at the beach. This parable would serve as the summation of everything Jesus taught the crowds that afternoon.

That final public parable was encapsulated in just one sentence.

# JUST A LITTLE

## 18

*Satan would build his own "church within the church," and would so permeate it that the false church would eventually be difficult to tell from the true one.*

The last of Jesus' first four mini sermons is the parable of the leaven, also known as the parable of the yeast.

It is as though with this one, easy-to-understand sentence, Jesus intended to sum up the message of the three parables that came before it. The teaching about the yeast should have been an obvious lesson; every Jewish person there that day was familiar with the commonly understood truth. The question was: Could they "see" and then apply the deeper spiritual truth it was meant to impart? More importantly, can *we* see it?

> He told them still another parable: "The kingdom of heaven is like yeast that a woman took and mixed into about sixty pounds of flour until it worked all through the dough." (Matthew 13:33)

To interpret this parable, we begin by affirming that *every other* figurative occurrence of "leaven" or "yeast" in Scripture *always* represents evil. There simply are no exceptions.[111]

This is especially true of the pervasive work of Satan and his human representatives.

> "Be careful," Jesus said to them. "Be on your guard against the yeast of the Pharisees and Sadducees." (Matthew 6:16)

The fact that yeast *always* represents evil when used figuratively is also declared in the ancient rabbinical writings. Even in the celebration of the orthodox Passover Feast, we find the tradition of purging every scrap of evil leaven from houses. Also, the bread eaten during that feast was specifically prescribed to be "without yeast" (1 Corinthians 5:8).

Likewise, Jesus Christ is acknowledged to be our *unleavened bread*—the bread of life—without sin. (Matthew 16:6–12; Luke 12:1; Galatians 5:7–10).

Additionally, the Apostle Paul never came close to suggesting that leaven had a connotation of anything but evil:

Do you not know that a little leaven leavens the whole lump? Therefore purge out the old leaven, that you may be a new lump, since you truly are unleavened. For indeed Christ, our Passover, was sacrificed for us. Therefore let us keep the feast, not with old leaven, nor with the leaven of malice and wickedness; but with the unleavened bread of sincerity and truth. (1 Corinthians 5:6–8, NKJV)

*The Numerical Bible* asserts:

And **this is in fact the meaning** of the leaven: **it is an energy, but alas,** *of evil from without*, **which** *transforms the character* more and more of what it works upon, and completes **the sorrowful** *picture of decline* [in the last-days church] at which we have been looking….

At once we see that **the parable falls into line with the previous parables in that it continues that thought of evil and opposition to the Word** which they all more or less exhibit. The woman, is doing what **the word of God prohibits: she is putting leaven into the meal-offering.**

God insists upon the feast being kept to Him with unleavened bread…and if *the Church is intended* by the woman,
then *the professing church is here seen as adulterating the pure
doctrine of Christ,* the bread of life, with impure admixture.[112]
(Emphasis and brackets added)

With these comments in mind, *Arno Gaebelein's Annotated Bible*
relates a particularly relevant truth about Jesus' kingdom parables, especially the parable of the leaven:

**These to whom** [Jesus] **speaks were Jews.** Now the hearers of
the parable certainly understood what was meant by leaven. *No
Jew would ever dream* that leaven, used in illustrating some
power of process, **could stand for** *something good.…* **Leaven**
with the Jews means *always evil.*

*It is impossible* that [the yeast, or leaven in this parable]
should mean only once something good, and **that the Lord
without any further comment, should use it here as a type of
the gospel** [as so many commentators attempt to do].

*Leaven is error, evil, corruption.* The good pure meal stands
for truth, for Christ and His Word. The *leaven corrupts* the
meal, it changes that which is good, and *attacks in a hidden
way its purity,* till it has pervaded the whole mass. The Lord
teaches in the parable **how** *evil doctrine will corrupt the fine
meal, the doctrine of Christ.* It follows the parable of the mustard seed.[113] (Emphasis added; brackets added to give proper
context to the entirety of his lengthy commentary.)

The *Cambridge Bible for Schools and Colleges* serves as an example of
the kind of erroneous commentary about which Gaebelein speaks—one
that attempts to interpret this parable as being about the *supernatural
growth of the church.* Yet even that interpretation has to finally admit the
indisputable biblical truth we have just illustrated:

*Except in this one parable*, **leaven is used** of the **working of evil;** cp. "A little leaven leaveneth the whole lump," Galatians 5:9; 1 Corinthians 5:6; and "purge out therefore the old leaven," 1 Corinthians 5:7. **So, too, in the Rabbinical writings.**[114] (Emphasis added)

*John Gill's Exposition of the Whole Bible* is also forced to acknowledge the obvious, even though he also desires for this parable to be about the *growth* of the church rather than the satanic infiltration of it. However, *Gill* has one little problem with which he must contend. But at least he acknowledges it:

Since the word "leaven" is **elsewhere *always* used in a bad sense,** deserves consideration; according to which, this parable expresses *not the spread of truth, but of error;* by "the woman" is thought to be meant, the Apocalyptic woman, the woman spoken of in the Revelations, ... the mother of harlots; and the "leaven" which she took, *the leaven of false doctrine and discipline;* by her "hiding" it, the private, *secret, artful methods, false doctrines, and bad discipline* were introduced, and **the gradual progress thereof.**[115] (Emphasis added)

## PICK AND CHOOSE

At the end of this candid admission, Gill adds a touch of his own exasperation. He seems to be unable to rectify the fact that the word "leaven" is always used in a negative sense. So he ends his narrative by declaring: "The *reader may choose* whichever interpretation *he likes best.*"

I understand Gill's anxiety. However, I have to take issue with his conclusion. We truly are *not* free to choose *whichever* interpretation we like best! In other words, we're not free to "sanitize" the Word of God to make it fit what we desire it to say, especially in the case of such an important teaching—and particularly when the interpretation of its meaning is given by Jesus Himself.

Can you imagine what the church would be like today, right in the midst of these deeply prophetic times, if the prevailing way Christian denominations developed their understanding of doctrine happened to be: "Just choose whatever you want to believe; whatever makes you the most comfortable will be just fine. *Whatever parts or understanding you like best.* Whatever you think will cause the least offense, just go with that one!"

Oh wait…never mind.

Sadly, that is precisely where most of today's visible church appears to be headed. A little leaven here and a little there, and soon it has spread throughout the whole batch, corrupting the purity of its foundation.

## ACCURATELY HANDLING THE WORD

The most excellent way to interpret Scripture, as F. W. Grant's commentary has already laid out, is to let Scripture interpret itself.

Since the biblically figurative use of leaven always speaks of evil—*with no exception*—then this parable must mean the same thing as well. The only exception would be if the speaker clearly stated that He had changed the well-known context of the previous usages. Of course, Jesus did no such thing on that day at Lake Galilee. The Jews listening to Him knew exactly what He meant.

The contextual truth of the first four kingdom parables of Matthew 13 is that Satan would pluck up the seed of the gospel wherever he found it sprouting. He would plant his weeds among the wheat, attempting to camouflage his secret agents of destruction. Satan would build his own "church within the church," and would so permeate it that the false church would eventually be difficult to tell from the true one.

It would be there, in the midst of the visible church, where his "birds of the air" would make their nests in an unnaturally growing "institution."

Satan's plan would be to sow *just a little* discord, or only a sprinkling of demented doctrine, and then merely a smidgeon of blasphemous thought into the midst of the churches.

Just like the elusive working of yeast, Satan planned to waltz right into the pews and ministry leadership positions—even into the pulpits. He would pull off the scheme under the alluring masks of tantalizing secret societies, the pressure cookers of political correctness, and the sparkling appeal of cultural accommodation. All of it would be wrapped in glittery packages designed to tickle the itching ears of a biblically deprived last-days population.

This is where the great apostasy would lower its roots and begin to flourish, like something abnormal, grotesque, and vile.

This diabolical plan makes perfect strategic sense.

The Word that was made flesh is Satan's primary target. Ever since the resurrection of Jesus, the *new* representative of the Body of Christ is now the church! Since the church is the Lord's first line of attack against Satan's doomed empire, it stands to reason that it would be at the center of Satan's target. This is exactly what Paul reveals as Satan's main strategy. It is also the message Jesus gave through His kingdom parables.

It all ties together.

Furthermore, the Apostle Paul identified that Satan's scheme would ultimately result in what he coined the "mystery of iniquity"…

…which brings us right back to 2 Thessalonians.

# A SCHEME OF ERROR

*For the mystery of iniquity doth already work:*
*only he who now letteth will let,*
*until he be taken out of the way.*
~2 THESSALONIANS 2:7 (KJV)

**19**

As a good number of classical scholars have noted, 2 Thessalonians 2:7 precisely aligns with Jesus' first four kingdom teachings. To keep this chapter brief, I have included only a sampling among those who express this pervasive truth.

Notice that the *Benson Commentary* weaves the main features of the kingdom parables into the understanding of the last-days "mystery of iniquity," especially as the mystery relates to the man of lawlessness setting himself up and worming his way into the "temple of God" through the "sowing of corrupt seed" and the "fermenting of the leaven":

> **The mystery of iniquity**, therefore, *is a scheme of error*, not openly discovered, whose influence is *to encourage iniquity*. Doth already work inwardly, in men's minds, or *in the church*, and perhaps *also secretly*. The *seeds of corruption were sown*, but they were not yet grown up to any maturity: *the leaven was fermenting* in some parts, but it was far from having yet infected the whole mass. To speak without a figure, the apostle means that the *false doctrines* **and bad practices**, which **he foresaw in after** times would be carried to a great height by the power which he denominates the man of sin, *were already operating* in the *false teachers*, who *then infested the church*.[116] (Emphasis added)

The *Pulpit Commentary,* among several other respected sources, mirrors *Benson's* observations:

Even at the time the apostle wrote, the *seeds of apostasy* were already sown; *the leaven of lawlessness* was fermenting [like leaven in dough] *inside Christianity;* the foundations of *a false Christianity* were being laid.[117] (Emphasis and brackets added)

*Barnes' Notes on the Bible* offers the following:

Any secret sources of iniquity *in the church* [Gnosticism, Freemasonry, etc.?]— Anything that tended to corrupt its doctrines, and to destroy the simplicity of the faith of the gospel, would correspond with the meaning of the word.[118] (Emphasis and brackets added)

The massive, fifty-six-volume commentary, *The Biblical Illustrator,* with entries by hundreds of renowned scholars of its day, such as Dwight L. Moody, Charles Spurgeon, J. C. Ryle, Charles Hodge, Alexander MacLaren, Adam Clark, Matthew Henry, and others, identified this "spirit" of iniquity to a tee:

Paul seems to prepare us, in passing from lawlessness to *the lawless one,* for a sort of incarnation of lawlessness—principle, power, or person, sitting, *as it were,* in the very temple of God, "showing himself that he is God."

"Lawlessness" is the predicted characteristic of the last age. May I not ask, Is it not now abroad? It *is in the family and the Church*—in the workshop and the study—in the literature of a "science falsely so called"—and in the lurking places of political fanatics.… It is working everywhere with ingenious industry among the time honored institutions of society itself.[119] (Emphasis added)

*John Gill's Exposition of the Whole Bible*:

**The doctrines and practices of antichrist may be called the mystery of iniquity,** especially as they were now *secretly spread*, imbibed, and practiced: the foundations of it were now *laying in the church* by false teachers; for **errors and heresies of every sort,** *respecting the person and offices of Christ*, and in opposition to them, were now broached.[120] (Emphasis added)

Notice how *Robertson's Word Pictures of the New Testament* also connects Paul's "mystery of lawlessness" with Jesus' Sea of Galilee parables:

This mystery means here the secret purpose of lawlessness already at work, **the only instance of this usage in the N.T.** where it is used of the kingdom of God—**Matthew 13:11.** [Jesus' kingdom parables][121] (Emphasis and brackets added)

*Wesley's Notes*:

*It began with* the love of honour, and the desire of power; and is completed in *the entire subversion of the gospel of Christ*. It seems to consist of…namely, *the adding to the word of God*. Already worketh—*in the church*.[122] (Emphasis added)

## LAWLESSNESS

Most modern, scholarly translations of the biblical text use either "iniquity" or "lawlessness" as the operating words in this passage. However, when we see the "lawlessness" used in an English translation, we're prone to think the term is speaking to the general breakdown of societal law and order.

Of course, we're told in other passages of the New Testament that this type of disorder, characterized by lawlessness, will indeed take place in the last days (2 Timothy 3:1). So, in a sense, that would be a correct assumption—but only partially.

That's because the Greek word *anomia* used by Paul also carries another specific *and much deeper* interpretation.

Are you ready for yet another surprise?

Have a look at how the Greek dictionary breaks down that word. *HELPS Word-studies*:

[The Greek word] *Anomía*—properly, without law; lawlessness; **the utter disregard for** *God's law (His written and living Word).*[123] (Emphasis added; parentheses in the original)

Just "who" would ultimately bring about this utter disregard for God's written and living Word at the same time he is provoking worldwide, societal lawlessness and civil unrest? Of course, it would be none other than the man of lawlessness himself. You know, the one who eventually will be sitting in the midst of an institution that pretends to be the "temple of God" and at the same time will be claiming that *he* is God.

Let no one in any way deceive you, for [the day of the Lord] **will not come unless** *the apostasy*[124] **comes** first, and *the man of lawlessness* **is revealed**, the son of destruction. (2 Thessalonians 2:3, NASB; emphasis added)

There can be no mistake. Paul is warning the church that this enigmatic event, already well on its way in his lifetime, not only involves a breakdown of societal order and rule of law in the last days, but also a *complete contempt* for the Word of God. In other words, the visible church of the end times will lose its biblical worldview.

# THE VANISHING BEDROCK  20

*A full 90 percent of Americans do
not have a biblical worldview.*

The "visible church" of America is already in a self-confessed and prophesied state of decay. For the first time in our storied history, there is now a statistically verified absence of a genuine biblical worldview among our population. It's vanishing right before our eyes.

As of late 2019, the Pew Research Center found that in only one decade, the percentage of American adults identifying as Christians dropped by a remarkable 12 percent, from 77 percent to just 65 percent. This was the lowest reported percentage of professing Christians in the nation's 243-year history.[125]

However, in an earlier poll, only a shocking 46 percent of Americans claimed they live from the standpoint of a *biblical worldview,* one that holds to an assessment of life that believes the Bible is accurate in all things and suitable for directing the affairs of our daily lives and societal norms.[126]

A biblical worldview is also marked by the belief that it is especially important for a true believer to openly speak to the vital issues of our times. These include, but aren't limited to, the biblical definition of marriage, radical agendas that support all manner of sexual perversions, gender identity, pornography, substance abuse, abortion, and obvious prophetic fulfillments within our lifetime, as well as the bold sharing of our faith as we attempt to shed biblical light upon these contentious issues.

But do these 46 percent of Americans who claim to see the world through the lens of a biblical worldview actually hold to that specifically defined context?

No, *they don't*. Not even close.

## ONLY ONE IN TEN

Consider the recent statistical assessment of the religious pollster George Barna:

> Our research collected information about attitudes and behaviors related to practical matters like lying, cheating, stealing, pornography, the nature of God, and the consequences of unresolved sin. It's what some might describe as "Christianity 101" substance. That's what makes the discrepancy between the percentage of people who consider themselves to be Christians—more than seven out of every ten—**and those who have a biblical worldview—just *one out of every ten*—**so alarming.[127] (Emphasis added)

This means that out of the 65 percent of Americans who claim to be Christians (*the visible church*), only 10 percent affirm that they hold a biblical view of life. That small percentage, according to Jesus, is the genuine *church.*[128]

Considering that even some of those 10 percent most likely *do not live* what they say they believe, you now understand where the church really is, and why.

This is a huge part of the last-days phenomenon that Jesus, Paul, John, and practically all other biblical writers were trying to warn us about. But it is a caution that has long been misinterpreted or flatly overlooked by the modern church. As a result, the mystery of iniquity is already slithering into our congregations and denominations. There is no longer a *coming* apostasy. The horrific leading edge of the last-days tsunami of false teaching is already here.

Like leaven leaching through a batch of dough, it has already spread throughout the visible church of the largest "Christian" nation on the planet. The swelling cultural demise burgeoning right in front of our faces testifies to this. And the yeast of its infecting power is proliferating across the entire planet—at the speed of our current instantaneous global-information-exchange delivery systems.

This phenomenon is proving to be Satan's grandest con job in human history, and we're the first generation to be living in the midst of that biblically prophesied spectacle.

> The Spirit clearly says that *in later times* some will **abandon the faith** and **follow deceiving spirits** and things **taught by demons.** (1 Timothy 4:1; emphasis added)

> But mark this: **There will be *terrible times in the last days.*** People will be…lovers of pleasure **rather than lovers of God—*having a form of godliness but denying its power*.** Have nothing to do with such people. (2 Timothy 3:1, 2–5; emphasis added)

This is exactly what Paul foretold, and in agreement with what Jesus outlined in His Capernaum parables of Matthew 13. Sadly, most of today's church doesn't even see it, much less understand that we were long ago warned it would happen.

Some of that misunderstanding is because today's church truly doesn't know the genuine nature of its enemy. He wears so many masks. He's the cosmic master of intrigue, and he is unimaginably vile.

Now we move to another *not-so-pretty* revelation, one that explains why all this is so.

# PART IV

# UNMASKING THE ENEMY

If you know the enemy and know yourself, you need not fear the result of a hundred battles. If you know yourself but not the enemy, for every victory gained you will also suffer a defeat.

~Sun Tzu, *The Art of War*[129]

# TREASON

*Satan wanted the garden for himself,*
*and every glorious thing it represented.*

**21**

Many books have been written regarding Satan, his biblical names, and the various theories regarding his creation and fall. However, our purpose here will be to take a closer look at his characteristics that are seldom written about. We will sweep away the myths and caricatures of the cosmic enemy of God's Word and expose him for what Scripture says he is.

Let's begin with this important truth: Nothing in the Bible indicates that God created Satan to become His eternal enemy. Rather, Satan (not his original name[130]) was initially created in absolute perfection and was subsequently placed in a trusted and exalted position.[131]

But, along with that divine gift of being created in glorious perfection also came the grand responsibility of having *free will*. Satan and the rest of the angelic host, like humanity, wasn't created to be a puppet or some lifelike robot. Nor was he created at the level of a lowly animal, creatures that respond to their surroundings based largely upon instinct.

Rather, Satan was endowed with the ability to freely decide his moment-by-moment actions in direct relationship to his environment and his communication with other freely choosing beings. He shared the company of all God's creation, both the angelic and the human.

Somewhere along the way (the Bible doesn't tell us specifically when it happened) Satan *chose* to become God's enemy.[132]

It is obvious from Scripture that sometime after the last verse of Genesis 1 and before the first verse of Genesis 3 were written, Satan was already plotting a scheme to "capture" God's throne for himself. The first chapter of Genesis ends with God declaring that everything He created—*everything* in its "vast array"—was "good." Therefore, Satan had not yet fallen.

## THE SNEAKY SNAKE

However, Genesis 3 opens with the introduction to a character not heretofore seen in the biblical narrative. It is here where three eternally important words jump off the page and slap us in the face: "*Now the serpent.*"

In that short chapter of Genesis 3, we begin to see the foundation of Satan's scheme. Even though his heart had already been corrupted, the working of his actual plan would commence in the Garden of Eden.

Satan desired for himself the garden and every glorious thing it represented. By the time of his exchange with Eve, he had already given himself over to a scheme of destruction. What he did in the garden was nothing short of a premeditated act of treason against the throne of God. The "serpent" was Satan. It was not a walking, talking snake.

In *the same way* Jesus is symbolically referred to as the Lion of Judah, the Lamb of God, the Lamb upon the throne, and the Lamb that takes away the sin of world, so Satan is also metaphorically identified as the serpent, or the dragon.[133]

*Benson Commentary*:

The serpent—*in reality* a fallen angel, or **the prince of fallen angels,** *Satan.*[134] (Emphasis added)

*Matthew Henry's Concise Commentary*:

*Satan assaulted our first parents*, to draw them to sin, and the temptation proved fatal to them. **The tempter** *was the devil....*

*Satan* **ruined himself** by desiring to be like the Most High, therefore *he sought to infect our first parents* with the same desire, that he might ruin them too.[135] (Emphasis added)

*Coffman's Commentaries on the Bible* puts the matter in the most scholarly and contextual light:

Here, at the outset of our studies in the O.T., it needs to be established that **the O.T. should be understood** *only in the light of what is revealed in the N.T. We reject* out of hand the **dictum laid down by Biblical interpreters that the text can have** *but a single meaning*.... To follow the arbitrary dictum mentioned above **would forbid any identification at all of** *Satan in this entire chapter*.... Thus, exploring the mind of the author should mean *exploring the mind of God* who is the **real author** *of the whole Bible.*[136] (Emphasis added)

There is no doubt: The garden usurper was not some "other" fallen being, as some scholars insist. It wasn't a literal ambulating, chatty snake, as still other scholars try to explain.[137] And the Genesis 3 account is not some mythological and ancient tale, as a handful of commentators through the ages have asserted.

The tempter in the garden was none other than Satan himself, a fallen but divinely created being of the highest order.

# THE FIRST MASQUERADE

## 22

*The one He entrusted with the apple of His eye betrayed Him.*

The third chapter of Genesis isn't the only place in the Bible where we're given clues as to what transpired in the Garden of Eden and who it was that caused the Fall. God Himself gives us even more detail through the prophet Ezekiel:

> You were the **seal of perfection**, full of wisdom and **perfect in beauty.** You *were in Eden, the garden of God….*
>
> You were anointed *as a guardian cherub*, for so I ordained you…. You were **on the holy mount of God** [where the Temple Mount is today; it's also the original location of the Garden of Eden[138]]; you walked among the fiery stones. *You were blameless in your ways from the day you were created till wickedness was found in you.* (Ezekiel 28:12–15; emphasis and brackets added)

Numerous scholars acknowledge that Ezekiel 28, although beginning with a lament against the king of Tyre, eventually morphs into a description of Satan himself—the real power at work behind the throne of the king of Tyre. The literary device of this mid-prophecy switch is known as a *compound prophecy.* As biblical scholar and commentator Dr. Lehman Strauss attests, the technique is common, and is found throughout the Scriptures.[139]

The work of Robert Jamieson, A. R. Fausset, and David Brown, *Commentary Critical and Explanatory on the Whole Bible*, explains Ezekiel 28 and its status as a compound prophecy:

> The language, **though primarily here applied to the king of Tyre**, as similar language is to the king of Babylon (Isaiah 14:13, Isaiah 14:14), **yet has an** *ulterior and fuller accomplishment in Satan* and his embodiment *in Antichrist* (Daniel 7:25, Daniel 11:36, Daniel 11:37, 2 Thessalonians 2:4, Revelation 13:6).[140] (Emphasis added)

*The Bible Exposition Commentary* also acknowledges the switch from the king of Tyre to Satan himself:

> The use of the word "cherub" (Ezekiel 28:4–6) suggests that **we're dealing here with an angelic creature**, also the fact that **he had been "upon the holy mountain of God"** (v. 14).
>
>     This sounds a great deal like the description in Isaiah 14:12 ff. *Satan began as an obedient angel but rebelled against God and led a revolt to secure God's throne.*[141] (Emphasis added)

Likewise, *Coffman's Commentaries on the Bible* also notes the "compound nature" of this prophetic passage:

> **There is not a line of this that can be applied to any other being who ever lived, except Satan!** It was **that garden where Adam and Eve had been placed by the Lord, and into which Satan appeared** as an intruder to seduce Eve and precipitate the fall of the human race.
>
>     *After this clause, the rest of the description* must be applied to Satan before his appearance in Eden. *The application is clear enough. Just as Satan lost his place* in the mountain of God, *the*

*king of Tyre,* **and all other proud kings,** *shall lose their place* in the destruction God prepares for them.[142] (Emphasis added)

*F. F. Bruce's New Layman's Bible Commentary* confirms the compound nature of Ezekiel 28:

This passage in Ezekiel **has contributed details** to the picture *of the fall of Satan.*[143] (Emphasis added)

Have a look at the *Guzik Bible Commentary—Enduring Word.* Guzik acknowledges the compound prophecy nature of both Ezekiel 28 and Isaiah 14:

**This chapter** [Ezekiel 28] **and Isaiah 14 throw light on** *the fall of Satan,* and indicate that he was a created being who fell through pride…. *Here we have the most graphic and illuminating portrayal of Satan to be found in the whole Bible.* His original power and greatness, wisdom and beauty, and exalted position are all set forth.[144] (Emphasis and brackets added)

The *Wells of Living Water Commentary* by Dr. Robert Edward Neighbour was published in 1939. His fourteen-volume commentary on the whole Bible includes a lengthy section on Ezekiel 28, where he deems *the whole chapter* as a compound prophecy.

The prince of Tyre, as discussed in Ezekiel 28:2–10 refers to the earthly ruler. [However], the king of Tyre in our verse [12ff], presents **Satan as the one who was the real power back of the throne.**
**Satan was full of beauty.** *Satan was far from the hideous monster* that he is usually pictured to the young. *It is his beauty which appeals,* and adds subtlety to every attempt he makes against the children of men.[145] (Emphasis added)

Again, we don't know how long the originally perfect cherub and Adam and Eve had enjoyed each other's company before sin entered the picture. Scripture doesn't fill in those details. The narrative of the third chapter of Genesis then moves right to the facts of the Fall.[146]

The point is this: The perfect, beautiful, and dazzlingly brilliant being God designed to be the guardian of the Garden of Eden, the one He entrusted with the *apple of His eye,* betrayed Him. Yahweh was betrayed by Satan, in the garden. That betrayal began with a false accusation against the Creator: *Did God really say?* And that is where Satan donned his very first mask.

And when the Creator put on flesh and came to us in the "fallen Garden" as *the second Adam* (1 Corinthians 15:45–49), He was once again betrayed by Satan—*in a garden*—the Garden of Gethsemane. This time, the betrayal came with a kiss planted on His cheek with a smirk of arrogance attached to it, and disguised in the person of Judas Iscariot.[147]

The puzzle pieces of the bigger picture are only just now beginning to fall into place.

# THE PLUNGE | 23

*Satan's stunningly pompous pride coveted
nothing less than God's own throne.*

The fourteenth chapter of Isaiah is couched with yet another compound prophecy. That chapter gives us additional information regarding the nature of Satan's plan on that fateful day in the Garden of Eden.

> **How you are fallen from heaven**, O *Day Star*, [or Lucifer][148] son of Dawn! How you are cut down to the ground, you who laid the nations low! **You said in your heart,** "*I will* **ascend to heaven; above the stars of God** *I will* **set my throne on high;** *I will* **sit on the mount of assembly** in the far reaches of the north; *I will* **ascend above the heights** of the clouds; *I will make* **myself like the Most High."** (Isaiah 14:12–14, ESV; emphasis and brackets added)

*Lange's Commentary on the Holy Scriptures: Critical, Doctrinal, and Homiletical* asserts that even Jewish scholars hundreds of years before Christ understood this portion of Isaiah to speak of Satan.

> Even as **early as the LXX [Septuagint]** this passage seems to have **been understood** of Satan. It points that way **that they change the second person into the third** [another compound prophecy]....

*And this is the aim of Satan* and of his earthly sphere of power, the world-power, *which culminates in Antichrist* (Daniel 11:36; 2 Thessalonians 2:3).[149] (Emphasis added)

Numerous respected biblical scholars see the obvious connection of Satan's fall with Isaiah 14. They understand it to be a compound prophecy.

*Arno Gaebelein's Annotated Bible*:

**Behind this…king…looms up Satan, who energized that wicked and false king.** The description of him who was "Lucifer," the light-bearer, **and his fall.**[150] (Emphasis added)

*E. W. Bullinger's Companion Bible Notes*:

[This is a] Divine revelation of Him Who knows what Satan "said in his heart."[151]

*Ironside's Notes on Isaiah*:

**The fall of Lucifer portrays the fall of Satan.** The passage *links very closely with Ezekiel 28*, which should be carefully considered in the effort to understand this fully. These words **cannot apply to any mere mortal** man. Lucifer (**the light-bearer) is a created angel of the very highest order, identical with the covering cherub of Ezekiel 28.** He was, apparently, **the greatest of all the angel host** and was perfect before GOD until he fell through pride. It is of him **our Lord speaks in John 8:44.**[152] (Emphasis added)

*The Bible Exposition Commentary* lays out the entire theme of this passage from Isaiah 14:

In the fall of the king of Babylon, *he saw the defeat of Satan*, the "prince of this world," who seeks to energize and motivate the leaders of nations (John 12:31; Ephesians 2:1–3). Dan 10:20 indicates that *Satan has assigned "princes"* (fallen angels) to the various nations *so that he can influence leaders* to act contrary to the will of God. *This highest of God's angels tried to usurp the throne of God* and capture for himself the worship that belongs only to God (Matt 4:8–10).[153] (Emphasis added)

In short, Satan's stunningly pompous pride coveted nothing less than God's own throne and all the power and glory that went with it. His desire would include not only being the ruler of the new creation of Eden, but also his craving to govern the inhabitants of the heavenly realm sometimes known in Scripture as the "stars of God."

The next three commentary entries give important biblical context to this symbolic phrase.[154]

*Barnes' Notes on the Bible*:

His object was…to exalt himself **above the stars**; to be elevated above all inferior beings; and to be *above the gods* [angelic beings].[155] (Emphasis and brackets added)

*Jamieson-Fausset-Brown Bible Commentary*:

**"The stars"** are often also used to express *heavenly principalities* (Job 38:7). (Emphasis added)

*Gill's Exposition of the Entire Bible*:

I will exalt my throne above **the stars of God**; which he has made and set in the heavens, and preserves; *meaning the angels, Job 38:7*. (Emphasis added)

The Scripture itself, in Revelation 1 and 12, as well as in Job 38, confirms that the word "stars," within a certain context, sometimes refers to the angelic host of God.

**The mystery of the seven stars that you saw** in my right hand and of the seven golden lampstands is this: *The seven stars are the angels...* (Revelation 1:20; emphasis added)

Where were you when I laid the foundation of my earth? While **the** *morning stars sang* **together** and *all the divine beings* shouted joyfully? (Job 38:4, 7, ISV; emphasis added)

[The dragon's] tail swept *a third of the stars* out of the sky and flung them to the earth.... The *great dragon* was hurled down— that ancient serpent called *the devil, or Satan*, who leads the whole world astray. He was hurled to the earth, *and his angels* with him. (Revelation 12:4, 9; emphasis and brackets added)

Isaiah 14 reveals that Satan's goal was not merely to rule a fallen earth, but to eventually capture Heaven's throne itself and to have all creation worship him, both in the heavenly realm and in the earthly realm. It seems his arrogance and pride know no boundaries.

This is our adversary.

The vileness of his wretched heart is unspeakable.

His masks are innumerable.

And for those who do not possess the spiritual discernment to see them for what they really are, his disguises are fiendishly mesmerizing.

In fact, Satan's greatest embarrassment is hidden behind the next mask that we'll reveal.

# THE CHARADE

*The "god of this age" has used this particular deception
for thousands of years in order to bring a certain level
of embarrassment upon the preaching of God's Word.*

ere's what Satan is really trying to cover up.

Through a verse found in Genesis 3, the Bible commences with an official indictment. That legal charge was issued from Heaven's throne against the cosmic thug of the universe, the one doomed to eternal destruction.

The curse of the Garden of Eden was pronounced upon the person of Satan. It was not proclaimed against a talking, walking snake, much less the entirety of *snakedom*. The metaphor of the garden curse should now be strikingly evident:

> So the LORD God said to the serpent, "Because you have done this, cursed are you above all livestock and all wild animals! You will **crawl on your belly and you will eat dust**[156] all the days of your life. And I will put enmity between you and the woman, and between your offspring and hers; *he will crush your head, and you will strike his heel.*" (Genesis 2:14–15; emphasis added)

The commentary of Bob Deffinbaugh, ThD, shines scholarly light on the garden narrative, neatly pulling the mask off the "serpent" metaphor and getting right to the heart of the account:

God began *by addressing Satan* and spelling out the punishment **for his sin**. This is appropriate in light of the fact that *Satan was the instigator*, **the tempter**.... As the promoter of sin, his punishment rightly comes first. *The first promise of a coming Messiah* in the Bible comes in God's *rebuke of Satan* in Genesis 3:15.

**The Messiah was to come**, then, both *to destroy Satan* and to deliver men from his dominion, **a theme which** *continues on into the New Testament.*[157] (Emphasis added)

The *Keil and Delitzsch Biblical Commentary on the Old Testament* explains the symbolic language of Genesis 3:14 like this:

The presumption of *the tempter was punished with the deepest degradation*; and in like manner his sympathy with the woman was to be turned into **eternal hostility**.... **And its crawling in the dust** *is a sign* [symbol or metaphor] that it will be defeated in its conflict with man.[158] (Emphasis and brackets added)

*Gill's Exposition of the Entire Bible* also sheds light:

As [crawling on the belly] respects the punishment of the devil, *may signify, that he being cast down from the realms of bliss and glory, shall never be able to rise more*, and regain his former place and dignity...

[That] this [eating dust] *is applicable to Satan, designs the mean and abject condition in which he is,* and the sordid food **he lives upon; no more on angels' food** and joys of heaven, **but on the base, mean, earthly,** *and impure lusts* of men; and this will be his case, condition, and circumstances, forever.[159] (Emphasis added)

*Coffman's Commentary on the Bible* puts the truth in very clear language:

The problem that stands at the head of this chapter is that of understanding what *the serpent* was.

*The near unanimous opinion of scholars* and commentators to the effect that he was a member of the animal kingdom is somewhat perplexing in view of *the fact that the grammar of our versions does not support such a view.*

*It is not stated* that the serpent was more subtle than any other **beast of the field**, but that he was more subtle **than** *any* **beast.**[160]

*This is an indication that he was not a beast at all.*[161] (Emphasis added)

*Dinsdale T. Young's* (1861–1938) commentary on Genesis 3 also snatches off Satan's serpent/dragon mask and exposes the heart of the matter:

Theologians have **a special name** for this text. They term it **the "Protevangelium,"** which being interpreted is **the "First Gospel."** Who uttered this first Evangel? God Himself. **To whom was the Protevangelium uttered?** *To Satan.*

The teachings of Christ verify this Gospel prophecy. *No marvel Satan loathes these heavenly oracles, and seeks to suppress them.*[162] (Emphasis added)

Dr. Young is correct. There should be no wonder as to why Satan so desperately wants to hide behind this mask. Because, without the proper contextual illumination of the rest of Scripture, his snaky-dragon masquerade simply becomes the stuff of fairy tales in the minds of the unredeemed world.

The masterful work of C. S. Lewis, *The Screwtape Letters*, exposes the enemy's plan. In that book, Lewis presents a senior demon by the name of *Screwtape* as he writes letters of diabolic instruction to his nephew *Wormwood,* a lesser demon.

Dear Wormwood. The fact that "devils" are *predominantly comic figures* in the modern imagination will help you. If any faint suspicion of your existence begins to arise in his mind, suggest to him a picture of *something in red tights*, and persuade him that **since he cannot believe in that** (it is an old textbook method of confusing them) he **therefore cannot believe in you.**[163] (Emphasis added)

# THE CHALLENGE TO THE CHURCH

Do you feel my angst here? I'm determined to keep Satan from getting away with this ruse among God's people any longer, especially within the unprecedented prophetic times in which we're living. We simply cannot afford to discredit or mischaracterize the enemy of humanity.

Consequently, the ignominy of Satan's garden sin is rarely exposed from the day-to-day proclamations of today's pulpits. This is Satan's goal. The ridiculous insistence upon the metaphorical image of the talking snake as a literal reality only serves as yet one more way of infusing the kingdom work with his "doctrines of demons."

The whole charade becomes a bit of leaven that eventually permeates the entire batch. Read through a collection of commentaries on Genesis 3 and the talking-snake scenario.[164] By now, you should be appalled by what you see in those writings. The leaven has certainly done its work; it truly is embarrassing to behold.

As a result of this demonic ruse, the seeds of biblical truth that are not held in their proper context are easily plucked off the often-rocky paths of our witnessing efforts. Christians are mocked and scorned for insisting on talking snakes and apples. As a result, the message of salvation is largely ignored by those who mock us. This is the work of the demonic *birds of the air* about which Jesus so clearly warned.

The Apostle Paul gave us the antidote for the problem:

**Do your best to present yourself to God** as one approved, a worker *who does not need to be ashamed* and who *correctly handles* the word of truth. (2 Timothy 2:15; emphasis added)

## A PLEA

Pastors, Bible teachers, and God's people everywhere, please hear this last-days warning. We must no longer allow Satan to relegate his abominable deed in the garden to a mere children's bedtime story, a mythical tale featuring a pretty little talking snake holding an apple and shoving it in the face of Adam and Eve.

We are playing right into Satan's subversive plans when we do so.

# THE MIGHTY ONE | 25

*The cherub is one of the most important positions
of authority among God's heavenly host.*

There is another important biblical description of Satan we've already
observed but haven't yet expounded upon. It is the designation of
Satan as having been created as a *cherub* (plural, *cherubim*).

Let's have another look at this truth, as expressed in Ezekiel 28:

> **You were in Eden, the garden of God**.... You were anointed as
> a *guardian cherub*.... Through your widespread trade you were
> filled with violence, and you sinned. So I drove you in disgrace
> from the mount of God, **and I expelled you,** *guardian cherub*.
> (Ezekiel 28:13–14, 16; emphasis added)

The word "cherub" or "cherubim" is used ninety-one times in Scripture, beginning in Genesis 3, in the account of the Garden of Eden.[165]

> After he drove the man out, he placed on the east side of the
> Garden of Eden cherubim and a flaming sword flashing back
> and forth to guard the way to the tree of life. (Genesis 3:24)

The complexity of the meaning of the name and the exact description of a cherub have been a matter of scholarly discussion for thousands
of years. According to some, the unique Hebrew word *cherub* most likely
means "Mighty One."[166]

Both Ezekiel and John's Book of Revelation give us descriptions of this category of exalted angelic beings. First, let's look at what Ezekiel initially calls "the living creatures."

> I looked, and I saw a windstorm coming out of the north—an immense cloud with flashing lightning and surrounded by brilliant light. The center of the fire looked like glowing metal, and in the fire was *what looked like four living creatures.* In appearance their form was human, but *each of them had four faces and four wings.* Their legs were straight; their feet were like those of a calf and gleamed like burnished bronze. *Under their wings on their four sides they had human hands.* All four of them had faces and wings, and the wings of one touched the wings of another. Each one went straight ahead; they did not turn as they moved. (Ezekiel 1:4–9; emphasis added)

Then, in chapter 10, Ezekiel states that the "living creatures" he described back in chapter 1 are in fact the *cherubim* of God.

> **Each of the cherubim had four faces:** One face was that of a cherub, the second the face of a human being, the third the face of a lion, and the fourth the face of an eagle. Then the cherubim rose upward. *These were the living creatures I had seen by the Kebar River.* (Ezekiel 10:14–15; emphasis added)

The *Benson Commentary* entry referencing Ezekiel 28:14–15 sheds more light on the matter, telling us that the cherub holds one of the most important positions of authority among God's heavenly host:

> The words allude to the **high advancement of Satan in heaven** before his fall, where he was placed in one of the **highest orders of angels,** such as were *nearest in attending upon the Divine Majesty.*[167] (Emphasis added)

This "highest order" that "attend upon the Divine Majesty" is shown to us again in the Book of Revelation through John's majestic vision of the throne room of God.

> He went and took the scroll from the right hand of him who sat on the throne. And when he had taken it, *the four living creatures* and the twenty-four elders fell down before the Lamb.... Then I looked and heard the voice of many angels, numbering thousands upon thousands, and ten thousand times ten thousand. They encircled the throne *and the living creatures* and the elders. (Revelation 5:7–9, 11; emphasis added)

Suffice it to say, a cherub is not the fat-little-baby angelic being as often depicted. Those fanciful caricatures are derived from Roman and Greek mythology, and they aren't even close to representing what the Bible describes.[168] Once again, Satan is trying to mask who he is, causing witnessing Christians and the biblical message to be mocked.

## THE ROYAL REGENT

Ezekiel 28 additionally informs us that not only was Satan initially placed in the Garden of Eden as *perfect*——but he was also assigned a specific purpose: to be its *guardian*—i.e., a holy and benevolent warden. He was appointed to be God's royal regent, His representative to the newly created human race. And he had come straight from God's holy mountain of assembly, the divine council of God.[169]

*The Expositor's Bible Commentary:*

> *The cherub is the warden* of the "holy mountain of God," and no doubt also *the symbol and bearer of the divine glory*.[170] (Emphasis added)

*The Pulpit Commentary*:

The splendor-of the King of Tyre of Ezekiel 28 had suggested the idea of Eden the garden of God. **This, in its turn, led on to that of the cherub that *was the warder of that garden*** (Genesis 3:24).[171] (Emphasis added)

Satan's assignment to guard the Garden of Eden is a huge clue indicating that the encounter between Satan and humanity's first couple in Genesis 3 most likely wasn't the first one.

Again, we see yet another example of what Satan doesn't want the modern church to know. The enemy steers us away from God's description of him as one of the mighty cherubim, yet *a despicably fallen one*. The evil one doesn't want us to focus on his miserably disgraced nature and his treasonous character.

He would much prefer us to identify him as a coloring-book character, like a walking, talking snake, a mythological dragon, a cartoon-like monster, or even a fat baby angel floating on a cloud. In so doing, Satan knows we're less apt to proclaim the plain truth of his vile nature and his soon-coming, horrendous demise.

But—there's still more.

For example, why in the world does Isaiah describe Satan as "Lucifer"?

The answer probably isn't what you're thinking now.

# HOWL!

**26**

*This trait is one of Satan's most hideous lying wonders.*

What you are getting ready to see is one of the most frequently disguised truths concerning Satan's actual identity and character.

However, it is only veiled because it hides behind the smokescreen of certain language and translation misunderstandings. It is a description of Satan's character that God Himself hung upon the evil one. Yet, for hundreds of years, the church has been largely deceived about the truth of this identification.

Let's straighten all that out.

## LUCIFER

English translations of the Old Testament have come to us only after they were first written in Hebrew. Also, the Hebrew versions might have been first translated into Greek and/or Latin, then into English. This process can make for some confusion, as in the case of a phrase found in Isaiah 14.

We've already seen that numerous scholars view Isaiah 14:12–17 as a compound reference to Satan and his treasonous fall from heaven. But, the problem lies in the very first verse of that passage:

How art thou fallen from heaven, *O Lucifer*, son of the morning! (Isaiah 14:12, KJV; emphasis added)

In a list of the twenty-eight most popular modern scholarly translations, *nine times* the designation of this "fallen one" is Lucifer.

However, within the remainder of the translations, we find the following alternative designations: "morning star," "shining star," "day star," "shining morning star," "bright morning star," and the "shining one." Why the discrepancy?

## NOT A NAME

The problem is that in the nine translations that use "Lucifer," it is always capitalized, suggesting that it is a proper noun—an alternative "name" for Satan.

But the word "Lucifer" isn't used as a name for Satan anywhere else in the Bible. Also, the term is not in the original Hebrew text of Isaiah 14. That's because *lucifer* is a Latin word that made its way into later Greek and English translations of the Hebrew text simply by being restated in its literal, Latin form.

However, it flatly is not a name for Satan. The Latin *lucifer* is a *description* of the evil one. And, this description isn't always used as a flattering one, as you will discover once we uncover the genuine word meanings and usages.

## HELEL AND HALAL

The original Hebrew word *helel*, which is actually used in the text, is a noun distinctly employed as an *attribute* of the one of whom it speaks. It is not meant to be a proper name. *Helel* translates to "the shining one."[172]

But there's more. The word *helel* comes from the Hebrew verb *halal*.[173]

*Keil & Delitzsch Commentary on the Old Testament:*

[*Helel*] … from *hâlal*, to shine, resolved from *Hillel* [Heb. to praise][174]

The relationship between the Hebrew words *helel* and *halal* would be similar to our English word "swimmer" and its verb form "to swim."

One word, the noun, defines something *about* a person: He is a *swimmer.* The other word, the verb, speaks of the specific *action* of that person: He loves *to swim.* But the person's name is not "Swimmer," nor is it "To Swim."

In the same manner, we can consider *helel* and *halal. Helel,* the noun, defines something about Satan: Satan is "the shining one." *Halal,* the verb, simply means to shine and refers to the action of Satan: Satan loves to shine.

The relationship between *helel* and *halal* is important because of the context of the entire Isaiah 14:12–17 passage. Satan is not being given a proper name; rather, he is being *described*…and not in a positive manner at all.

## CRY OUT!

Here's the most helpful fact in determining what we are dealing with in this verse. The verb form *halal* is also the word from which we derive the term "hallelujah." That word translates to "praise unto the Lord." In its most literal sense, we are proclaiming, "Cry out! Shine the light of praise upon the Lord!"

*Barnes' Notes on the Bible:*

Lucifer "Day-star" (he yle l, **from hâlal, "to shine"). The word in Hebrew occurs** *as a noun* **nowhere else.** In two other places Ezekiel 21:12; Zechariah 11:2, it is **used as a verb in the impera-**

tive mood of Hiphil, and *is translated "howl"* from the verb *yālal,* "to howl" or "cry."[175] (Emphasis and parentheses added)

*Clarke's Commentary on the Bible* gives us a translation that's probably closest to its intended meaning:

*Heilel,* **which we translate Lucifer,** comes from *yalal,* yell, howl, or shriek, *and should be translated, "Howl, son of the morning;"* · and so the Syriac [translation] has understood it.[176] (Emphasis and brackets added)

## SHINING A LIGHT ON HIMSELF

As we draw ever closer to the genuine meaning of this verse, consider the following. In its distinctly negative sense, which would be determined by context, *halal* can also mean to "shine one's own light" or "to boast. Especially as in an extremely arrogant manner."[177]

Used in that fashion, *helel* would be seen as a negative description of a person. For example, the word might speak of a "boastful one," someone who shines the light on his or her own accomplishments and strengths.

Forgive me for being a bit technical in this chapter. However, by now, you've probably seen the importance of what we've discovered. In Isaiah 14, the context is that Satan is boasting about how he will "take" the throne of God. In fact, five different times, Satan pronounces that he *will* ascend to the highest place in Heaven. He is taunting Yahweh!

## THE BRAGGART

It's now plain to see. Yahweh is calling Satan the "shining one" in the sense of saying something like, "You are a despicable, arrogant, prideful, and lying braggart! You, who *howls* to the heavens, shaking your fist in *my* face—beaming your arrogance throughout the unseen realm and proclaiming that *you* will be its rightful ruler!"

Truly, the Hebrew designation *helel* is the perfect one to use! While describing Satan's perverted and fallen nature, Isaiah 14:12 also becomes a brilliant play on words. Satan was indeed originally created in light and splendor! He formerly was the "shining one" in the most positive sense of the phrase.

Once again, back in Ezekiel 28, we find the truth.

Your heart became proud on account of your beauty, and you corrupted your wisdom *because of your splendor.* (Ezekiel 28:17; emphasis added)

The word "splendor" in Hebrew is *yiphah,* which means "brightness."[178] It is directly related to the Hebrew verb form *yapha,* meaning "to shine out or forth, to send out beams, to cause to shine."[179]

## THE MASK OF "LIGHT"

This trait is one of Satan's most hideous lying wonders. It is a mask of feigned innocence. With a childlike grin and a twinkling of the eye, he puts his finger in his mouth, lips pooched out, and seems to say, "*Who? Me? But…look how shiny and pretty I am. I am an angel of light!*"

No. His name is not Lucifer. He is no longer the "shining one" of heaven. And he certainly is not pretty. He is not an angel of light either; although Scripture clearly states that he still prefers to masquerade as one.

Satan is the cosmic braggart. He is so full of himself that he will stop at nothing to destroy everything in his path to get to the throne of God. And I mean everything: You. Me. Nations. Homes. Families. Marriages.

Children. Babies in the womb. Loved ones and friends. The church. *Everything*.

However, there's still something else about this *lucifer* we must explore, something that might explain his subtle but hideous exploitations, planted deep within today's institutional church.

# THE MUSIC MAN | 27

*It is a distinct possibility that Satan led Heaven's worship before his fall.*

A number of scholars and biblical researchers have put forth the thought that Satan may have indeed been the royal worship leader among the heavenly host. The Bible doesn't pointedly make this declaration, but there is enough evidence in the context to prompt us to investigate further.

Consider the suggestion that angels worship God in perpetuity.[180] It is a distinct possibility that Satan led that worship, before his fall.

First, have a close look at Psalm 150. Take special note of the highlighted portions indicating words and phrases found in other passages that are related directly or indirectly to Satan's pre-fallen state:

*Praise the Lord* [Hebrew, *Hallelujah*]. Praise God in his sanctuary; *praise him in his mighty heavens.* Praise him for his acts of power; praise him for his surpassing greatness. Praise him with the sounding of the trumpet, *praise him with the harp* and lyre, *praise him with timbrel* and dancing, *praise him with the* strings and *pipe*, praise him with the clash of cymbals, praise him with resounding cymbals. Let everything that has breath praise the Lord. Praise the Lord. (Psalm 150; emphasis and brackets added)

Now, look at Ezekiel 28 again.

**Thou hast been in Eden the garden of God**; every precious stone was thy covering, the sardius, topaz, and the diamond, the beryl, the onyx, and the jasper, the sapphire, the emerald, and the carbuncle, and gold: **the workmanship** *of thy tabrets* [tambourines] *and of thy pipes* **was prepared in thee in the day that thou wast created.** (Ezekiel 28:13, KJV; emphasis and brackets added)

The Hebrew word for "tabrets" is *toph*—the same word used in Psalm 150 and translated as "timbrel." It most correctly translates to our English word "tambourine" or some other percussion-type instrument. This is the *only meaning*[181] of this Hebrew word, no matter how it's colored by various English translations.

## SETTINGS AND SOCKETS

A few Bible translations indicate that Ezekiel 28:13 refers to something along the lines of "settings and sockets" or "mountings and settings"—i.e., a jeweler's terminology rather than the lingo of musical instruments.

And the gold, the workmanship of your *settings and sockets*, was in you. On the day that you were created they were prepared. (Ezekiel 28:13, NAS 1977; emphasis added)

However, out of twenty-eight of the most popular Bible translations, twenty-four translate the text to indicate musical instruments. So, obviously, there is some scholastic disparity.[182]

Note the highlighted words in the following examples of those who see the "instruments" rather than a jeweler's settings. (Note: See the endnotes for a list of nine other commentary entries that present this same position.)[183]

Dr. John McArthur—*Grace to You*:

[Satan is] identified as the covering cherub, in verse 14 [of Ezekiel 28], "...the cherubim, the **specially singled out angels
involved in worship**, according to Isaiah. It may be that the
anointed cherub—of all the cherubs who were given to worship,
the anointed one, and *the singled out one was heaven's praise
leader.*[184] (Emphasis and brackets added)

*Guzik Bible Commentary—Enduring Word*:

The workmanship of your *timbrels and pipes* was prepared for
you: Before his fall, **Satan had a significant role in the** *music of
heaven*, **surrounding God's throne.**[185] (Emphasis added)

*Christian Apologetics and Research Ministry* (CARM):

It is quite possible that...**Satan, was originally an angel whose
purpose was to be involved in the worship of God.... The
case can be made from Ezekiel 28.** In the Hebrew, the word
for "settings" is *toph* which means timbrel, which is *a musical
instrument*. Likewise, the Hebrew word for "sockets" is *neqeb*
and means "pipes, grove, hole."[186] (Emphasis added)

*Commentary Critical and Explanatory on the Whole Bible -Jamieson,
Fausset, and Brown Commentary*:

**Tabrets—***tambourines*. **Pipes**—literally, "**holes**" in *musical
pipes or flutes*. Created—that is, in the day of thine accession to
the throne. **Tambourines and all the marks of joy were ready
prepared** for thee ("in thee," that is, "with and for thee").[187]
(Emphasis added)

*Keil & Delitzsch Commentary on the Old Testament*:

The meaning timbrels, **tambourines**, is **well established**, and in 1 Samuel 10:5 and Isaiah 5:12 *flutes are mentioned* along *with the timbrels.*[188] (Emphasis added)

Here's the Carl Gallups interpretation: Since the Hebrew word *toph* always means a timbrel, a tambourine, or a percussion instrument, and since the Hebrew word *neqeb* is most comfortably translated as "a setting for gem stones," why can't the two be directly relating to each other?

It seems the most natural and literal translation would be that the guardian cherub of Ezekiel 28 was entrusted with a magnificent, gem-studded percussion instrument, one used for leading the praise and worship of his Creator. This translation also fits with Psalm 150, describing the use of tambourines in worship leadership and connected with praise and worship-dance.

## ANOTHER HINT FROM ISAIAH

As Dr. David Guzik's *Enduring Word Commentary* correctly indicates, even Isaiah 14, another compound prophecy that proves to be ultimately concerned with Satan also mentions the musical instruments associated with his previous station in Heaven. Here is that verse:

All your pomp has been brought down to the grave, along with *the noise of your harps.* (Isaiah 14:11; emphasis added)

*Guzik Bible Commentary* explains:

Isaiah 14:11 also makes mention of the stringed *instruments associated with Satan* before his fall. Some take this to say that *Satan was the "worship leader" in heaven* because there *are songs of worship mentioned* in the Bible. (Job 38:7; Revelation 5:9, 14:3, and 15:3; emphasis added)[189]

# THE THRONE ROOM IN HEAVEN

Another apparent connection to the potential pre-fall role of Satan's worship-leadership position comes with the imagery of the living creatures in the fifth chapter of Revelation:

> He went and took the scroll from the right hand of him who sat on the throne. And when he had taken it, *the four living creatures* and **the twenty-four elders** fell down before the Lamb. *Each one had a harp* and they were holding golden bowls full of incense, which are the prayers of God's people. *And they sang a new song.* (Revelation 5:7–9; emphasis added)

For some grammatically unexplainable reason, a number of the classical commentators attempt to explicate that the living creatures of Revelation 5 could *not have been* playing the harps—only the "elders," so they claim.

However, no grammatical structure in the Greek translation of this verse demands that the harps are to be *only in the hands of the elders.*

The *Greek Testament Critical Exegetical Commentary* addresses this odd interpretation found in so many of the commentaries:

> [Some say that the playing of harps] apparently applies only to the elders: *not for any grammatical reason*, but on account of the symbolism.[190] (Emphasis and brackets added)

Consequently, a number of commentators summarily assert that the living creatures weren't playing the harps, even though the text clearly says they were. Some try to make the ludicrous case that it would be "impossible" for these creatures to even "hold a harp." However, the *Cambridge Greek Testament* flatly debunks these peculiar theories:

> If we attempt to carry the image into detail it is obvious that it was as impossible for the elders literally to play their harps and hold their bowls as it would be to speak while holding a two-edged sword in the mouth; up to a certain point *it is not more difficult to picture the Living Creatures holding harps* than the Lamb taking the Book and breaking the seals.[191] (Emphasis added)

Dr. Harry A. Ironside, a friend and contemporary of evangelist Billy Sunday and Dr. Dwight L. Moody, also addressed the proper interpretation of this passage in his *Ironside's Notes on Selected Books*:

> The moment that the Lamb takes the book, **the four living ones and the four and twenty elders** fall down before Him. *Every one of them has harps* and golden bowls full of odors [incense], which are the prayers of saints.[192] (Emphasis and brackets added)

## THE BOTTOM LINE

Thus far, we've uncovered several of Satan's most prominent and devastating charades. First, there is the mask of the "temple of God," whereby Satan keeps the outward institutional church in a state of spiritual stupor while he infiltrates it and corrupts it to the very core. It seems to be a sleight-of-hand act. *Look for that…while I'm really doing this.*

Then, there are the masks of long-established caricatures: a walking, talking snake, a flying dragon, impish creatures with pitchforks—cartoon-like representations of Satan and the demonic realm. And we certainly must not forget the misnomer "Lucifer"—"the shining, bragging, obnoxious one."

And now, we discover that Satan might have been a trusted worship leader in the heavenly realm. That would surely explain a few more things.

However, there are still several other convincing disguises Satan uses. And, in these last days, it appears he is using them with increasing frequency. Perhaps—as many prophecy watchers are coming to believe—we are now in the beginning stages of Satan's attempt to "deceive even the very elect…if that were possible."

# PART V

# PERSPECTIVE

For there shall arise false Christs, and false prophets, and shall
shew great signs and wonders; insomuch that, if it were possible,
they shall deceive the very elect.

~MATTHEW 24:24, KJV

# WHO TURNED OUT THE LIGHTS?

*The Bible has not hidden the truth from this fallen world.*

**28**

There is a burgeoning, worldwide phenomenon of unmitigated anxiety. Billions around the planet believe something is about to snap. They can't quite place their finger on the exact mechanism that might cause the anticipated rupture; nonetheless, they truly believe it's on the way.

In many different ways, all appear to express the same concern: *Someone, or something, has drastically dimmed the light.* What light is actually left appears to be fading to black with unprecedented speed.

Some are convinced the global shift will take place through a disastrous incursion of cataclysmic "climate change." A 2019 *Live Science* article emphasizes this position, and even attempts to set a date for it:

> **There's a good chance society could collapse as soon as 2050** if serious mitigation actions aren't taken in the next decade....
> At this point, the world's **ice sheets vanish**; brutal **droughts kill many of the** trees in the Amazon rainforest (removing one of the world's largest carbon offsets); and *the planet plunges into a feedback loop* of ever-hotter, **ever-deadlier conditions.**
>
> "Thirty-five percent of the global land area, and *55 percent of the global population,* are subject to more than 20 days a year of **lethal heat** conditions, **beyond the threshold of human survivability,**" the authors hypothesized.

**Meanwhile, droughts, floods and wildfires regularly ravage the land.** Nearly **one-third of the world's land surface turns to desert.** *Entire ecosystems collapse.*[193] (Emphasis added)

Also in 2019, *Newsweek* expressed the worldwide fear that we may already be in the edges of a soon-coming World War III:

**So far, history recounts two mass conflicts categorized as world wars,** both of which involved two major multinational factions battling it out on multiple continents and the latter of which resulted in what was likely **the most widespread man made death and destruction the planet has ever known. Both were sparked by a series of destabilizing events** that followed mounting tensions and successive failures in diplomacy.

**The fallout of World War I and World War II left only two remaining superpowers**—the United States and the Soviet Union—mounting tensions between the two countries once again risk driving rival proxy wars in the 21st century. **Officials current and former from both sides have even suggested that the situation today was worse as communication channels collapsed.**[194] (Emphasis added)

The UK publication, *Independent*, echoed the World War III forecasts:

There are **three key fronts** emerging that make **the prospect of a third global conflict alarmingly conceivable….**

**The first** is the Europe-Russia front with a new cold war triggered by the Ukrainian conflict. **The second** is the Middle East cauldron centered around Isis and the Syrian war. **The third** is the Asia-Pacific front with a face-off between the United States and China.[195] (Emphasis added)

## SUMMONING THE DEMON

How about the world of artificial intelligence (AI)? Are our technologi
cal advancements aimed at the ultimate goal of creating real-time artificial robotic learning going to be our ruination? An ever-growing pool of
famous tech experts believe so.

In a 2019 piece put out by *CBInsights*—a technology and research
company with financial backing from the National Science Foundation—declared in its headline, "How AI Will Go Out of Control
According to 52 Experts."

Those experts, ranging from the late Stephen Hawking to the
renowned technology writer James Vincent, weighed in on the "destructive" threat that AI poses to the future of humanity. The article began by
referring to our hyper-rapid growth in AI technologies as "summoning
the demon." This appears to be a fitting description, in light of what
we've uncovered thus far, wouldn't you agree?

"Summoning the demon." "The new tools of our oppression."
"Children playing with a bomb." These are just a few ways the
world's top researchers and industry leaders have described the
threat that artificial intelligence poses to mankind. There's no
way around it—artificial intelligence is changing human civilization, from how we work to how we travel to how we enforce
laws…. As AI technology advances and seeps deeper into our
daily lives, its potential to create dangerous situations is becoming more apparent.[196]

## PLAGUES AND PESTILENCE

Then there's always the outpouring of plagues and pestilences. The
*Atlantic* expressed the fears of billions of people across the globe with
these alarming words:

*The Next Plague Is Coming.* The epidemics of the early 21st century revealed **a world unprepared**, even as the **risks continue** to multiply. *Much worse is coming.*[197] (Emphasis added)

Yes, indeed. Even the Word of God assures us that much worse is on its way. Jesus warned that the coming dark days that humanity innately dreads will indeed arrive.

- "As long as it is day, we must do the works of him who sent me. *Night is coming*, when *no one can work*. While I am in the world, I am the light of the world" (John 9:4–5; emphasis added).
- "And there shall be signs in the sun, and in the moon, and in the stars; and **upon the earth distress of nations, with perplexity;** the sea and the waves roaring; **Men's hearts failing them for fear, and for looking after those things which are coming on the earth: for the powers of heaven shall be shaken**" (Luke 21:25–26, KJV; emphasis added).

## GET RID OF BILLIONS

Let's not forget the following ever-present threat hanging over the heads of the world's population. In September 2019, *World Watch Institute* updated its most current research under the headline, "Global Population Reduction: Confronting the Inevitable." Have a look at some of the opening words of this organization's agenda:

Looking past the near-term concerns that have plagued population policy at the political level, it **is increasingly apparent that the long-term sustainability of civilization will require not just a leveling-off** of human numbers as projected over the coming half-century, *but a colossal reduction in both population and consumption.*

**The Earth's long-term sustainable human carrying capacity**, at what might be defined as an "adequate" to "moderately comfortable" developed world standard of living, **may not be much greater than 2 to 3 billion.**

It is past time to think boldly about the midrange future and to **consider alternatives that go beyond** merely slowing or stopping the growth of global population

Obviously, a demographic change of this magnitude will **require a major reorientation of human thought, values,** expectations, and lifestyles.[198] (Emphasis added)

So, what will be the ultimate end of us all?

Will it really be global warming or climate change? Ecological devastation? Human population reduction? Artificial intelligence run amok? Pestilence, disease, and plagues? All of it? Some of it? None of it? Something else entirely?

The bottom line is this: The Bible has not hidden the truth from this fallen world. Like it or not, there is coming a generation of humanity that will see and experience something cataclysmic—so much so that humanity will reel in pandemonium.

However, before those days bloom into reality, Satan will first attempt to lull the world into a spiritual stupor.

Many believe he will accomplish it by flooding the world with fakery.

What do you think? Is our current world largely a *fake* one?

# IT'S A FAKE-FAKE WORLD

**29**

Do you ever get the feeling that practically everything about our world and our own personal earthly life is bogus?

If you do, you're not alone. It seems a sizable number of everyday folks, as well as a number of scientists and philosophers, have the same nagging feeling. Their posts, papers, books, and articles are all over the Internet.

## LET'S CHAT

As an anecdotal example of this phenomenon, consider the following musings of a chatboard user who, at the time of the post, was identified as *u/bringmedamuffin*. The poster claimed to be married, with a child, and serving in the US military. The person also asserted, "I'm not religious at all."

> Now more than ever, I have **this persistent feeling** inside.…
> *Everything feels fake and foreign (almost like everything is a lie),*
> the media, politics, war, just day to day life. Sometimes I stop
> to look around and feel like I am surrounded by robotic sheep.
> I feel like *everything is a lie and an illusion.* I can't shake *this*
> *feeling of there being something way more than what we know*
> *or can sense.*

**Why do I feel like everything is an illusion or a lie?** Why do
*I have this burning desire to know the truth* and experience real
reality? Am I alone?[200] (Emphasis added)

Regardless of *u/bringmedamuffin's* potential underlying issues, a
number of other people across the globe are offering these same kinds of
observations and concerns. The point is, this world is filled with fakery,
illusions, and deceit. It doesn't surprise me that people are beginning to
sense it in a very real way—perhaps more than ever before. Again, Satan
is the "prince of this world"; how else would one expect his world to
"feel?"

## COUNTERFEITS

I'm going to present a few of the everyday elements of our lives that have
a healthy dose of fakery at their core. Scan through the list and see if you
can think of other items to add.

For example, our current fallen "shadow world" is filled with fake
intelligence (AI), fake people (robots), and fake security (ubiquitous spy
technology). Then there's fake sex (porn), fake love (unbridled lust), a
planet full of fake religions, fake churches, fake denominations, and fake
preachers. Heck, we even gulp down fake foods—billions of us, every
single day, with hardly a thought (GMOs, artificial additives, etc.).

But we're not finished. There are fake robotic priests,[201] fake marriages, fraudulent genders, and tons of *fake science* (pseudoscience):[202]
man-made global warming, accidental-explosion-to-humanity "evolution," human embryos not being human lives, males being "turned
into" females (and vice versa), and so forth. Of course, fake science then
leads to a world full of fraudulent knowledge and so-called truth.

Some people are even earning fake degrees in areas of fake science,
then teaching this fake knowledge to others in centers where fake education is promoted as the genuine article. They do this so that even more

people can earn the same fake degrees! Many agree that we're already many miles down the road of abject fakery.

But there's still more. Wouldn't combining the DNA of humans with that of various other animal species (chimera-tech), also fit this category of our fake world?[203] Sure it does! In fact, it ranks right up there with the "days of Noah" and the corruption of all flesh.

What about the fake biotech *birth method* that is currently being developed? I'm speaking of the laboratory manufacturing human embryos using skin stem cells, hoping to bypass the true human birth process altogether.[204] Or, what about the newest technology of "genetically modifying people," beginning in the womb?[205]

Another disturbing technology upon us is the field of "deepfake" media applications. This is a nightmare scenario wherein video and audio clips can be created to look and sound like *anyone* we wish to mimic—or to put fake words into their fake mouths. Furthermore, the claim is that this new technology might soon be utterly impossible to distinguish from reality. *Good grief!* What could go wrong with *that*?[206]

But, we're still not finished. And remember, this is just my own short list.

We haven't yet mentioned fake news, fake documents, fake currency, and fake identities. What about fake and manipulated elections? That used to be something relegated only to third-world nations. Apparently, not anymore! And, how do we not consider in this list what we now know about fake governments—Deep-State and shadow governments?

What about fake medicines? How about fake water,[207] fake economies, fake free markets, fake justice systems, and fake free-trade agreements, not to mention fake morality, along with fake spirituality?

Dare I mention fake history taught to our children every day in a mostly fake government-education system? How about the fake war on terror or the fake war on drugs?

Many insist that most of the "social media" genre also qualifies as fake—at least in respect to what it is supposed to represent in our lives. For example, social media is not genuine *media*. Nor is it very *social*. In

fact, it is often downright *antisocial,* and holds at least correlational connections to horrendous societal ills.[208] Therefore, the whole ruse of social
media could also fall into the category of fake friends and fake human
relationships, wouldn't you agree?

If you're beginning to think that I'm sensationalizing the idea of our
fake world and the dangers thereof, look at excerpts from a July 2019
article published by the otherwise hard-left *Politico.*

The article is titled "How Fake News Could Lead to Real War."

Who really bombed the oil tankers in the Gulf of Oman three
weeks ago...?

*Here's a confession* from *two former senior government officials:* "For days after the attacks, *we weren't sure.* Both of us
believed in all sincerity there **was a good chance** these actions were
part of *a false flag operation,* an **effort by outsiders to trigger a
war** between the United States and Iran. *Even the film* of Irani-
ans hauling in an unexploded limpet mine from near the side of
tanker, we reasoned, **might be a fabrication**—*deep fake footage*....

**For the two of us,** with 30 years of government service and
almost 20 more as think tankers between us, **this was shocking....** *We weren't sure whether to believe our government.*

**Imagine waking up one morning and catching yourself
thinking** that...perhaps the Sandy Hook shooting was faked
or that the 9/11 attacks were really an inside job?

**But the whole unsettling episode opened our eyes to a
deeply troubling reality:** The current *fake news epidemic* isn't
just shaking up U.S. politics, it *might end up causing a war,* or
just as consequentially, *impeding a national response* to a genuine threat."[209] (Emphasis added)

I could go on and on, yet, I think I hear you begging me to stop.
However, the "idea" gets even larger than you might think. Even the
science community is getting on board with the notion of cosmic fakery.

# IT'S A FAKE, FAKE UNIVERSE?

*Our Creator has been revealing these truths to us
since Adam drew his first breath.*

30

In case you're still thinking that I'm making too big of a deal over the fake-world idea, consider the following excerpts from a Space.com article entitled "Is Our Universe a Fake?" and published in the "Science and Astronomy" section.

> Nick Bostrom, director of the Future of Humanity Institute at Oxford University, describes a fake universe as a **"richly detailed software simulation of people**, including their historical predecessors, by a very technologically advanced civilization."
> **It's like the movie "The Matrix,"** Bostrom said, except that "instead of having brains in vats that are fed by sensory inputs from a simulator, the brains themselves would also be part of the simulation. It would be *one big computer program simulating everything,* including human brains down to neurons and synapses."[210] (Emphasis added)

Science.com isn't the only mainstream source of science and news reporting on the computer-simulation theory of life. Look at a sampling of recent headlines:

- "Are We Living in a Computer Simulation?" (*Scientific American*)[211]

- "Are We Living in a Simulated Universe? Here's What Scientists Say" (NBC News)[212]
- "Is Our World a Simulation? Why Some Scientists Say It's More Likely Than Not" (*The Guardian*)[213]
- "Even if Life Is a Computer Simulation…" (*New York Times*)[214]
- "We Might Live in a Computer Program, But it May Not Matter" (BBC)[215]
- "Are We Living in a Computer Simulation? Let's Not Find Out" (*New York Times*)[216]
- "20 Years after The Matrix…Many Scientists and Philosophers Still Think We're Living in a Simulation" (*Business Insider*)[217]

But, not all scientists are convinced that our universe is a fraud.

*Cosmos Magazine* ran a piece attempting to refute the idea of a computer-simulation universe titled, "Physicists Find We're Not Living in a Computer Simulation."

However, the end of the article had an interesting qualification. It almost sounded biblical, even though I seriously doubt that was the intention.

> *There is a caveat* **to this conclusion**: if our universe is a simulation, **there is no reason** that the laws of physics should apply outside it. In the words of Zohar Ringel, the lead author of the paper, "*Who knows what are the computing capabilities of whatever simulates us?*"[218] (Emphasis added)

The author of the article asks, "Who knows the capabilities?" He also addresses the mystery of "whatever simulates us." Yet, the Word of God has given us the genuine answers to that question all along:

- "How precious to me are your thoughts, God! *How vast is the sum* of them! *Were I to count them, they would outnumber the grains of sand*—when I awake, I am still with you" (Psalm 139:17–18; emphasis added).

- "By faith we understand that the universe was formed at God's command, so that what is seen was not made out of what was visible" (Hebrews 11:3; emphasis added).

So, without knowing it, the *Cosmos* article's caveat was correct. Our Creator does not exist within the universe. He *created* the universe! He created the "unseen" elements and the universal laws that hold it all together. He exists outside of our reality.

Therefore, the "laws of the universe" are externally fabricated constructs that enable our lives and existence to work only within our physical and current state of being. Those laws are barriers or fences. We are allowed to go so far, then no farther.

God existed before the laws; therefore, there would almost have to be *other laws* in play in the grand scheme of things that do not necessarily need to line up with our own laws of existence. And the computing capabilities of God's mind are, in fact, not even remotely graspable by our extremely limited brainpower, especially regarding understanding the totality of all "that is."

However, we are without excuse. Our Creator has been revealing these truths to us since Adam drew his first breath. We are the ones, as a society, who have rejected Him and looked for other ways to explain our existence.

About the best we've come up with so far is the accidental, cosmic-soup, fish-to-man evolution model. Or, something along the lines of the following: Preexisting intelligent beings developed us as their own twisted entertainment project, within a cosmic computer program that is merely simulating our universe of existence.

## I'M NOT BUYING IT

You've probably figured out by now that I don't buy into the "computer-simulation" theory at all. This is because my view of life is not based upon *The Truman Show*[219] or *The Matrix*[220] paradigms, or any other delusion that Satan dangles in front of our faces. I'm not biting.

My reality is based on a biblically contextual worldview. Because of my relationship with God's Word, and more importantly, my relationship with the *Living Word* of God—Jesus Christ—I know how we arrived here. I also know where we're going, and what all the fakery in which we are daily immersed is really all about. And, hopefully, so do you.

> If ye continue in my word, then are ye my disciples indeed; and ye shall know the truth, and the truth shall make you free. (John 8:31–32, KJV)

## THE FOUNDATIONAL RUSE

As we delve deeper into that Space.com article, we begin to get the sense of where all this "computer-simulation reality" tripe is headed. It's pretty easy to identify who's behind it all. Here's another excerpt from the article:

> Bostrum said, "The simulation hypothesis is…*independent of whether God exists*." While the simulation argument is "not an attempt to refute theism," he said, *it would "imply a weaker form of a creation hypothesis,"* because *the creator-simulators* "would have some of the attributes we *traditionally associate with God* in the sense that *they would have created our world*."
>
> *They* would be *superintelligent*, but *they* "wouldn't need unlimited or infinite minds." *They* could "intervene in the world, our experiential world, by manipulating the simulation. So *they* would have *some of the capabilities of omnipotence* in the sense that *they could change anything they wanted about our world*."[221] (Emphasis added)

Aha! Sounds like someone is familiar with the account of the Garden of Eden, wouldn't you say?

That article seems to carry with it the shades of *"Did God really say? You could be like us! He knows that you could be like the gods! He's keeping something from you! You could know what they know! If you would just do this one little itsy bitsy harmless thing...it could all be yours."*

Yet, the articles you just read or were given references to represent the kind of nonsense that often passes for "science" and "philosophy" in our world of *fake knowledge.* A huge chunk of humanity gobbles this stuff up, unquestioningly accepting it as "truth."

- "It prospered in everything it did, and *truth was thrown to the ground*" (Daniel 8:11; emphasis added).
- "Since what may be known about God is **plain to them,** because God has made it plain to them. **For since the creation of the world God's invisible qualities—his eternal power and divine nature—have been clearly seen, being understood from what has been made,** *so that people are without excuse.* For although they knew God, they neither glorified him as God nor gave thanks to him, but **their thinking became futile and their foolish hearts were darkened. Although they claimed to be wise, they became fools**" (Romans 1:19–22; emphasis added).
- "*The god of this age has blinded the minds of unbelievers*, so that **they cannot see** the light of the gospel that displays the glory of Christ, who is the image of God" (2 Corinthians 4:4; emphasis added).

Do you recognize the ruse?

Think about it: If there's so much fakery in our world—*and there truly is*—from where does that massive amount of counterfeit "truth" come? It certainly doesn't originate from the throne of Heaven.

Believe me. What is really happening in our world gets so much darker than what you've read about in the preceding chapters. But think of the multiple generations that have been steeped in the mire of fake information about life itself, with no real knowledge of the truth of God's Word.

Think of the young people who are being raised in the midst of our own prophetic times. Consider the institutions of education, entertainment, "science," information and communication technology, and even "the church" that have been distorted and/or completely usurped by the demonic realm. Contemplate the sheer deluge of the "doctrines of demons" that continue to pour forth upon humanity from all of these sources. And think of the younger citizens of this planet who have only known this kind of diabolical fakery—for their entire lives.

Is it any wonder that so much confusion reigns across the planet? What kind of *world-to-come* is being created by this torrent of filth and fraud? Actually, the Bible gives us that answer as well. It's all hurtling toward the kingdom reign of the *man of lawlessness*.

> *The coming of the lawless one will be in accordance with how Satan works*. He will use all sorts of displays of power through signs and wonders that serve the lie, and all the ways that wickedness deceives those who are perishing. They perish because they refused to love the truth and so be saved. For this reason God sends them a powerful delusion so that they will believe the lie and so that all will be condemned who have not believed the truth but have delighted in wickedness. (2 Thessalonians 2:9–12; emphasis added)

The deception continues to unfold before us every single day.

It commenced ages ago with a steady *drip, drip, drip*. Then it evolved into a rapidly flowing stream. Then it blossomed into a raging river.

Now it's bearing down upon us like a devastating tsunami, and much of today's church is sound asleep as it approaches.

# PART VI

# THE PRETEND GODS

I am the LORD your God…You shall have no other gods before me.

　　You shall not make for yourself an image in the form of anything in heaven above or on the earth beneath or in the waters below. You shall not bow down to them or worship them; for I, the Lord your God, am a jealous God, punishing the children for the sin of the parents to the third and fourth generation of those who hate me, but showing love to a thousand generations of those who love me and keep my commandments.

-EXODUS 20:2–6

# TEST THE SPIRITS

## 31

*They are doing the bidding of the prince of demons.*
*Their mission is to ultimately prepare the world*
*for the coming Antichrist kingdom.*

We have once again reached one of those subjects about which there is already a massive amount of material published. Again, I will not reproduce what's previously been written. Rather, in the next few chapters, I will focus on answering questions that are less frequently addressed or are often misunderstood.

The Bible counsels that we must learn to discern the spirits, especially in these last days. The elderly apostle John wrote the following to the churches of his day:

> Dear friends, **do not believe every spirit**, but *test the spirits* to *see whether they are from God*, because many false prophets have gone out into the world. (1 John 4:1–5; emphasis added)

The implication of John's warning was that through wicked men and circumstances, and behind all the thrones of power, there are demonic forces operating in the unseen realm. Those demonic powers are consistently about the business of undermining the truth of God's Word and work. They are doing it primarily by infiltrating the very core of the last-days church.

This was the truth Jesus expressed in His kingdom parables. Satan's work is like planting weeds in a wheat field or permeating an unspoiled batch of dough with yeast. John was clear: If we're not tuned into this fact, then navigate our lives merely in the flesh and only by what we can see with our physical eyes, we will be extremely susceptible to being deceived.

Because demonic principalities work in and through various thrones of earthly power as well as through individual human beings, they're able to wear many different masks. In this manner, they're masters at concealing themselves. The seriousness of this truth is no small matter. This is what makes demonic warfare so treacherous.

## REAL OR FAIRY-TALE?

When we get into the area of demonology, I know a number of folks in today's "enlightened" culture and "modern" church who balk at the notion. More than likely, you're not one of those, or you wouldn't be this far into the book. Or perhaps the more you read through these pages, the more you're becoming convinced of the reality of the unseen realm.

Let me assure you, it's real. As of this writing, I've now spent more than forty years of my life either working in criminal law enforcement or in full-time ministry as a senior pastor. I've seen, heard, and spoken to manifestations of the demonic realm, even with multiple witnesses present.

While belief in organized faith systems has greatly diminished in recent decades, belief in the paranormal perseveres. As reported in November 2019, Gallup and Harris polls showed more than 60 percent of Americans still believe in the devil, regardless of their understanding of "religion" in general.[222]

I find it fascinating, though, that the mainstream media has been quite fond of mocking those of us who accept what the Bible reveals about the demonic realm. Yet, only a couple of years back, some in the media were giddy as they reported that even the "highly educated" were now professing to *believe in demons*.

CNN published a piece titled "When Exorcists Need Help, They Call Him" which touted the work of Dr. Richard Gallagher, an Ivy League-educated, board-certified psychiatrist who teaches at Columbia University and New York Medical College.

> Fighting Satan's minions wasn't part of Gallagher's career plan while he was studying medicine at Yale. He knew about biblical accounts of demonic possession but thought they were an ancient culture's attempt to grapple with mental disorders like epilepsy. He proudly calls himself a "man of science."
>
> Yet today, Gallagher has become something else: *the go-to guy for a sprawling network of exorcists* in the United States. **He says demonic possession is real. He's seen the evidence:** victims suddenly speaking perfect Latin; sacred objects flying off shelves; people displaying "hidden knowledge" or secrets about people that they could not have possibly have known.
>
> "There was one woman who was like 90 pounds soaking wet. She threw a Lutheran deacon who was about 200 pounds across the room," he says. "That's not psychiatry. That's beyond psychiatry."
>
> Gallagher calls himself a "consultant" on demonic possessions. For the past 25 years, he has helped clergy distinguish between mental illness and what he calls "the real thing." He estimates that he's seen more cases of *possession* than any other physician in the world.[223] (Emphasis added)

In spite of their largely positive presentation on Dr. Gallagher's work with the demonic, it seemed CNN just couldn't help itself. So, the article ended with these words:

> Is Gallagher doing God's work, or does he need deliverance from his own delusions? Perhaps only God—and Satan—knows for sure.[224]

Even after this earlier article, various mainstream media sources continued, for years, to refer to Dr. Gallaher's ongoing attestation to the reality of the demonic world.[225]

## AN ANCIENT TRUTH

Think of this. In Exodus 20, within the words of the very first commandment, God warned His people: "You shall have no other gods before me." When we read that English word "gods," please understand that this is not a reference to nonexistent, make-believe entities.

In the thirty-second chapter of Deuteronomy, we're warned of the reality of what we're truly up against and why that particular commandment was the first among all the others.

> They made him jealous with **their foreign gods** and angered him with their **detestable idols**. *They sacrificed to demons*, **which are not God**—*gods* they had not known, *gods* that recently appeared. (Deuteronomy 32:16–17; emphasis added)

The *gods* about which Yahweh warns His people are therefore demonic entities. Professional posers. They pretend to be the genuine powers to which humanity must bow and worship. They're perfectly satisfied to hide behind the mask of an idol's altar, or a human's face, or the diabolical edicts of an earthly despot, or even a totem pole. They do not mind ruling from behind the dimensional curtains of humanity's thrones of power and influence. They are, after all, doing the bidding of the prince of darkness and deceit.

Apparently, the demonic have no real interest in "being seen" by humans—*as humans*. They would rather operate in the shadows and mysteries of every day human life and societal affairs. In that manner, their allurement becomes much more intoxicating to those who are interested. And for those who don't even believe in their existence in the first place: *that's all the better!*

Their ultimate mission is to prepare the world for the coming kingdom reign of the Antichrist—Satan's counterfeit kingdom—his ultimate masquerade. It's all a part of the grand illusion. This is the cosmic battle that rages around us, largely fought in the unseen realm but fleshed out in the daily affairs of humanity, just like Jesus' ministry in the region of Galilee.

## MASKS OF THE FAKE GODS

From *Matthew Poole's Commentary*, consider the entry for Deuteronomy 32:17:

> *Unto devils, i.e. unto idols,* which *the devils* brought into the world in opposition to God, in and by which *the devils oft-times manifested themselves unto men,* and gave them answers, and received their worship…. *The devils* which *inspired* them *deluded* the nations **with false pretenses that they were *a sort of lower gods.***
>
> Moses therefore *takes off this mask,* and shows the Israelites that **these *pretended gods were really devils,*** those great enemies of mankind, and therefore that it was *the height of madness* to honour or worship them.[226] (Emphasis added)

And when the ancient people of God made their sacrifices unto these so-called *gods,* the LORD of Heaven made it clear to them what it was that they were actually doing:

> They *worshiped their idols,* which became a snare to them. They **sacrificed their sons and their daughters** *to demons.* (Psalm 106:36–37; emphasis added)

The New Testament further solidifies the truth of what we're up against. There's really no room for misunderstanding. Note the emphasized words:

- "No, but the *sacrifices of pagans are offered to demons*, not to God, and I do not want you to be *participants with demons*. You cannot drink the cup of the Lord and the *cup of demons* too; you cannot have a part in both the Lord's Table and *the table of demons*" (1 Corinthians 10:20–21).
- "The Spirit clearly says that in later times some will abandon the faith and follow *deceiving spirits* and *things taught by demons*" (1 Timothy 4:1–2).
- "Put on the full armor of God, so that you can take your stand against the devil's schemes. For our struggle is *not against flesh and blood*, but *against the rulers*, against the authorities, against the *powers of this dark world* and against the spiritual *forces of evil in the heavenly realms*" (Ephesians 6:11–12).

Now that we've settled these biblical truths, let's go a little deeper.

Let's find out exactly what we're dealing with when we speak of the demonic realm.

What can they *do, and* what can they *not* do?

# FALLEN OR UNFALLEN?
# THAT IS THE QUESTION

**32**

*We observe the demonic realm to be working primarily through the subtle crafts of manipulation and supernatural influence.*

What is a demon?

This question has been debated among scholars and students of the Bible for ages. Since no single passage contains a precise definition of a demon, we have to pull together various biblical references that address the subject in order to get the clearest picture.

Again, entire encyclopedic volumes have been written on this sometimes controversial and always complex topic. Therefore, for the purpose of our study, we'll settle on a general yet biblical definition. Demons are "fallen ones." Specifically, they are fallen, heavenly entities that exercised their original freedom of choice and followed Satan's rebellion. Satan, of course, is now the ruler of that fallen spiritual dimension.[227]

But, since we're talking about demonic deceptions and Satan's most frequent modes of operation, we'll address the question that a number of Bible students frequently ask: Can Satan or his demons appear in the form of a fleshly human being in the same way that we sometimes see the "good angels" appearing in the Old and New Testaments?

# THE UNFALLEN

Let's first consider the entities from the unseen realms that can indeed appear upon the earth in the form of human beings.

More than twenty earthly interactions with angels are listed in the Gospel accounts and in the rest of the New Testament, from Gabriel appearing to Mary and another angel appearing to Peter in prison right on through to an angel appearing to John on the Isle of Patmos, preparing him to receive the scroll of Revelation. There are many more such accounts in the Old Testament as well.

We are also assured that "good angels" still appear among us today in human form.

Are not all angels ministering *spirits sent to serve* those who will inherit salvation? (Hebrews 1:14; emphasis added)

Do not forget to show hospitality to strangers, for by so doing some people *have shown hospitality to angels without knowing it.* (Hebrews 13:2; emphasis added)

*Barnes' Notes on the Bible* (Hebrews 1:14):

*What* [angels] *do now may be learned from the Scripture* account of **what they have done**—as it seems to be a fair principle of interpretation **that they are engaged in substantially** *the same employment in which they have ever been.*[228] (Emphasis added)

*Barnes' Notes on the Bible* (Hebrews 13:2):

For thereby some have *entertained angels unawares*—**Without knowing** that *they were angels*. As Abraham (Genesis 18:2 ff), and Lot did; Genesis 19.[229] (Emphasis added)

*Meyer's New Testament Commentary* (Hebrews 13:2):

The author was certainly, in connection with this statement, **thinking specially of Abraham** and Lot (Genesis 18:19).[230] (Emphasis added)

*Gill's Exposition of the Entire Bible* (Hebrews 13:2):

As Abraham, Genesis 18:1, **he knew them not to be angels *at first; they appeared as men***, and he treated them as such; ***but they were angels***, yea, ***one of them was Jehovah himself.***[231] (Emphasis added)

I've previously written about two distinct and biblically legitimate angelic encounters I've had during my ministry years. One is related in my book *Gods of Ground Zero*, and the other one is told in my book *Gods of the Final Kingdom*. In each of those cases, there were other people around. The angelic beings did not exalt themselves. They gave only glory to Yahweh, and each had a message of biblical comfort and instruction. In each case, only some people saw them—others didn't. Each appeared in undeniable human form, and neither one was at first recognized to be an angel.

In the second encounter, the angelic messenger spoke to me and revealed a piece of information only my wife and I were intimately familiar with. The angel further expanded upon what we already knew and gave me much more insight into the matter, thus comforting me, encouraging me to not give up, urging me to continue in ministry. That visit came at a critical time in my life.

I didn't ask the Lord for either of those encounters, nor will I ever seek another. I am keenly aware that there is a stated biblical danger in seeking such manifestations. The demonic realm might be all too glad to oblige.

This is why we're warned that the spirits must be "tested."

# THE FALLEN ONES | 33

*This is how we "discern the spirits."*

There appears to be a biblical divide between the fallen and unfallen angels and their abilities—or "divine allowances"—regarding whether they can appear to humans in a distinctly human form.

While there are numerous New Testament manifestations of human-like, "good" angels, we're not introduced to a single human-like *fallen one* in those same books of the Bible. Nor are we informed that a demon might even *be able* to appear as though it is in human flesh—at least, not *after* the Flood of Noah's day. Even so, we *are* assured of their reality as well as their deeply sinister power and influence over fallen humanity.[232]

For the most part, we observe the demonic realm working primarily through the subtle crafts of manipulation and supernatural influence, preying upon humanity's fallen condition and even our own self-induced choices and resulting weaknesses.

## MANIFESTATIONS

Sometimes, in the pages of the New Testament, we find demons "inhabiting" or "infesting" the body of a human being and/or that person's thought processes.

181

- "Jesus turned and **said to Peter, 'Get behind me, Satan**! You are a stumbling block to me; you do not have in mind the concerns of God, but merely human concerns'" (Matthew 16:23; emphasis added).
- "**Then Satan entered Judas**, called Iscariot, one of the Twelve" (Luke 22:3; emphasis added).
- "Then Jesus replied, 'Have I not chosen you, the Twelve? **Yet one of you is a devil!'**" (John 6:70; emphasis added).

We're also told that, in some instances, demons are the culprits behind certain mental illnesses, self-mutilation, and even superhuman strength exhibited along with the demonic infestation. This kind of possession may, in fact, involve more than one demonic spirit, and the demons might even be assigned to territorial areas referred to as "principalities."

When Jesus got out of the boat, *a man with an impure spirit came from the tombs* to meet him. This man lived in the tombs, and **no one could bind him** anymore, not even with a chain. For he had often been chained hand and foot, **but he tore the chains apart and broke the irons on his feet. No one was strong enough to subdue** him. Night and day among the tombs and in the hills he **would cry out and cut himself with stones.** Then Jesus asked him, "What is your name?" "**My name is Legion**," he replied, "**for we are many.**" And he **begged Jesus** *again and again* not to send them out of the area. (Mark 5:2–5; emphasis added)

We also see that demons can be the culprit of certain physical maladies:

- "Jesus was driving out a demon that was mute. When the demon left, the man who had been mute spoke, and the crowd was amazed" (Luke 11:14).

- "And there was a woman who for eighteen years had had a sickness caused by a spirit; and she was bent double, and could not straighten up at all" (Luke 13:11, NASB).

The Scriptures inform us that demons can inhabit or communicate with people in order to give them "demonic power or knowledge."

As we were going to the place of prayer, we were met by a slave girl who had a spirit of divination and brought her owners much gain by fortune-telling. (Acts 16:16, ESV)

We're even introduced to the possibility that demons posing as angels of light might appear in a dream or some sort of ethereal vision. They may even be able to play upon the vain imaginations of human minds.

Do not let anyone who delights in false humility and the *worship of angels* disqualify you. Such a person also goes into *great detail about what they have seen*; they are puffed up with idle notions by *their unspiritual mind.* (Colossians 2:18; emphasis added)

*Vincent's Word Studies* (Colossians 2:18):

Used here of the **false teachers** who **professed** *to see heavenly truth in visions,* and to investigate and discuss philosophically **the revelation they had received.**[233] (Emphasis added)

*Ellicott's Commentary for English Readers*:

The thought is that *Satan is ever so transforming himself.* If we are to look for any special allusion [to this fact], we may find a possible explanation in the words "*though we, or an angel from heaven,*" in Galatians 1:8.[234] (Emphasis and brackets added)

The uncovering of the truth, of "what" it is that people might think they are seeing, actually lies within the *message* the supposed demon/angel brings. If that communication is a perversion of God's Word, we can be certain that the "revelation" is demonic, regardless of whether the "visitation" is real or imagined. This is how we "discern the spirits."

> Evidently some people are throwing you into confusion and are *trying to pervert the gospel* of Christ. But *even if we or an angel from heaven should preach a gospel other than* the one we preached to you, *let them be under God's curse*! (Galatians 1:7–8; emphasis added)

The Book of Acts gives us an example of demonic possession causing violence and superhuman strength. It also portrays a demon-possessed man as the primary vehicle through which the demons might speak to other human beings.

> Some Jews who went around driving out evil spirits tried to invoke the name of the Lord Jesus *over those who were demon-possessed.* They would say, "In the name of the Jesus whom Paul preaches, I command you to come out."
> Seven sons of Sceva, a Jewish chief priest, were doing this. One day the *evil spirit answered them*, "Jesus I know, and Paul I know about, but who are you?" **Then the man who had the evil spirit** *jumped on them and overpowered* **them all**. He gave them *such a beating* that they ran out of the house naked and bleeding. (Acts 19:13–16; emphasis added)

And, believe it or not, there was once an Israeli king who attempted to conjure up a certain dead prophet. But, in order to do so, he had to arrange a visit with a witch.

*Gee.* What could go wrong with that?

# THE KING, THE WITCH, AND THE ROBE | 34

*It's amazing how the Bible can actually interpret itself, if we would only allow it to do so.*

At times, the demonic realm manifests as "familiar spirits"—that is, it works through a family line or through specific occult rituals.[235]

Often, in this role, the demonic have been known to masquerade as a deceased family member, a familiar acquaintance, or some other loved one. This type of manifestation frequently occurs in the private setting of an occult ceremony or within the context of an unwitnessed personal encounter. The apparitions are usually described as appearing in a wispy, ghostlike fashion rather than as a distinguishable human body that can be differentiated by a human-like "feel." Of course, some of these "appearances" are nothing more than abject human fakery and money-making chicanery. However, some are genuine.

Evidence and Answers is a teaching ministry specializing in Christian apologetics. The founder, Dr. Patrick Zukeran, holds a degree from Dallas Theological Seminary (ThM) and Southern Evangelical Seminary (DMin). On the topic of "familiar spirits," Dr. Zukeran's website attests:

> **The Great Masquerade**—If a person is encountering any spirit entity at all—for example, a person who is involved in the occult—*it is a demonic spirit that apparently has the ability to imitate a dead human*. There is scriptural support for the idea that Satan and his horde of *demons have the ability*

185

*to impersonate dead humans*, and they do so in order to give credence to the false religion of Spiritualism, thereby **leading millions of people astray**. We must not forget that Satan is a masterful counterfeiter.[236] (Emphasis added)

The *Expository Notes of Dr. Thomas Constable* states:

Mediums and spiritists **do not have access to the dead** but communicate *with evil spirits posing as people* who have died. That is why these spirits are called "*lying spirits*" (1 Kings 22:22; emphasis added).[237]

# THE NECROMANCER

We see a biblical example of the strictly forbidden practice of the conjuring of the dead in the account of Israel's King Saul. The ancient king sought out the occult assistance of the witch of Endor (1 Samuel 28), demanding that she "bring up" the prophet Samuel for him, so he might seek the departed prophet's advice. A ghostly figure did "arise" amidst the incantations, startling both the witch and the king. The ghost appeared to be the prophet Samuel, dressed in his well-known robe.[238]

A number of respected commentators have attempted to convey this "appearance" of Samuel as genuine. To do so, however, they also have to make this instance an "exception" to God's otherwise pointed commands about such wicked practices.[239]

However, when we read God's own words regarding this precisely defined practice, we quickly realize that what happened to King Saul was not an "exception." Rather, this instance was clearly of an evil nature, in that a demon was masquerading as Samuel.

First, have a look at God's prohibition against *anyone* participating in this occult ritual. Notice the condemnation given against those who violate the commandment. Also note that there are no stated exceptions.

When you enter the land the Lord your God is giving you, *do not* learn to imitate *the detestable ways of the nations* there. *Let no one be found among you* who sacrifices their son or daughter in the fire, *who practices divination* or sorcery, interprets omens, engages in witchcraft, or casts spells, or who is a medium or spiritist **or who consults the dead.** *Anyone* who does these things is detestable to the Lord; because of *these same detestable practices the Lord your God will drive out those nations before you.* You must be blameless before the Lord your God. (Deuteronomy 18:9–13; emphasis added)

I'd say the Bible is pretty clear, wouldn't you? And this is not the only passage issuing such weighty prohibitions. Thankfully, there are also a number of scholars who understand this truth. Following are a few examples of the proper contextual understanding of King Saul's egregious sin.

*Matthew Poole's Commentary*:

Samuel said to Saul; **as the devil appeared in Samuel's shape** and **garb, so also he speaketh in his person,** that he might **ensnare Saul,** and **encourage others to seek to him in this wicked way.** And God permits him to do so for Saul's greater condemnation and punishment.[240] (Emphasis added)

*Gill's Exposition of the Entire Bible*:

*This was not the true Samuel*; and it was *not in the power of men and devils* to disquiet [Samuel's departed soul]; **much less would [Samuel] have acknowledged that he was brought up by Saul,** by *means of a witch*, **and** *through the help of the devil.*[241] (Emphasis and brackets added)

*Lange's Commentary on the Holy Scriptures: Critical, Doctrinal, and Homiletical*:

We have no hint that Saul saw the appearance that was visible [only] to the woman… [And] According to the preceding
words: "God has left me and answers me no more," Saul cannot
regard the answer which he asks from Samuel as God's revelation and declaration; in fact there is in his words a contrasting,
or at least a distinction between the divine revelation no longer
granted him and the supernatural magic-gotten answer which
he expects from Samuel.[242] (Emphasis and brackets added)

Besides all this, God's Word has one final thing to say about this
incident:

So Saul died for his transgressions which he committed against
the LORD, even against the Word of the LORD, which he kept
not, and also for asking counsel of one that had a familiar
spirit, to enquire of it. And inquired not of the LORD: therefore
he slew him, and turned the kingdom unto David the son of
Jesse. (1 Chronicles 10:13–14; emphasis added).

For these distinctive biblical reasons, God's children are forbidden
to participate in the rituals of séances, communicating with the dead,
occult services of "worship," and the like. These *dark arts* are especially
fertile areas of demonic infestation and attachments.

This particular arena is Satan's playground of demonic infiltration.
Do not be deceived. God makes no exceptions in this matter.

# MESSENGERS OF DECEPTION | 35

*We are the first generation of humanity to be
in the midst of this prophetic occurrence.*

If we pay close attention to passages that speak of the demonic outpouring of the last days, we'll notice they speak mainly of manifesting their "presence" through the words of false prophets and false teachers. These, of course, are humans who are demonically manipulated. But they're not demons that are merely appearing in the form of humans.

- "For such men are **false apostles**, deceitful workmen, *masquerading* as apostles of Christ. And no wonder, for **Satan himself masquerades** as an angel of light. It is not surprising, then, if *his servants masquerade* as servants of righteousness" (2 Corinthians 11:13–15; emphasis added).
- "The Spirit clearly says that *in later times* some will abandon the faith and *follow deceiving spirits and things taught by demons*. Such teachings *come through* hypocritical liars, whose consciences have been seared as with a hot iron" (1 Timothy 4:1–2; emphasis added).

In other words, the demonic have the ability to inhabit people and/or to manipulate their thought processes and words. They do this so that false biblical teaching might pour forth throughout the visible church and its institutions, sending the truth of God's Word into a delusional disarray.

*Meyers' New Testament Commentary* on 2 Corinthians 11:15 affirms the summation of what Jesus spoke on the shores of Galilee in Matthew 13:

> *The kingdom of God*, is naturally that which Satan and his servants seek to counteract.[243] (Emphasis added)

*Barnes' Notes on the Bible*:

> It is not to be deemed surprising. You are not to wonder if *people of the basest, blackest character* put on the appearance of the greatest sanctity, and even become eminent *as professed preachers of righteousness*.[244] (Emphasis added)

## WOLVES IN SHEEP'S CLOTHING

As evidence of these truths in our own days, think of the men and women wearing ecclesiastical collars, badges, and titles—*all in the name of Jesus and His church*—who, at the same time, debase the very biblical definitions of marriage, sexuality, home, family, gender identity, masculinity, and femininity, as well as the sanctity of the womb and of life itself.

Additionally, consider those who profess to be teachers of the "Word of God," yet question some of its most foundational truths, such as the deity of Jesus, the inerrancy of the Bible, and the supremacy of genuine salvation being found only in the Person of Jesus Christ.

And what about those "preachers" and "teachers" who attack and call into question the existence of the prophetically returned nation of Israel? They question or outright deny Israel's biblical and historical right to even exist. All the while, they ignore prophecies declaring that Israel's return would be God's own sign to the nations of the last days—a sign that He alone is God.[245]

Jesus warned us of such teachers:

Watch out for false prophets. They come to you in sheep's cloth-ing, but inwardly they are ferocious wolves. By their fruit you will recognize them. Do people pick grapes from thorn bushes, or figs from thistles? Likewise, every good tree bears good fruit, but a bad tree bears bad fruit. A good tree cannot bear bad fruit, and a bad tree cannot bear good fruit. Every tree that does not bear good fruit is cut down and thrown into the fire. Thus, by their fruit you will recognize them. (Matthew 7:15–20)

What did Jesus say would be the tactic these false ones would employ? You got it! They would put on a *masquerade*! They are wolves, but they pretend to be sheep. This is how we will know that Satan has a grip upon them. This is one of the clearest and most present dangers for today's last-days church.

Remember, all of this is happening right *now*, smack in the middle of the rise of the age of instantaneous communication and information technologies. The demonically inspired perversions of God's Word now spread worldwide at the speed of light. We are the first generation to witness such an all-out demonic outpouring. In reality, it appears that our days are in fact the beginning of the time about which Jesus and Paul were warning.

This is how Satan's agenda moves forward—not in a human-like body of flesh and blood, but behind the veils of everyday human life. He works in the shadows. He works through the institutions presently in place and through the hearts of people who are already infested with a fallen nature, ripe for his diabolical abuse. He especially delights in working through the institutions and pulpits of the visible church. All of this is just as Jesus warned.

These truths are why the Apostle Paul so passionately cautions God's people not to look for flesh-and-blood manifestations of demons. They are much smarter than that! They work through the powers of earthly principalities and regional dominions of spiritual authority (Ephesians 6:10–12; my paraphrase).

Thus, the demonic realm remains largely hidden to the human eye. Its agents move in the unseen realm. Their primary work is to destroy. Their mission is to thoroughly denigrate the Word of God and His people until they are finally able to enthrone their own prince, the fallen one of heaven.

# PERSPECTIVE

Let me offer a word of caution and perspective.

All in all, I do not think that believers should be looking for a demon under every rock or behind every evil motive or activity, sickness, or mental ailment. That is not a healthy way to carry out the Christian life. Sometimes, evil manifests through our own depraved human condition and in the guise of our own evil desires. Practically everything we observe is in a downward spiral because of humanity's rebellion toward its Creator. Ultimately, the responsibility for the choices we make fall squarely upon our own shoulders.

Yet we must always be mindful that the demonic *are* among us, behind the veil, picking and pulling at the threads and hastening the deterioration process. They poke, they prod, searching out our weaknesses, looking for open doors of opportunity. This is one of the major themes of caution given to the New Testament church throughout the pages of Scripture. It is why we are reminded to daily put on the armor of God so we can take our stand in the midst of the onslaught (Ephesians 6:10ff).

While every malady that waltzes into the midst of our lives might not be the result of a demonic attachment or infestation, nonetheless, the battle is real.

And it is exceedingly vile and vicious.

# AN ABANDONED HOUSE

## 36

*They crossed a line that Yahweh would not permit,
and their judgment was particularly dreadful.*

The New Testament holds a vital clue as to why demonic entities apparently are unable *or are no longer allowed* to manifest themselves in physical, human-like bodies.

According to a number of reputable scholars, a passage in Jude appears to give us the essential information.

> And the angels who did not keep their positions of authority but *abandoned their proper dwelling*—these he has kept in darkness, bound with everlasting chains for judgment on the great Day. (Jude 1:6; emphasis added)

The highlighted words tell us that the presently imprisoned *fallen ones* somehow, and sometime in the primordial past, abandoned their "proper dwellings."

Other translations have the word "dwelling" translated as "abode" or "habitation." Some versions render the word as "place," as in leaving their preassigned locality of existence; they simply moved from one realm to another.[246]

So, why are there nuances of translation in this verse? Because the Greek word with which the various versions are grappling is used *only twice* in the New Testament in this form. The word is a noun, and the form used in both of those places is in the *neuter* form. That Greek word is *oikétérion* (oy-kay-tay'-ree-on).

Have a look at the definition of the word, especially noting the highlighted portion:

*Thayer's Greek Lexicon* (3613: *oikétérion*):

A dwelling-place, habitation: Jude 1:6; *of the body as the dwelling-place of the spirit, 2 Corinthians 5:2* [As it is in other distinctly Greek sources as well] (2 Macc. 11:2; 3 Macc. 2:15; (Josephus, contra Apion 1, 20, 7); Euripides, Plutarch, Cebes tab. 17).[247] (Brackets and emphasis added; parentheses in original)

Now you understand the problem.

That Greek word might sometimes mean a literal house or even a specific *locale*—a designated sphere of existence. However, *oikétérion* can also mean a physical body. As *Thayer's* attests, *oikétérion* is frequently translated to mean a literal *body* in other examples of Greek literature, including medical texts.[248]

## ONE OTHER PLACE

Most important, though, is that when the word is examined in the *only other place* it is used in the New Testament, it indicates a physical body, not a literal house or a specific locale. To some scholars, this is a huge clue regarding the proper interpretation of Jude 1:6.

That additional use of *oikétérion* is found in 2 Corinthians. Take a look at Paul's use of the word, then look at Jude's use of the word again. The highlighted words in both passages indicate the underlying original Greek word *oikétérion*:

- "For we know that if the tent that is our earthly *home* is destroyed, we have *a building* from God, *a house* not made with hands, eternal in the heavens. For in this tent we groan, longing to put on our heavenly *dwelling*" (2 Corinthians 5:1–2, ESV; emphasis added).

- "And the angels who did not keep their positions of authority but abandoned their proper *dwelling*—these he has kept in darkness, bound with everlasting chains for judgment on the great Day" (Jude 1:6; emphasis added).

Some scholars would rather translate Jude's use of *oikétérion* to mean that these uniquely punished angels had left their specific "place" of existence; namely, they merely left the *heavenly realm*.

But it seems to others to be much more likely that Jude is using the word *oikétérion* in the same manner as Paul did: as a real, physical "body." Somehow, these angels had taken upon themselves some type of human form and function. In that form and by that function, they sinned in a vile and damaging way. They crossed a line that Yahweh would not permit, and their judgment was particularly dreadful.

There are respected biblical commentators who understand Jude's use of *oikétérion* in this manner. Note that each of the following examples either directly or indirectly relates Jude's declaration to a pre-Flood passage in Genesis 6. We'll have a closer look at that passage a bit later.

*Meyer's New Testament Commentary*:

What Jude says of the angels **corresponds with the doctrine of the angels**[249] contained in the **Book of Enoch.**[250]

Jude [speaks of] **a definite class of angels**, to whom, in agreement with the Book of Enoch, **he refers Genesis 6:2.** This is correctly observed by Hofmann, Wiesinger, and Schott, with whom Brückner appears to agree.[251] (Emphasis and brackets added)

*Pulpit Commentary*:

**The sin alleged as the reason for the penalty** which the writer recalls to the minds of his readers is that they **failed to keep… their proper habitation**; by which latter clause a descent to a **different sphere** *of being* is intended.… The reference, therefore, is taken to be to the Jewish idea *that amatory passion is not limited to the creatures of earth, and that some angels, yielding to the spell of the beauty of the daughters of men* [Genesis 6], *forsook their own kingdom, and entered unto unnatural relations with them.*[252] (Emphasis and brackets added)

*Lange's Commentary on the Holy Scriptures: Critical, Doctrinal, and Homiletical:*

Their own habitation, *not heaven in general*, but *their own dwelling of light* [original bodies] assigned to them by the Creator. Their fall and guilt seem to have been the consequence of their *leaving that habitation* and arbitrarily going beyond the sphere allotted to them…

"*They made themselves at home on earth* and exchanged the power belonging to their vocation in heaven with an earthly exhibition of power *usurped for the sake of selfish sensual indulgence* [Genesis 6]."[253] (Emphasis and brackets added)

The *Cambridge Bible for Schools and Colleges* expounds on the passage in 2 Peter 2:4–5, which is considered by the majority of scholars to be speaking of the event referenced in Jude 1:6:

We may think either of a *rebellion of angels* headed by Satan… *or of the degradation of their spiritual nature by sensual lust, as in Genesis 6:2.*

Looking to the *more definite language of Jude, 2 Peter 2:6-8, where the guilt of the angels is placed on a level with that of*

*Sodom, it seems probable that the Apostle had the latter* [sexual perversion] **in his thoughts**.[254] (Emphasis and brackets added)

If you've never seen this connection or heard its contextual explanation, I can empathize with your trepidation. While I'm not dogmatic about the specific interpretation of what Jude intended, I do know that what we have laid out here makes sense, and several scholars agree. Additionally, that particular understanding becomes much more personal as we continue to explore its implications in other verses.

For example, Jesus addressed the issue of "demons and houses" on the day He delivered the first kingdom parables. He spoke those words near the shores of Galilee…where our journey began.

Do you get the sense that everything seems to keep going back to that specific day?

# THE GALILEE CONNECTION | 37

*There is no doubt Satan had access
to that knowledge.*

The neuter form of the Greek noun *oikétérion* is used only in Jude and 2 Corinthians. However, there is also an interesting use of that same Greek noun in the masculine form—*oikos*.

We heard Jesus use that word by the shores of Galilee in the opening pages of this book. He was warning the crowds of the demonic battle we face as true ambassadors for His kingdom.

Have a look at that narrative again:

> [Jesus said to them] When *an impure spirit* comes *out of a person*, it goes through arid places seeking rest and does not find it. Then it says, "I will return to the *house* [*oikos*] I left." When it arrives, it finds the *house* [*oikos*] unoccupied, swept clean and put in order. Then it goes and takes with it seven other spirits more wicked than itself, and they go in **and live** [verb form, "to dwell"—*katoikeó*] there. And the final condition *of that person* is worse than the first. (Matthew 12:43–45; emphasis and brackets added)

Here we find yet another use of the Greek word for "house" or "dwelling." And, again, metaphorically refers to a physical, human body. That body or house (*oikos*), is identified as the potential habitation of demonic spirits. In this passage, Jesus assures us that evil spirits can "come and go" from one human body to another.

Based on all we've uncovered in this matter thus far, it would appear Jude is saying that, in the pre-Flood days of Genesis, a certain genre of the angelic realm somehow "abandoned their proper, or divinely assigned, *oikétérion*." They left one bodily form and put on another— or, at least, they assumed the *appearance* of another. That new body was human-like.

The Bible doesn't give any more information than this. It doesn't describe the mechanics of such an operation, nor does it detail when or how the abandonment of their original *oikétérion* occurred, other than suggesting that it seems to have occurred before the Flood. Jude seems to be stating that this capability was well known among the angelic realm, and this knowledge was absolutely forbidden.

It also makes sense to conclude that this divine understanding was more than likely related to the "fruit" of the tree of the "knowledge of good and evil." That offer was beguilingly made to Adam and Eve by the master of deceit himself.

In Genesis 3, Adam and Eve are presented with the tantalizing ability to somehow "transform" themselves so that they, too, could possess this power, and thus *become* "like the gods" or be "like God" Himself.

There is no doubt Satan had access to that knowledge, and still does. The Bible is clear:

And no wonder! For Satan *transforms* himself into an angel of light. (2 Corinthians 11:14, NKJV; emphasis added)

And no marvel; for even Satan *fashioneth* himself into an angel of light. (2 Corinthians 11:14, ERV; emphasis added)

And no wonder, for even Satan *disguises* himself as an angel of light. (2 Corinthians 11:14, ESV; emphasis added)

*Gill's Exposition of the Entire Bible*:

Now Satan, the enemy of mankind, sometimes appears in the form of one of these [angels of light]; *as he did to Eve in the garden*, and *to Christ in the wilderness*.[255] (Emphasis and brackets added)

*Barnes' Notes on the Bible*:

We are not to expect that Satan will appear to man to be as bad as he is. He never shows himself openly to be a spirit of pure wickedness; or black and abominable in his character; or full of evil and hateful. He would thus defeat himself. It is for this reason that wicked people do not believe that there is such a being as Satan. Though continually under his influence and "led captive by him at his will," yet they neither see him nor the chains which lead them, nor are they willing to believe in the existence of the one or the other.[256] (Emphasis added)

*Ellicott's Commentary for English Readers*:

The thought is that *Satan is ever so transforming himself.* If we are to look for any special allusion [to this fact], we may find a possible explanation in the words *"though we, or an angel from heaven,"* in Galatians 1:8.[257] (Emphasis added, brackets added)

The Greek word for Satan's "transforming" of himself is *metaschématizó*, a straightforward term that doesn't leave much room for translation variations.

*Thayer's Greek Lexicon*:

To transform oneself *into someone*, to assume one's appearance, 2 Corinthians 11:13f; so as to have the *appearance of someone*

[else], 2 Corinthians 11:15…. As expressing "transition but no absolute solution of continuity," **the *spiritual body being developed from the natural*, as the butterfly from the caterpillar.**[258] (Emphasis and brackets added)

*Strong's Concordance*:

**To *change the outward appearance*** (the dress, the form of presentment) of something, *transfigure*.[259] (Emphasis added)

For the angels that disobeyed Heaven's decree regarding the malevolent use of this divine knowledge, God summarily imprisoned them.

Now, let's have a quick look at how Jude's declaration ties directly to Genesis 6—the days just before Noah's Flood.

# THE GENESIS 6 CONNECTION  38

*The Hebrew term* bene elohim *always means
"created, divine beings from the heavenly realm."*

As we've seen, to a number of respected biblical scholars, it is apparent that Jude 1:6 ties the sin of these specific angels directly to what happened in Genesis 6:4.[260]

Note the highlighted portions of that passage, as the *International Standard Version* renders it:

> The Nephilim were on the earth at that time (and also immediately afterward), **when those *divine beings* were having *sexual relations* with those human women**, who gave birth to children for them. These children became the heroes and legendary figures of ancient times. (Genesis 6:4, ISV; emphasis added)

Among the most-referenced modern English translations of that verse, the *Contemporary English Version* and the *Good News Translation*, along with the *International Standard Version*, state that certain rebellious divine beings involved themselves in this boundary-breaking interrelationship.[261]

Even the scholastically revered Greek translation of the Hebrew Scriptures, the Septuagint, interprets the "divine beings" as "angels" that came unto the daughters of men.[262] Other modern translations, however, have it as "the sons of God," preferring only to indicate in the English what the Hebrew says in its literal rendering (*bene elohim*).

# SONS OF GOD

Here's the crux: The Hebrew term *bene elohim* always means "created, divine beings from the heavenly realm." In the handful of places in the Old Testament where this phrase is used, it *never* indicates human men. Have a closer look at this truth, as it is stated by both modern and classical biblical scholars.

*The Guzik Bible Commentary*:

**The sons of God** saw the daughters of men: It is more accurate to see **the sons of God as either demons** (angels in rebellion against God) or **uniquely demon-possessed men**, and the daughters of men as human women.... The phrase *"sons of God" clearly refers to angelic creatures* when it is used the three other times in the Old Testament (Job 1:6, 2:1, and 38:7). *The translators of the Septuagint translated sons of God as "angels."* **They clearly thought it** *referred to angelic beings*, not people descended from Seth.[263] (Emphasis added)

*Cambridge Bible for Schools and Colleges*:

Sons of the Elohîm [God], i. e. *angels.* The name Elohim *or sons of the Elohim* is a *name given directly to angels* in contrast with **men.**[264] (Emphasis and brackets added)

Dr. C. Fred Dickason, *Names of Angels*:

**Bene elohim** *is a technical term for angels* and is...the sense in which "the sons of God" in Gen 6 is used. It *refers to angels as a class of mighty ones or powers*. It is used of angels in Job 1:6; 2:1; 38:7. Some say that this term is also used of *God's own people*; **but close inspection of the passages usually listed (Deuteron-**

omy 14:1; Hosea 1:10; 11:1) will show that *the exact term is not* bene elohim.[265] (Emphasis added)

Dr. Michael Heiser, *The Unseen Realm*:

When it comes to **Genesis 6:1–4**.... **The truth is** that the writers of the New Testament *know nothing of...any view that makes the sons of God in Genesis 6:1–4 humans.*[266] (Emphasis added)

*Barnes' Notes on the Bible*:

The sons of God—*Angels*—called the *sons of God* from their resemblance to him, or their being created by him.[267] (Emphasis added)

*Matthew Poole's Commentary*:

**These** [angels] **are called the** *sons of God*, partly because they had their whole being from him, and partly because they were made *partakers of his Divine and glorious image.*[268] (Emphasis and brackets added)

*Keil and Delitzsch*:

[**That sons of God mean divine beings**] *may be defended on* **two plausible grounds**: first, the fact that the "sons of God," in Job 1:6; Job 2:1, and Job 38:7, and in Daniel 3:25, are unquestionably angels (also בני אלים in Psalm 29:1 and Psalm 89:7); and secondly, the antithesis, "sons of God" and "daughters of men." ... *these two points would lead us most naturally to regard the "sons of God" as angels*, in distinction from men and the daughters of men.[269] (Emphasis added)

## THE RESET BUTTON

We're meant to understand from the context of the verses that follow Genesis 6:4 that this unholy interaction between the "sons of God" and the "daughters of men," and its consequences, was one of the main reasons Yahweh eventually destroyed everything with the Flood.

In those ominous days, God pushed the "reset" button. He killed everything upon the earth that had breath, except for those beings that He specifically singled out for deliverance from His coming wrath. Apparently, it was some time during this period when God imprisoned the angels who were largely responsible for the disastrous outcome resulting from the "abandonment" of their *oikétérion*.

> The earth also *was corrupt* before God, and the earth was *filled with violence.* And God looked upon the earth, and, behold, it *was corrupt; for all flesh had corrupted* his way upon the earth. (Genesis 6:11–12, KJV; emphasis added)

The Apostle Peter speaks of the same angels and their punishment, as does Jude. However, some scholars also note that Peter appears to tie that angelic punishment event directly to the days of Noah's Flood:

> For if God **did not spare angels** when they sinned, but **sent them to hell**, putting them **in chains of darkness to be held for judgment**; if he did not spare the ancient world **when he brought the flood** on its **ungodly people**, but protected Noah, a preacher of righteousness, and seven others. (2 Peter 2:4–5; emphasis added)

*Ellicott's Commentary for English Readers:*

In the Book of Enoch *the Flood follows closely upon the sin of the angels,* as in Genesis 6 upon that of the sons of God, so that in either case *the first instance would naturally suggest the second.*[270] (Emphasis added)

*Meyer's New Testament Commentary:*

It cannot be doubted that the sin meant here is the same as that of which Jude speaks.[271]

Dietlein insists that this verse is intimately connected with 2 Peter 2:4, so that *"the judgment of imprisonment on the angels must be considered as one and the same event with the Noachic flood"*[272] (emphasis added).

Considering that Jude was Jesus' half-brother,[273] and Peter was a part of Jesus' "inner three" circle of closest relationships and the pastor of the first church at Jerusalem, it's hard to believe they could have gotten this wrong. Again, their theology teacher was Jesus Himself, the Creator and Sustainer of the universe![274]

As we think about everything else we've uncovered in the last several chapters, we begin to get a clearer understanding of how and why those in the demonic realm operate in a veiled manner. Even though they can "manifest" themselves in different ways, it appears that, through God's sovereign decree, they're not allowed to manifest as physical human beings and thus casually walk among us. However, that certainly doesn't eliminate their arsenal of malevolent capabilities.

It is apparent from Scripture and human history that the demonic realm possesses certain proficiencies enabling them to directly affect humanity. The Word of God assures us that the modes of impact they *do* have are going to be magnified in the last days. We are, at least, in the beginning stages of those days now.

With these truths in mind, it is imperative that we understand the main entry points through which so much of the world's demonic infestation and harassment finds its way into human life.

# PART VII

# GATEWAYS

With all Satan's views, his far end is to diminish from the glory of God.

You are wrong, if you think his far end is to destroy your soul: you are wrong, if you think his far end is to destroy the universe of souls.

He takes these—but only as a means to his highest ambitious end: his final object is to derogate something from the Majesty of God.

~J. Vaughan, (1874)[275]

# A MAGICAL POWER

## 39

*They claim to have talked with demons and to have sometimes been directly influenced and manipulated by demonic entities.*

Several surefire vehicles through which one might open the doors of demonic infestation are actually listed in the Bible, grouped together in one passage in the Book of Revelation and identified as the prevailing sins of the very last days.

> The rest of mankind who were not killed by these plagues still did not repent...of worshipping demons...nor of their murders, ***their magic arts***, their sexual immorality or their thefts. (Revelation 9:20–21; emphasis added)

## THE WORDS

As you see, I emphasized the phrase "magic arts."

Here's why: That phrase comes from a precise Greek word found in the original New Testament text. No matter which English translation we use, we're sure to miss out on the gravity of that word unless we dig a little deeper into its meaning.

Most modern English translations interpret that word as "witchcraft or sorceries," or, as this translation has it, "magic arts."

At this point, you might say "What's the big deal? I don't practice witchcraft, sorceries, or magic arts, so, *I'm good to go!*"

Perhaps. But maybe not.

## THE DARK APOTHECARY

The Greek word used in that verse is *phármakos.* It's the word from which we get our words "pharmacy" and "pharmacist," and it's found only three times in the New Testament, and only in the Book of Revelation—which deals primarily with the time of the end. Have a look at how the Greek dictionaries and word studies define the term:

*Helps Word Studies*:

Cognate: 5333 phármakos—properly, a sorcerer; **used of people** *using drugs* **and "religious incantations"** *to drug people into living by their illusions*—like having *magical (supernatural) powers to manipulate God* into giving them more temporal possessions.[276] (Emphasis added; parentheses original)

*NAS Exhaustive Concordance*:

Word Origin: From *pharmakon (a drug).* Definition*: a poisoner,* sorcerer, magician.[277] (Emphasis added; parentheses original)

*International Standard Bible Encyclopedia*:

The word translated "witchcraft" in Gal 5:20 (pharmakeia) is the ordinary Greek one for "sorcery"…though **it means** *literally the act of administering drugs* **and then of magical** *potions.*[278] (Emphasis added; parentheses original)

*The Complete Word Study Dictionary—New Testament*:

Pharmakeia, from pharmakon, *a drug*, which in the Greek writers is used both for a curative *or medicinal drug*, **and also as a poisonous one.** Pharmakeia means the occult, sorcery, witchcraft, **illicit** *pharmaceuticals*, trance, magical incantation with *drugs* (Gal. 5:20; Rev. 9:21; 18:23; Sept.: Ex. 7:22; Is. 47:9, 12).[279] (Emphasis added; parentheses original)

There's little doubt concerning the truth of what we're dealing with here. Few Christians know that the Bible addresses the issue of substance abuse and the demonic doors it opens.

## POISON

You probably noticed one of the terms that defines *pharmakon*, according to the *NAS Exhaustive Concordance*, is "poisoner." The earliest apothecaries were little more than ancient medicine men or even witch doctors. They were famous for formulating special elixirs of poisons, potions, and herbal drugs. As the art and science of *pharmakon* advanced, apothecaries gradually began to earn more professional respect.

Philippus Aureolus Paracelsus (1493–1541) is known as the father of modern pharmacology because of his work in the chemical management of medical disorders.[280] He espoused the proposal that "*like*-cures-*like*," explaining: "A *poison* in the body will be cured by a similar *poison*. *Solely the dose* determines that a thing is *not a poison*."[281]

But there's more. The Greek word *pharmakeia* has an equivalent word in the Hebrew. That Hebrew word is *kesheph*, often translated into English as "sorcery" or "witchcraft." When the Hebrew Old Testament was being translated into Greek, sometimes called the *Septuagint* or LXX, *pharmakeia* was the Greek word used for the Hebrew *kesheph*. This is because *pharmakeia* and *kesheph* represent the same meaning.

*A Biblical Dictionary—James Austin Bastow214*:

The word *mecashsheph*, rendered "sorcerer," (Exodus 7:11, Jeremiah 27:9, Daniel 2:2, and Malachi 3:5), like the Greek *pharmakos*, (Revelation 32:8; 22:15) designates one who **uses magic formulas**, [elixirs of drugs, alcohol, and mind-altering herbs] incantations, a magician; also a woman of like practices, rendered "a witch."[282] (Brackets and emphasis added)

Imagine that.

The Bible, *you know,* that ancient, two-thousand-year-old, irrelevant book, as so many unbelievers label it today, foretold that one way the demonic realm would connect with humanity in the last days would be through substance abuse, which is apparently tantamount to intentionally ingesting *a poisonous dose* of mind-altering drugs or liquid and chemical elixirs.

No one in his or her right mind would intentionally do such a thing. But that's just the point: Satan has to get that person "out" of his or her right mind. He knows it can't be done in a mask of ugliness or through a state of immediately realized misery.

So instead, he pulls on his disguise of light, beauty, and a promise of god-like *ecstasy*.

# TALKING WITH THE GODS | 40

*Some claim to have actually talked with demons.*

As of this writing, my son, Brandon Gallups, is an associate pastor of a church family in Alabama, just north of Birmingham.[283] The church and its primary ministry—a substance-abuse clinic and program—are helping people with deliverance from addiction to pharmaceuticals, among other substances.

Brandon and the church's senior pastor, Chris Gortney, have spent years ministering to substance abusers and their families. They have related to me that a number of drug abusers independently testify to practically the same thing: *They have all seen the "other side" in person.*

Pastor Brandon Gallups says:

> To state the fact plainly, a number of them speak about seeing demons. Some claim to have actually talked with demons, and to have sometimes been directly influenced and manipulated by demonic entities. A number of them speak in vivid detail about demonic encounters that were so real, they swear they will never forget them.
>
> We are faced with this phenomenon on a regular basis as a result of our ministry in the realm of substance abuse.[284]

The abuse of alcohol sometimes goes hand in hand with drug abuse and addiction. Also, the same type of demonic portal-opening capabilities that exist in drug addiction often manifest in alcohol addiction as well. Even Dr. Carl Jung, a Swiss psychiatrist and psychoanalyst, spoke of the spiritual connection to alcohol abuse. He founded what is today's practice of analytical psychology. Jung apparently was not a *believer*, in the biblical sense of the word, but was raised in a "religious" home early in his life and had several family members who were clergy.[285]

Some of Jung's principles of discovery led to the creation of Alcoholics Anonymous. He labeled alcohol addiction as partly caused by "the ***spiritual thirst*** of our being, for wholeness…the ***union with God.***" Dr. Jung is even mentioned in some of AA's literature.[286]

When speaking of chronic alcohol abuse, Dr. Jung asserted:

Once in a while, alcoholics have had what are called ***vital spiritual experiences***. I call them ***phenomenon***.

**Guiding** *forces* of the lives of these men are ***suddenly cast to one side***, and a ***completely new set*** of conceptions and motives **begin to *dominate* them.**[287] (Emphasis added)


## THE OTHER SIDE

This truth is precisely why the ancients often identified themselves as being able to communicate with the gods during drug or alcohol-induced states of ecstasy. And it is why there are so many warnings throughout God's Word against substance abuse, especially regarding how that abuse is connected to opening up other demonic portals of entry, including areas of vile sexual perversion.

Dr. Martti Nissinen, professor of Old Testament studies at the University of Helsinki, is an expert on drug-induced, prophetic phenomena in the ancient Eastern Mediterranean. He is known for his monumental work, *Ancient Prophecy: Near Eastern, Biblical, and Greek Perspectives*. As Dr. Nissinen addresses the very issue we're exploring, note the specific elements often involved in conjuring up the so-called communication with gods:

Further **commonalities with the shamanic practice** include the *altered state of consciousness* and its occasional triggers, *such as liquids or drugs,* and *music* or sounds, as well as the *ambiguous gender roles* of some of the prophets and shamans... ['I'hrough these] they were *focused on the transmission of divine knowledge.*[288]

*The Pythia*[289] [is presented] as the prime example of someone **experiencing** *spirit possession* as the *mouthpiece of a deity* and indeed entering into an *altered state of consciousness*...the Pythia and her colleagues were believed...*to transmit divine knowledge* to their consultants.... In whatever way **the divine speaker's** *mania* became noticeable.... It was [considered to be] *a god-given skill to be the mouthpiece of the divine*, and persons with such skill were *not expected to behave like anyone else*, and *certainly not while transmitting* the *divine knowledge.*[290] (Emphasis and brackets added)

Considering what we've learned about Satan thus far, it's pretty easy to pull back the mask of today's international, crisis-level blight of substance addiction. The fallen race of humanity has an empty hole that can only be satiated through a personal, born-again relationship with Jesus Christ. Satan seeks to fill that void with himself, so he opens the door to his realm, largely through substance addiction. These "poisons" open spiritual portals of the darkest kinds.

## THE SCOURGE

There is no doubt that the spiritual, mental, and physical issues of alcohol and drug addiction are deeply related. They're now at the levels of "global concern," regardless of the economic status of the nations involved. The National Center for Biotechnology Information states:

Drug addiction is a chronically relapsing disorder that has been characterized by the compulsive use of addictive substances. *Addiction to drugs and alcohol* is increasingly becoming *a worldwide trend* in lifestyle that is **prevalent in rich and poor countries alike.** Addiction *to alcohol…and drugs* is now regarded as **a major [global] health problem.**[291] (Emphasis added)

When the epidemic proportions of drug addiction were recently addressed at a United Nations conference, it was noted that the entire planet is now dealing with a rapidly mushrooming opioid-abuse epidemic.[292] In fact, drug overdoses in 2017 killed an unprecedented 72,287 US residents—nearly three times the number of people killed by global terrorism and ten thousand more than the number of Americans killed in the Vietnam War. Nearly fifty thousand of those deadly overdoses were caused by either heroin or fentanyl.[293]

# LINKS

Think about the ramifications of what we have uncovered.

Chemical abuse, certain types of music or sounds, ambiguous gender roles, the desire for divine knowledge, and the manic goal of inducing an altered state of consciousness are all deeply connected. Each hearkens back to the Garden of Eden and continues right on through to the days of Noah and the other side of the Flood through the platform elements of the most ancient—and modern—pagan worship practices.

And, the scourge is not going away. In fact, it appears to be getting worse, almost exponentially.

# DEPRAVITY

*It is a forbidden fruit, now fully consumed,*
*with very little method to turn*
*back the clock and shut the lid.*

In the same passage of Revelation 9 we've been looking at, we discover another illuminating Greek word. It, too, offers a much broader understanding of an unquestionable portal of demonic attachment. The phrase representing that specific Greek word is highlighted below.

> The rest of mankind who were not killed by these plagues still did not repent...of worshipping demons...nor of their murders, their magic arts, *their sexual immorality* or their thefts. (Revelation 9:20–21; emphasis added)

The Greek word often translated as "sexual immorality" is *porneia*. Like *phármakos,* the subject of the last chapter, it's pretty easy to discern the word's root meaning. Right away, we can see where the English word *pornography* is derived. However, *porneia* carries a much broader scope of significance than only pornography.

*HELPS Word-studies*:

> 4202 porneía (the root of the English terms "pornography, pornographic"; cf. 4205 /pórnos) which is derived from pernao, "to sell off")—**properly, a** *selling off* **(surrendering) of sexual purity;** *promiscuity of any (every) type.*[294] (Emphasis added)

*Strong's Exhaustive Concordance*:

From porneuo; harlotry (including adultery and incest); figuratively, idolatry—fornication.[295]

# PORNEIA AND PROPHECY

Consider the following prophetic truth: We are now the first generation in human history to have enabled the global epidemic of pornography addiction and the horrors that this blight inflicts upon women and children, along with their marriages, homes, and families.[296]

In the United States alone, 66 percent of men and 41 percent of women consume pornography on a monthly basis. An estimated 50 percent of all Internet traffic is related to pornography. Porn addiction is now a *mass phenomenon* that directly, and negatively, impacts our culture.[297] This scourge has direct prophetic connections to Revelation 9.

Before us is yet another Pandora's box of demonic deluge unleashed upon a new generation. It is a forbidden fruit, now fully consumed, with very few options to turn back the clock and shut the lid. From this point forward, the curse is practically unstoppable. A number of prophecy watchers see the relatively new global pornography addiction epidemic as yet another marker indicating that we are nearing the very last days before the return of the Lord.

> [Jesus said to them] "It was the same **in the days of Lot**.... But the day Lot left Sodom, fire and sulfur rained down from heaven and destroyed them all. *It will be just like this* on **the day the Son of Man is revealed**." (Luke 17:28:30; emphasis and brackets added)

This powerful portal of demonic grip is now immediately accessible, even to our youngest children, through the latest technological wonders.

Often, the implements necessary for our loved ones to inadvertently connect their minds and souls to this demonic battleground are given to them as gifts.

With the almost universal proliferation of instantaneous information and communication transfer, pornography addiction has genuinely become a global plague—and only in *our* immediate historical generation.

Consider again the study of our last chapter concerning the demonic doors that are undeniably opened through liquid and chemical drug addiction. Then have a look at the following excerpt from an article published online by NPR titled, "National Review: Getting Serious on Pornography."

> Imagine *a drug so powerful* it can *destroy a family* simply by distorting a man's perception of his wife. Picture an *addiction so lethal* it has the potential to *render an entire generation incapable of forming lasting marriages* and so widespread that it **produces more annual revenue**—$97 billion worldwide in 2006—**than all of the leading technology companies combined.**
>
> Consider a *narcotic so insidious* that *it evades serious scientific study and legislative action* for decades, **thriving instead under** the ever-expanding banner of *the First Amendment.*[298] (Emphasis added)

In fact, the article asserts that, according to two addiction experts, pornography addiction often holds a *more powerful* grip than that of drug dependency:

> Indeed, *two authorities* on the *neurochemistry of addiction*, Harvey Milkman and Stanley Sunderwirth, claim **it is the *ability of this drug*** to influence *all three pleasure systems* in the **brain**—arousal, satiation, and fantasy—**that makes it "*the* piece de resistance** *among the addictions.*"[299] (Emphasis added)

That assertion is further backed up by several institutions of scientific research. Just a few years ago, the National Center for Biotechnology Information (NCBI) released the following, indicating a dramatic "shift" in its stance regarding porn addiction:

> *A revolutionary paradigm shift is occurring in the field of addiction* that has great implications for assessment and treatment.
>
> While *"addiction" has historically been associated* with the problematic overconsumption *of drugs and/or alcohol*, the *burgeoning neuroscientific research in this field has changed our understanding* over the last few decades.
>
> **It is now evident** that **various behaviors**, which are repeatedly reinforcing the reward, motivation, and memory circuitry **are all part of the disease of addiction.** Common mechanisms among addiction involving **various psychoactive substances** such as *alcohol, opioids and cocaine*; and *pathological behaviors such as…pornography and sexual acting out* have also been delineated.
>
> The review **leads to the conclusion** that *Internet pornography addiction fits into the addiction framework and shares similar basic mechanisms with substance addiction.*[300] (Emphasis added)

A unique study from Cambridge University concurs:

> *People who are addicted to pornography show similar brain activity to alcoholics or drug addicts….*
>
> **The research by Cambridge University** assessed the brain activity of 19 addictive pornography users against a control group of people who said they were not compulsive users.
>
> **Lead scientist Dr Valerie Voon, an honorary consultant neuropsychiatrist**, told the *Sunday Times*: "*We found greater activity in an area of the brain* called the ventral striatum, which

is a reward center, involved in processing reward, motivation and pleasure…. *We are seeing this same kind of activity in users of pornography.*[301] (Emphasis added)

In November 2019, a researcher at Canada's University Laval, Rachel Anne Barr, warned:

**People who regularly watch** adult movies often fall victim to *brain damage*, more specifically to a region of it known **as the prefrontal cortex, which is not formed until adulthood and is responsible for willpower, morality, and impulse.**
*She has likened those who binge on porn-watching to drug addicts and their crash effects:* "**When a person uses cocaine,** their brains give off a rush of dopamine, the 'feel-good' hormone. **The same happens with sex and arousal,**" Barr said, adding that **the same neurotransmitter is in charge** of memories.[302] (Emphasis added)

## THE STARK FACTS

The following facts are listed, along with their original references, by the National Center on Sexual Exploitation. I have reproduced excerpts that offer a brief synopsis of the information unearthed in these last several chapters. Notice how often the abuse of drugs is compared with pornography and other sexual addictions.

**The Research Is In:** Since 2011, there have been 26 major studies which reveal pornography use has negative and **detrimental impacts on the brain.**
**Shrinks Brain:** A 2014 study of the brain scans of 64 pornography users found that increased pornography use is linked to **decreased brain matter**[303] in the areas of the brain associated with

motivation and decision-making, and contributed to impaired impulse control and desensitization to sexual reward. Thus the study demonstrated that **pornography use** can produce physical, anatomic **change in the brain**—a **hallmark of addiction**.

**Hijacks the Brain's Reward System**: addiction occurs when the pleasure/rewards **pathways of the brain are hijacked by drugs** such as cocaine or by natural process vital to survival such as eating and sex…. Growing evidence suggests that **pornography use hijacks the brain's** reward system in the **same way that drug** use does.

**The Addiction Gets Worse**: Using functional MRI, a 2015 study from Cambridge found that compulsive sexual behavior is characterized by novelty-seeking, conditioning, and habituation to sexual stimuli in males—meaning users need more extreme content over time in order to achieve the same level of arousal… a finding **consistent with theories of incentive motivation underlying drug addiction**.[304] (Emphasis added)

A number of Christian professionals—ministers, counselors, clinical workers, and the like—already suspected that these biological connections existed. It is helpful, however, to now possess the scientific data behind that practical knowledge, especially in this age of so much fakery and false information.

It's also refreshing to know that certain credible scientific institutions, and their academic studies, are also acknowledging what we believe to be the most important element of all: the *deeply spiritual connections* often involved in addiction.

There's no longer any doubt: This area of darkness is one of Satan's most hideous masks—especially as the times are rapidly approaching the Day of the Lord.

# CAMOUFLAGED CONNECTIONS  42

*It seems that, once again, "science" is slowly catching
up to what the Word of God has declared all along.*

Here's the real shocker: The American Society of Addiction Medicine
acknowledges the truth that we've unmasked throughout our own
study. Take special note of the highlighted parts in the passage below,
especially the last couple of words:

> As a result of the *growing neuroscientific evidence*, the Ameri-
> can Society of Addiction Medicine (ASAM) *formally expanded
> their definition of addiction* in 2011 to include both *behaviors
> and substances*:
>
> Addiction is a primary, chronic disease of brain reward,
> motivation, memory and related circuitry. *Dysfunction in these
> circuits* leads to *characteristic* biological, psychological, social
> and *spiritual manifestations.*[305] (Emphasis added)

In other words, just like substance addiction (*pharmakos*), pornography (*porneia*) is yet another one of Satan's diabolical masquerades. It is
a hook that, once embedded, goes to the very core of one's body, mind,
personal relationships, and soul. And, it can induce a decidedly demonic
attachment and infestation (or, as the ASAM puts it: "characteristic spiritual manifestations").

It seems, once again, that "science" is slowly catching up to what the
Word of God has declared all along. *Who knew?*

Perhaps this is why we find these heartfelt scriptural admonitions warning us to stay away and to even flee these open doors of diabolical activity, not allowing them into our lives. The Word of God is clear in this regard. Sadly, much of the today's church not only ignores the warnings but continues to eat the fruit.

> **Flee from sexual immorality**. All other sins a person commits are outside the body, *but whoever sins sexually, sins against their own body*. Do you not know that *your bodies are temples of the Holy Spirit*, who is in you, whom you have received from God? You are not your own; you were bought at a price. Therefore *honor God with your bodies*. (1 Corinthians 6:18–20; emphasis added)

Did you see it? There's that "temple of God" theme again!

As we discovered in earlier pages, we—*our bodies*—are declared by God's Word to be *the temple of God*, and/or the *temple of the Holy Spirit*. What does *porneia* addiction do to that temple? It sets up Satan to take a seat upon the throne of one's soul and mind so he can become the true "god" of that person's life. This is known as idolatry.

## THE TEMPLE LINK

These addictive behaviors open the doors for the "birds of the air" to fly in and build their vile nests within the core of our spirit. Does any of this sound familiar, in light of what we've learned in earlier chapters of this book?

Then there's the following admonition, which connects directly back to the warning of 1 Corinthians 6:

> Therefore, *I urge you*, brothers and sisters, in view of God's mercy, to **offer your bodies** as *a living sacrifice*, holy and pleasing to God—this is *your true and proper worship*.

Do not conform to the pattern of this world, but *be transformed by the renewing of your mind*. Then you will be able to test and approve what God's will is—his good, pleasing and perfect will. (Romans 12:1–2; emphasis added)

Here is yet another passage connecting the definition of the "true temple" with our bodies. It does so by insisting that our bodies and minds encompass the entire *sacrificial system*, and the type of New Testament sacrifices we are to offer in that true and spiritual temple of God.

What eventually happens to those who allow Satan to occupy this particular throne of idolatry? Paul says in the first chapter of the Book of Romans that God eventually gives over to a depraved mind those who continue to travel the ever-downward-spiraling road of sexual degradation (*porneia*). And a depraved mind is yet another portal allowing the entrance of even more demonic infestation.

Here are excerpts from that first chapter of Romans:

Therefore **God** *gave them over* in the sinful desires of their hearts **to sexual impurity** for the **degrading of their bodies** with one another.... Because of this, *God gave them over* to shameful lusts.... Furthermore, just *as they did not think it worthwhile* **to retain the knowledge of God**, so *God gave them over* to a *depraved mind*, so that **they do what ought not to be done**. (Romans 1:24–28; emphasis added)

## EVEN IN THE CHURCH

Do you want to know how pervasive this demonic portal has become, even in the church? The sad truth is shocking. Following is a short sample of statistics gathered at an online resource called the Conquer Series. I have arranged and edited the material for ease of use in this chapter.[306]

As you look at the heart-wrenching statistics, please remember that Jesus warned us, especially in His Galilee parables, that these insidiously vile, last-days demonic encroachments are sure to come. Again, we are the first generation to experience such a deluge of this kind of filth pouring into the church. Especially note the emphasized portions.

- There are around **42 million porn websites**, which totals around 370 million pages of porn.
- The **porn industry's annual revenue** is more than the NFL, NBA, and MLB combined. It is also more than the combined revenues of ABC, CBS, and NBC.
- Eleven is the **average age that a child** is first exposed to porn, and 94% of children will see porn by the age of 14.
- 56% of **American divorces** involve one party having an "obsessive interest" in pornographic websites.
- 68% of **churchgoing men** view porn on a regular basis.
- Over 50% of **pastors** view porn on a regular basis.
- Of **young Christian adults** 18–24 years old, 76% actively search for porn.
- **59% of pastors** said that married men seek their help for porn use.
- Only 13% of **self-identified Christian women** say they never watch porn.
- 87% of **Christian women** have watched porn.
- 55% of **married men** and 25% of **married women** say they watch porn at least once a month.
- 57% of **pastors say porn addiction** is the most damaging issue in their congregation. And 69% say porn has adversely impacted the church.
- **Only 7% of pastors say** their church *has a program* to help people struggling with pornography.[307]
- **93% of pastors** see porn as an increasing problem in the church.

It appears we have, once again, gone right back to Jesus' seaside kingdom parables.

These last couple of chapters have demonstrated how the process of injecting "just a little" leaven into the otherwise pure batch of dough eventually permeates the entire loaf. They demonstrate how Satan's demonic hordes—*the birds of the air*—roost right in the middle of the visible kingdom work of Jesus Christ. All of it is meant to debase and spiritually cripple the people of God, but it is especially meant to grieve the heart of God Himself.

How in the world can these addictions be so debilitating? Why are they so unbelievably difficult to escape? How can they be so pervasive in their grip upon this planet, especially within the church?

The next chapter reveals the key to Satan's knowledge in this area.

# WHAT HAPPENS

## 43

*If people have immersed themselves in addictive behaviors and substances, their brains have been biologically and chemically rewired.*

When Satan has trapped a person in the throes of addiction, he has basically kidnapped them. He has commandeered key information centers of that person's brain. Of course, first, he has to *beguile* the person to succumb to his baited hooks.

> When tempted, no one should say, "God is tempting me." For God cannot be tempted by evil, nor does he tempt anyone; but each person is tempted when they are dragged away by their own evil desire and enticed.
>
> Then, after desire has conceived, it gives birth to sin; and sin, when it is full-grown, gives birth to death. Don't be deceived, my dear brothers and sisters.
>
> Every good and perfect gift is from above, coming down from the Father of the heavenly lights, who does not change like shifting shadows. (James 1:13–17)

## HIJACKED

The following excerpts are from a Harvard Medical School publication titled, "How Addiction Hijacks the Brain."

Today we recognize **addiction** as a chronic disease that *changes both brain structure and function*. Just as cardiovascular disease damages the heart and diabetes impairs the pancreas, *addiction hijacks the brain*.

Genetic vulnerability contributes to the risk of developing an addiction. *But behavior plays a key role*, especially when it comes to reinforcing a habit.

*The brain registers all pleasures* in the same way, whether they originate *with a psychoactive drug…or a sexual encounter*. In the brain, pleasure has a distinct signature: the release of the neurotransmitter dopamine in the nucleus accumbens, a cluster of nerve cells lying underneath the cerebral cortex (see illustration). **Dopamine release** in the nucleus accumbens *is so consistently tied with pleasure* that neuroscientists refer to the region as the brain's pleasure center.

**Dopamine** not only contributes to the experience of pleasure, but *also plays a role in learning and memory*.… Addictive behaviors…stimulate the…circuit—and then overload it.[308] (Emphasis added)

Even *National Geographic* acknowledged the very real process of the literal brain reshaping that addiction causes. In doing so, its article made an important theological point—unwittingly, I'm certain:

**Addiction** causes *hundreds of changes* in **brain anatomy**, chemistry, and cell-to-cell signaling, including in the gaps between neurons called synapses, which are the molecular machinery for learning. *By taking advantage* of the brain's marvelous plasticity, **addiction remolds** neural circuits *to assign supreme value* to cocaine or heroin or gin, **at the expense of other interests** such as health, work, family, *or life itself*.[309] (Emphasis added)

Did you see the ultimate outcome of addiction? It reassigns the objects of *supreme value* in a person's most deep-seated worldview. Interestingly, true biblical worship is often defined as assigning the highest worth, or *supreme value*, to the person and character of God, our Creator and Savior.

So, if an addictive substance or behavior ultimately usurps a person's *supreme value* regarding his or her worship of Jesus Christ, guess who's behind that door? Of course, it's none other than *Nachash*, the beguiling serpent.

The bottom line is this: For those who have immersed themselves in addictive behaviors and substances, their brain has been biologically and chemically rewired to crave that thing. The addiction becomes "learned" by the brain. Before long, the focus of that person's *worship* goes directly to the dark side, whether they acknowledge it or not.

Humanity is just now learning these biological truths. But Satan has known them all along, from the beginning. He is the master practitioner of witchcraft and sorcery. He knows the buttons to push. He knows how to cause the epigenetic changes in our entire makeup, the changes he needs in order to enslave us. Once again we discover how vile and thoroughly appalling Nachash really is.


## THANKS BE TO GOD

The plain truth is that *every one of us* is fallen. And every one of us has the tendency within our own fallen nature to lower ourselves into all kinds of debauchery and debasement, given the necessary contributing environment and circumstances and the often resulting poor choices. *Each of us* struggles with our thought life, our flesh, and our sin nature to one degree or another practically every single day. Those who will not admit this truth are not being honest with themselves or the Lord (1 John 1:7–9; emphasis added).

It's helpful to remember that even the great Apostle Paul admits this:

I find this law at work: *Although I want to do good, evil is right there with me.* For in my inner being I delight in God's law; but I see another law at work in me, *waging war against the law of my mind* and *making me a prisoner* of the law of sin at work within me. What a wretched man I am! *Who will rescue me from this body* that is subject to death? **Thanks be to God, who delivers me through Jesus Christ our Lord!** (Romans 7:21–25; emphasis added)

And there is the key!

Thanks be to God—I can win the battle through Jesus Christ!

We do not have to engage in this fight alone with only our own strength. Just as supernatural forces constantly come against us, we also have supernatural forces in our favor—*mega-supernatural forces!* We have power that emanates from God's throne itself. Through Jesus Christ, we have the opportunity for real and complete release.

We do not have to be taken captive by Satan's masquerade of beguilement any longer.

———

**Note:** At the end of this book is an addendum titled "Deliverance," a brief chapter designed for those who are suffering under the bondage of addictions and demonic oppression or for those who have a loved one or other aquaintance who is trapped. Repentant people *can* be delivered, and their brains and spirit-lives *can* be rewired and set free! It is not easy, but with the Lord's infusion of His holy power, it can be done.

That chapter includes Scripture passages about healing, which readers can meditate upon. It also contains a list of reliable resources that provide visual media, reading material, courses, and recovery center contact information for those seeking additional help. I pray that you find all of this information useful.

Please be sure to have a look at that section. Perhaps you'll be able to pass it on to someone who might be blessed by it.

# THE GARDEN LINK | 44

*He simply took it and claimed it as his own.*

At this point, you might be asking, "What about murder and thievery? Aren't they listed in Revelation 9 as well?"

Yes, they are. I doubt anyone reading this book would question how both of those crimes could easily open many other doors to demonic infestation and continued depravity of mind and soul. However, there's something more to the list in Revelation 9 that I want to be sure you see.

Each of the elements mentioned in that passage is a factor in the original Fall in the Garden of Eden.

## BEGUILING

The sorcery, witchcraft, and devil-worship that took place in the Garden of Eden ought to be rather obvious by now. After all, Eve admitted that she was "beguiled" or "seduced" by the tempter.[310]

Paul addressed the issue in his letter to the church at Corinth:

> But I am afraid that *as the serpent deceived Eve* by his *cunning*, your *thoughts will be led astray* from a sincere and pure devotion to Christ. (2 Corinthians 11:3; emphasis added)

Even more interesting is the Hebrew word translated as "serpent" in the third chapter of Genesis: *nachash*.[311] That word can mean a literal snake, or it can be used in the obvious metaphorical sense of *a person*—in the sense of, "Look at that snake in the grass! He's such a liar!"

However, *nachash* is also used for an "enchanter, a diviner, one who casts a magic spell, one who whispers *like a hiss*, and an interpreter of omens."[312] And, of all things, the word is associated with the practice of *sorcery*, referring to "one who mixes potions, elixirs, and drugs."[313]

## THE CRAFTY ONE

Paul also uses another interestingly nuanced Greek word, *panourgia*, when he mentions Nachash's "cunning" nature. That word, in the negative sense, means "an unscrupulous *scheming* that stops at nothing to achieve a selfish goal; ready to do anything. Equivalent to a specious or false wisdom. Employing trickery or sophistry."[314]

Surely, you see where this leads us.

The "serpent" in Eden was not a literal walking, talking snake, as we've already learned. Originally, he was the divinely appointed and majestic *mighty one* from Heaven—the anointed cherub of Yahweh. Satan was also the father of witchcraft, enchantment, sexual immorality, deceit, lying, and sorcery. Likewise, he was undoubtedly the father of what would actually become the worship of the *fallen ones*—later known as idolatry. And all of that started in the Garden of Eden.

## HOMICIDE

We also know that Satan introduced another iniquity to the world through the garden Fall. He introduced the specter of death. It came to us by a long, slow process of purposely induced murder. To be sure, he didn't kill Adam and Eve with one stroke. That would have defeated his purpose.

Rather, Satan murdered them *and the entire human race* by injecting the curse of corruption. Every other vile thing that happened in the garden on that fateful day was the result of a continual string of lies uttered from the mouth of Nachash, the lying, murdering serpent.

[Satan] was *a murderer from the beginning*, not holding to the truth, for *there is no truth in him*. When he lies, he speaks his native language, for he is a liar and *the father of lies*. (John 8:44; emphasis added)

In other words, by calling the tempter "Nachash," the entirety of his wicked personality is unmasked. He is the genuine "snake in the grass." He is also the father of witchcraft and the mixer of magic potions. He is the designer of beguiling intoxications. He is the originator of deceit and lies. And through all of these crafts, Satan had one grand goal in mind.

## THEFT

Satan's entire plan involved *theft*. He wanted the garden and all of its future potential for his very own. So, in effect, he stole it. He simply took it and claimed it as his own. With that larceny, he stole our original, pristine relationship with the Creator, thus corrupting our *divine nature*.

That theft was the reason Jesus went to Calvary's cross. He had to pay the ransom, wherein we were redeemed, *bought back*.

**The thief [Satan] comes only to steal** and kill and destroy. I came that they may have life and have it abundantly. (John 10:10, ESV; emphasis added)

Praise be to the God and Father of our Lord Jesus Christ! In his great mercy *he has given us new birth into a living hope* through the resurrection of Jesus Christ from the dead, *and into an inheritance that can never perish,* spoil or fade. This inheritance is *kept in heaven for you.* (1 Peter 1:3–4; emphasis added)

**According as his divine power** hath given unto us all things that pertain unto life and godliness, through the knowledge of *him that hath called us to glory* and virtue: by which have been given to us exceedingly **great and precious promises**, that through these *you may be partakers of the divine nature*, having **escaped the corruption** that is *in the world through lust.* (2 Peter 1:3–4, KJV; emphasis added)

Think of it! To be able to "participate in the divine nature" is our glorious promise! If we are "in Christ Jesus," then we're assured that the same nature originally possessed by Adam and Eve before the Fall, thus the nature that was to be rightfully ours from the beginning, will soon be fully restored!

*Meyer's New Testament Commentary*:

*The thought* that man is intended *to be partaker of the divine nature*, or *to be transfigured into the divine being*,—which is accomplished in him through faith in the promises,—is, though in other terms, *often enough expressed in the N. T.* (Hebrews 12:10; 1 Peter 1:23; John 1:12–13, and many other passages.)[315] (Emphasis added)

*Expositor's Greek Testament*:

**Man becomes either regenerate or degenerate.** Either his spiritual and moral powers are **subject to slow decay** and death, the wages of sin, **or he rises to** *full participation in the Divine.*[316] (Emphasis added)

Do not be misled by the word "divine." Its use in this passage does not mean we will become "gods" of some sort. After all, the promise of becoming more "like God" was one of the elements of Satan's temptation in the first place! No, "divine" denotes not only the condition of *restored perfection*, but also a specific "location." For example, there is the *divine realm* and then there is the *fallen, earthly realm*. Through salvation in Jesus Christ, we will soon be participators in everything that is *divine!*

This glorious promise is why Revelation 21 assures us that in *that day*, "all things will be made new." In *that day*, there will be "no more crying, or death, or pain." The Garden of Eden will be restored. Our originally intended divine nature will be returned to us. Everything Satan took will be given back to us—*forever*.

# BEGUILED 45

*Never have any of these dark elements in the Fall
in the Garden of Eden skipped a generation.*

*I know. I know.* Now you want to know about *porneia*. You're probably
asking, "How does *porneia* play into the garden coup and the list of the
last-days demonic hooks found in Revelation 9?"

There's simply not enough room in this book for a thorough study
of that topic. However, I produced a systematic investigation of the
matter in my previous book, *Gods of Ground Zero: The Truth of Eden's
Iniquity.*[317] That work examines every passage in the Word of God—
from Genesis to Revelation—that might have anything to do with the
subject, in its complete and proper context. I urge you to read it; it will
open your eyes to a number of striking connections you might not have
seen before.

I'll only state here that a stunningly sizable number of classical and
modern scholars, along with Hebrew and Greek language experts and
even a number of the most ancient Jewish scholars, agree that at least
a degree of *porneia* was present in the garden in one form or another.
Again, those possible forms are explored in *Gods of Ground Zero*.

As we've already seen, something along those very same lines happened in Genesis 6, just three chapters after the account of the Garden
of Eden, for which angels are held in the deepest recesses of prison to
this very day.

That devastating brand of *porneia* happened sometime before the
Flood. In fact, the Bible declares that the earth was destroyed through

the deluge *because* of this sin and its demonic connections. And it's probably because of its connection to the garden and the days before the Flood that God's entire Word so vehemently warns us to stay clear of this category of sin.

## CONCLUSION

From the Garden of Eden to the Flood, and from the Flood to our very own day, all of these Revelation 9 sins and their evil consequences have continued. They've been unfailingly pervasive throughout every generation. Never have any of the dark elements in the Fall skipped a generation. No culture or nation has ever been immune to their allure.

But, by the time we reach the Book of Revelation, lo and behold, we discover that even near the very end of it all, these same foundational sins not only are still with us, but are profoundly magnified. However, in those days, they will reign *throughout the planet*—and there's the big difference. They will become global epidemics. God, through the Book of Revelation, calls a special and focused attention to those scourges—drawing our attention all the way back to the Garden of Eden.

Again, please don't lose sight of the fact that never before in history have each of those markers of humanity's depravity—*demonic intrusion, substance abuse, vile sexual perversion, murder, and thievery*—been so ubiquitous…only in our lifetime.

Their inclusion in the Book of Revelation indicates they are prophetic indicators, specifically meant for the very last-days generations. Those last days apparently started less than a double handful of decades ago. Shouldn't this be a prophetic clue? Certainly, *it should*! How is it then, that so much of the church misses this sign? It's because the church has been fooled. *Beguiled.*

A masquerading angel of light has entered and sits among us. We've been infiltrated. Like yeast working through a batch of dough. Like weeds planted among the wheat. Like an unseen snake slithering through the grass right at our feet. Like vile vultures making their nests in the branches of the institutions of the visible church, looking down upon those they yearn to drown in their cesspool of filth and heartache.

It's as if the foundations of the genuine truth of God's Word have been supplanted…with the doctrines of demons.

But it's not like we weren't warned.

# PART VIII

# CLASH OF KINGDOMS

One of the things that saves us is that the demons are divided against themselves. Because they are a kingdom divided against themselves, they cannot stand—they cannot get their act together because their character is such that they are always in competition with each other.

We can understand this when we recognize that the governments and most of humanity has been subject to and deceived by demons.

~JOHN W. RITENBAUGH[318]

# GODS AND THRONES

*Satan's scheme to seek out and finally destroy
that prophesied Seed has always lurked
in the shadows of history.*

## 46

Ever since the Garden of Eden, Satan's war against the coming "Seed" of God's redemptive plan has been waged against the throne of God. That war has been largely played out through the demonically manipulated seats of earthly power.

The conflict is generally laid around three specific fields of battle, each lurking behind Satan's psychoses of unmitigated arrogance and fury. Through these masquerades, Satan is telegraphing his message of intended dominance over the entire planet. They are meant to be an affront to the throne of God.

The main stratagem Satan uses is his abject hatred for the returned nation of Israel and the genuinely born-again people of God—the true church. Further, particularly devastating is Satan's destructive focus upon the "womb of the woman" and the "Seed" it produces.

All three of these battlefronts blossomed into full-blown global scourges only a few short decades ago. We are the first generation to witness the outrageous carnage and insanity that accompanies them. Sadly, only a few pulpits in America give these matters even a casual mention, though the planet is awash in the blight of their existence. Yet, the Scriptures prophesied each of them.[319]

First, let's discover how this all began…

## EDEN'S LINK

These global plagues trace straight back to the Garden of Eden and Yahweh's pronouncement of judgment upon the head of *Nachash*—the original murderer, liar, thief, and sorcerer.

> So the LORD God said to the serpent, "***Because you have done this***, Cursed are you.… And I will put enmity between you and the woman, and between your offspring and hers; ***he will crush your head***, and you will strike his heel." (Genesis 3:14–15; emphasis added)

With this declaration, God told Satan that his day was coming. He would eventually "die" for what he had wrought in the Garden of Eden.

In that decree, God foretold that Satan's demise would come through the womb of a woman. Furthermore, that *Seed* would appear among humanity in the personage of a male child, one who would ultimately destroy Satan's stolen kingdom and accomplish the restitution of all things.[320]

Not only that, but this Seed would eventually appear in the world through the nation of Israel. Out of that nation would also emerge the true church, the body of Christ on earth, until Jesus' literal return. So the Seed of the woman, the nation of Israel, and the church are linked all the way back to the Garden of Eden. And each is what Satan despises the very most.

## NACHASH'S DILEMMA

From the moment the decree was handed down, Satan understood the "what" and "how" of God's judgment upon him. *But*—this is monumental—Satan didn't know the "when, where, and *through whom*" of the matter.

His scheme to hunt down and destroy that prophesied Seed[321] has always lurked in the shadows of the history of humanity. But, the church has largely missed this truth. Satan has been hiding behind the cosmic curtains of interdimensional principalities, pulling the strings of authority and influencing the sin-darkened hearts of powerful people and the institutions they control.[322]

## THE DISCOVERY

Satan first discovered that the Seed of his destruction would come through the line of Abraham. From that point forward, Satan put the children of Israel and everything they represented in his crosshairs.

[God said to Abraham] **In your seed** all *the nations of the earth shall be blessed*, because you have obeyed my voice. (Genesis 22:18; brackets and emphasis added)

So Nachash went to work. He had to find and eliminate the singular Seed that would be used to bring about his own destruction. Satan would eventually arrange for Abraham's descendants, the Israelites, to be enslaved in the land of Egypt. From Egypt, Nachash would pull the strings of his puppet, Pharaoh, so that a murderous edict would be issued through him: *Kill all the newborn male children among the Israelites.*[323]

By this murderous plot, Satan believed he might be able to prevent the pronouncement of Yahweh's garden punishment prophecy. But in spite of the demonically inspired proclamation emanating from the mouth of Pharaoh, God spared a little boy by the name of Moses—the one who, in years to come, would be used to lead Israel's deliverance from Pharaoh's clutches.

However, even after the Exodus and throughout the forty years of the Israelites' wilderness wandering, the ancient civilizations of the surrounding nations came against the nation, time and time again, seeking to destroy the newly emerging children of Israel.

Once they were settled in the land, Satan continued to manipulate the emerging world empires toward his diabolical goal. From the beginning of the Assyrian Empire in 722 BC and through the Babylonians, Persians, and then the 449 BC rise of Alexander the Great's Greek empire, Satan relentlessly endeavored to hunt down and destroy the Seed. A huge portion of humanity's history was being crafted by Nachash, the serpent, with this one goal in mind.

When we examine those national histories under the microscope of biblical context, the homicidal pattern of the cosmic criminal becomes evident. Through those empires, Nachash would enslave the people of God, kill their children, and even attempt to eradicate all the Jews— not to mention tear down Solomon's Temple and destroy Jerusalem. Satan would specifically focus on the male children through Pharaoh of Egypt and Nebuchadnezzar of Babylon. Then he would finally set out to destroy the entire Jewish race through a man named Haman, the Persian assistant to the emperor.

Even in the wake of his psychopathic rants, Satan's plan to destroy that one path to the arrival of the Seed was thwarted by Heaven's throne every single time.

## IN SIGHT OF THE GOAL

By the turn of the first century, the Roman Empire had spawned one of the most brutal war machines and far-reaching kingdoms the planet had ever seen. The Jewish people were swallowed up in the global melee that had brought about its birth.

But, by bowing and scraping to the new and overwhelmingly powerful Roman government, Israel's priests and rabbinic officials gained enough power to become sufficiently comfortable and highly influential. They were even assigned their own "king" who would rule over them within the Roman province of Judea. The king's name was Herod.

The ubiquitously hated King Herod, who wasn't much more than a political puppet of the Roman government, became especially susceptible to the demonic powers behind the thrones of his Roman despotic overlords. Herod's brutality, murderous heart, and arrogant pomposity soon became the foundation of his infamous reputation.

So it was that the degenerate king would be the one Satan would manipulate into focusing on the little village of Bethlehem, less than six miles from Jerusalem's gates and Herod's palace. It was time for Satan's plan to repeat itself.

Once again, Satan supposed he might have the Seed cornered, ready for slaughter. To make certain his plan succeeded, Herod ordered the murder of all of Bethlehem's male children, two years old and younger. These children were said to have been birthed in Bethlehem during the same period as the one who was being called the new king of the Jews. And the newborn king was reported to have arrived through the womb of a woman with a lineage tied directly to David's ancient throne.[324]

Once again, Satan's *modus operandi* was in play: Kill the children, Find the Seed, and destroy Him!

> *Cambridge Bible for Schools and Colleges:*[Herod's treachery] symbolizes the ***enmity of the serpent against the seed of the woman…*** including also the malice that pursued [Jesus] through life, the temptation, and at last the Cross.[325] (Emphasis and brackets added)

> *Gill's Exposition of the Entire Bible:*

> ***Just as the dragon Pharaoh*** lay in the midst of his rivers, in the river Nile, Ezekiel 29:3; ***to slay the male children of Israel*** as soon as born; and ***as the dragon Herod*** sought to take away the life of Jesus quickly after his birth; and as Satan is like a roaring lion, seeking whom he may devour, so the Pagan empire, or ***the***

*Pagan emperors, took every opportunity to stifle the kingdom of Christ in embryo.*[326] (Emphasis added)

One more time, Satan thought he had finally destroyed the ultimate Seed of God—that is, until Nachash heard yet another disturbing announcement about thirty years after the Bethlehem massacre. It was exclaimed from the serene shores of the Jordan River: *Behold the Lamb!*

The proclamation was shouted from the lips of a desert preacher, an ill-dressed fanatic with a pauper's diet—but one the people of the surrounding regions were pouring into the Jordan River valley to see. They were coming to be baptized by him. They were there to repent and turn back to Yahweh. They had gathered to welcome the *days of Messiah*, the promised Seed of Abraham.

John the Baptizer shouted the announcement as he pointed to Jesus, his voice rolling through the desert and across the placid river waters, "Behold! *Here* is the Lamb of God! The one sent from Heaven's throne! The one who has come to take away the sins of the world!"

The serpent was enraged. But at least now he finally knew *the who* of Yahweh's garden death sentence.

This was war.

It was time to bring this to an end...

# THE DARK GOD SPEAKS

**47**

*The persecution of Christians across the globe is more common in our generation than in any other before us.*

**A**fter three long years of battle...*there was a cross.*

Next...there was an empty tomb.

And that's when Satan knew. *He had been defeated.* His time was quickly running out.

When Satan's plan to destroy Jesus failed, he went off to make war against the *seed of the Seed,*[327] those who belong to the prophetically revenant nation of Israel and, most importantly, those who belong to Jesus Christ and His present earthly body, the true, *born-again, inner* church.

Told in metaphorical terms, Revelation 12 recounts the drama. Following is a relevant portion of that chapter:

> Therefore rejoice, you heavens and you who dwell in them! But woe to the earth and the sea, because **the devil has gone down to you!** He is **filled with fury**, because he *knows that his time is short."*
>
> When the dragon saw that he had been hurled to the earth, he pursued *the woman who had given birth to the male child.*
>
> **Then the dragon** was enraged at the woman and *went off to wage war against the rest of her offspring—those who keep God's commands and hold fast their testimony about Jesus.* (Revelation 12:12–13, 17; emphasis added)

The woman in Revelation 12 is Israel, the ultimate "mother" of the Seed of prophecy, as well as the "mother" of the true church. Jesus Christ was brought to this earth through a literal, human woman. That woman was Mary of Nazareth, who was also of the people of Israel. This "woman" of Revelation 12 also points us back to the very beginning, to the Book of Genesis.

*Cambridge Bible for Schools and Colleges*:

**Who then, or what, is** the typical or **mystical Mother** of Christ? *Not the Christian Church*, which in this book as elsewhere is represented as His wife.... *More certain is the reference...to Genesis 37:9*, where "the eleven stars," represent Jacob's eleven sons, bowing down to Joseph, and the twelfth. **Here,** *the ideal Israel appears* in the glory of all the patriarchs.[328] (Emphasis added)

The "rest of the woman's offspring"—those who keep God's commands and hold fast their testimony about Jesus—especially as the image relates to the last days of Revelation's subject matter, is none other than the "true" and "invisible" church.

Note how all of these links consistently return us to Jesus' kingdom parables of Matthew 13 and Paul's declaration in Thessalonians 2:4 concerning the "temple of God."

*Jamieson-Fausset-Brown Bible Commentary*:

**Satan's first effort** was *to root out the Christian Church*, so that there should be no visible profession of Christianity. Foiled in this, **he wars against the** *invisible Church*, namely, "those who keep the commandments of God, and **have the testimony of Jesus.**" These are "the remnant," or **rest of her seed, as distinguished from her seed, "the man-child."** Unable to destroy Christianity and the Church as a whole, *Satan directs his enmity against true Christians*, the elect remnant: the others he leaves unmolested.[329] (Emphasis added)

Today, right in front of the world, Satan's fury is unquestionably aimed directly toward the prophetically returned nation of Israel. That nation stands as God's last-days sign of His glory and the truth of His eternal Word. Sadly, most of that anti-Israel hatred comes right out of today's visible church. And, of all things, that institutional church, the *fake church* that poses as the real church, accuses the presciently returned Israel of being a "fake Israel." The demonic hypocrisy is appalling.[330]

However, just as striking is still another prophetic image embedded in Revelation 12. It is the prophecy of Satan's concentrated global assault on anything that represents Christianity.


## THE REST OF HER OFFSPRING

The persecution of Christians across the globe is more common in our generation than in any other before us. It is widely reported that more believers have died as a result of proclaiming their faith within the last century alone than in the previous two thousand years *combined.*[331]

We, the body of Christ, are *the seed of the Seed.* We are what Satan fears the most as a potential disruption to his kingdom agenda. We are in his sights of destruction. It is the church that Nachash wishes to denigrate and destroy, and in which he desires to "set himself up" as God.

*Orthodox Christian Network*:

> **The outlook for Christians in countries around the world is looking "*worse than ever before,*"** according to a new report from Aid to the Church in Need. According to the report, "*persecution against Christians is at an all-time high.*"[332] (Emphasis added)

Open Doors USA is one of the most trusted and consistent sources of reporting concerning global Christian persecution. By 2019, that organization documented that the statistics on persecution had grown even higher than just a few years earlier.[333]

Their latest figures, as of this writing, state there are now *eleven* countries with Christian persecution rates at the "extreme" level. Just five years prior, only *one* country ranked at that level—North Korea. In the top fifty nations most notorious for killing and/or persecuting Christians, there was a 14 percent rise over the numbers of the previous year. Most of the persecution against Christians comes from the Muslim nations.

Open Doors USA also reported that in the top fifty of its "world watch list" of persecuting countries in 2018 alone, there were 4,136 Christians killed for faith-related reasons. In that same year, among those same top fifty nations, 2,625 Christians were detained without trial, arrested, sentenced, and imprisoned—and that's not to mention the 1,266 churches or Christian buildings that were attacked and/or destroyed in those same countries.

The bottom line is this: On a global basis, there is a Christian man, woman, boy, or girl killed for his or her faith approximately every two hours *of every single day*.

We're now the first generation to be living in at least the leading edges of the fulfillment of what Jesus declared would happen just shortly before His return, making us the most profoundly prophetic generation since His First Coming.

> Then you will be handed over to be persecuted and put to death, and you will be hated by all nations because of me....
>
> For then there will be great distress, unequaled from the beginning of the world until now—and never to be equaled again. (Matthew 24:9, 21)

In America, however, where our designer coffee shops are open every day and our favorite sports teams are playing, Satan veils what he's doing elsewhere around the world by hiding behind his façades of loveliness and the shiny things of life. We are sometimes like the citizens of ancient Rome, cheering on their favorite gladiators while Christians were being rounded up and executed.

We don't really "see" what Satan's doing, nor do we "hear" what he's screaming at Heaven's throne, because most churches don't even acknowledge that it's happening. So it's fairly easy for Satan to conceal the true depth of his diabolical rage. He is, after all, the father of lies and the grand master of illusion. It is his nature. It is his specialty.

As the bodies of our brothers and sisters continue to pile up around the world, Nachash merely smiles—like the innocent angel of light he pretends to be.

However, the most prolific carnage that Satan exacts upon the planet is specifically focused on the human womb. It was from the womb of a woman wherein a Seed was brought forth that started the certain downfall of his entire kingdom.

And he is filled with rage because of it.

# THE TARGET

## 48

*Nachash's rage against the womb
of the woman extends all the way
back to the Garden of Eden.*

The leading cause of death on the planet for more than the last three decades is nothing short of murder.

More specifically, it is the wanton, almost unrestrained murder of children—the little ones—those who are still in their mother's wombs.

Think about that! All of the annual global deaths *combined* that are associated with AIDs, cancer, automobile accidents, smoking, alcohol, and heart disease don't come close to totaling the number of the "seed of the womb of the woman" who are put to death through abortion. In fact, the total of those combined causes of death still falls at least ten million short of the number of abortions around the world each year.[334]

According to the World Health Organization figures, the *top ten* causes of combined annual global death still don't approximate the total count of abortion-related deaths worldwide.[335] This is staggering.

And, in the United States alone, an estimated 99 percent of abortions are not carried out because of medical necessity; the most frequently cited reason for abortion is "convenience."[336]

*The Washington Examiner:*

In 2018, 41.9 million pregnancies were prematurely terminated, **making abortion the leading cause of death in the world.** The staggering figure was tallied by Worldometers, a site which aggregates **statistical data from sources such as the World Health Organization.**

259

Yet unlike most of the other leading causes of death in the world, abortion is almost 100 percent preventable. Case in point: *In the U.S., 9 out of 10 abortions are elective. That is to say they are performed not for medical reasons but because the baby is not wanted.*[337] (Emphasis added)

As a measurement of how monumental the scourge really is, consider these facts. Between the years 2010 and 2014, an average of almost sixty million abortions each year were performed around the world[338] That yearly total is about the same number of abortions it has taken the United States to *aggregately* tally over a *fifty-year* period.[339]

Sixty million is precisely ten times greater than the total number of Jewish people who were exterminated in the Holocaust of World War II. It is also about the same number of deaths recorded throughout the entire Second World War.[340]

But, even those annual global abortion numbers are most likely *much lower* than the actual total, since large swaths of the nations of the world do not even record, much less report, abortion statistics. The most accurate estimates we *do* have are compiled from a variety of sources, including the United Nations (UN), the World Health Organization (WHO), the Guttmacher Institute (AGI), and the Center for Reproductive Rights.[341]

Here's another way to statistically analyze the horrors of the epidemic of *abortion murder*. Since 1980, well over a billion and a half children have been killed in their mothers' wombs worldwide. That figure represents at least 21 percent of the world's current population.[342] The vile scourge of abortion is of pandemic proportions.

## DIABOLICAL MADNESS

By God's design, the womb of a mother-to-be should serve as the safest place on earth for the unborn child. But it is not. It has become the laser-focused target of Satan, *the murderer from the very beginning*.

What is the *mask of excuse* that Satan hides behind as he uses the slaughter of children as a way to thumb his nose at Heaven's throne? The self-proclaimed "false information debunking" site, Snopes, answers that question the most succinctly, without even recognizing what it has actually exposed.

> Stating that abortion is the **"leading cause of death" worldwide is a problematic pronouncement**, because that stance *takes a political position*, one that is **at odds with the scientific/medical world**.
>
> **The medical community does not** *confer* **personhood upon fetuses that are not viable outside the womb**, so counting abortion as a "cause of death" does not align with the practices of health.[343] (Emphasis added)

In other words, Snopes admits that the horrendous global abortion numbers are correct! That is a fact Snopes knows it simply can't argue. Instead, it offers an adjustment to the truth by asserting that the medical industry says fetuses are not really "persons."

*Viola*! If the fetus is not a person, then it's not illegal. And, if it's not illegal, then it certainly isn't murder! In fact, it's not really even a genuine "death." How perversely convenient.

## THE YEAR THE MUSIC DIED

In 1973, the floodgates for Satan's agenda were opened with the Supreme Court decision in *Roe v. Wade*. However, in that same year, when it was made a nationally legal practice to purposely invade the womb of a woman and destroy the infant within it, the United States government also passed the Federal Endangered Species Act. That decree made it against the law to molest an eagle's nest or to destroy a turtle's egg.[344] And that's when the madness truly began to flood upon us and spill into the rest of the world.

I am convinced that, in 1973, our nation was given over to yet another degenerate doctrine of demons. Think about how far down that cavernous abyss we've traveled since then.

Now, by decrees of the Supreme Court, federal edicts, and national political correctness, we don't even know what true marriage is anymore. We also seem to be thoroughly confused as to what constitutes gender. Is the identification of gender a psychological issue, an emotional matter, or a physical malady that needs to be "corrected" or accommodated? Or, is it a deeply spiritual issue? Perhaps it's *all of the above*.

Additionally, it seems we no longer remember what constitutes a true home and a real family. Manhood is debased, womanhood is smeared, and the sanctity of childhood is in a constant state of gender confusion. It's a dysphoria that is permeating the minds of our little ones through an increasingly befuddled culture that is literally going mad.

> *They exchanged the truth about God for a lie, and worshiped and served created things rather than the Creator*—who is forever praised.
>
> Therefore, just as they did not think it worthwhile to retain the knowledge of God, so *God gave them over to a depraved mind*, so that they do what ought not to be done. (Romans 1:25, 28; emphasis added)

As we've seen in Revelation 9, the Word of God tells us that the pervasive last-days global "spirit" would be that of unabashed demonic worship. That worship would come through the vehicles of the global epidemics of substance abuse, sexual perversion, murders, and thievery. We've now seen the links between all of these. We are the first generation in human history to see the worldwide scourge paraded before us on a daily basis.

Right after Revelation 12, in the very next chapter, we're introduced to the rise of the Antichrist kingdom. This was the ultimate warning of Paul's second letter to the Thessalonians. It was also the thrust of Jesus' revelations on the shores of Galilee through His kingdom parables. That kingdom-beast will culminate in the worldwide, brutally enforced and diabolically demanded worship of Satan's "man"—the *man of lawlessness*.

The world is now close to those days, but most don't even see it. The church has been anesthetized. It's been drugged. It's been seduced. It has been infiltrated.

Satan is orchestrating an inglorious masquerade.

However, the Word of God assures us that Nachash has saved his most diabolical and grandest ruse for the days yet to come.

Perhaps those days are just around the corner. Many believe we are currently right in the midst of the "setup."

# PART IX

# ARRIVAL OF THE GODS

It has been said that human history is little more than a chronicle of man's wars. These wars are the result of men being influenced by invisible, evil spirit beings ever since Adam and Eve sinned and were cast out from the presence of God.

~GENESIS 3:22–24

No people and no generation have ever been immune from Satan's attempts to keep men separated from God.

~EARL L. HENN (1934–1997)[345]

# MANIFESTATION | 49

*It seems the world is thoroughly infatuated
with the idea of a visitation.*

Did God create intelligent life forms on other planets? If so, could these intelligent entities be behind what humans call UFO visitations?

Since antiquity, dating back as far as 1440 BC, we've been in possession of the transcripts of famous military commanders and still-revered historians who purportedly observed (or reported upon) strange flying objects in the skies over the earth. Some of those otherworldly "flying craft" were even said to have been engaged in "battle." These "UFO" sightings continued to be reported worldwide long before humanity recorded its very first flight in 1903. And, of course, UFO sightings are still being reported today in record numbers.[346]

This ubiquitous phenomenon has been a primary catalyst for the age-old questions: Are we alone in the universe, or is there life elsewhere? If so, is that life genuinely visiting us? And if it is actually visiting us, then, to what end?

First, if we stay strictly with what the Bible says, there is no direct mention whatsoever of intelligent life having been created on other planets. However, that is not to say God couldn't have done such a thing. Of course He *could* have. I consider it a highly unlikely prospect simply because of the lack of biblical information to the contrary.

However, if it was ever 100 percent, scientifically verified that there is intelligent life on other planets, that fact would do nothing to destroy the biblical message. Yahweh would be their Creator also.

267

Dr. Michael Heiser[347] addresses the matter in a similar fashion:

> I would argue that **if there ever turns out to be alien life**, then *God was its creator like everything else*. While **I don't think there is any evidence** for truly extraterrestrial life from other planets, I **don't rule it out.** God is under no obligation to tell us everything in the Bible about his creative output.[348] (Emphasis added)

Now we are left with the question about UFOs and the manifestations of so-called alien beings that are supposedly visiting earth—or stranger yet, about the reports of aliens that have allegedly abducted a number of humans over the last decades.

## UFOS

In late September 2019, Tucker Carlson of Fox News' *Tucker Carlson Reports*, started his program with the following:

> Not so long ago, anyone that used the term UFO was considered a crank or a conspiracy nut, but now a growing number of military pilots and serious professionals are discussing their own encounters with strange encounters in the sky. Those experiences are unpacked in some length in an upcoming History Channel AME special called "Unidentified."[349]

So, what are we "enlightened ones" to think concerning these strange encounters in the heavens?

The term UFO, which, of course, stands for "unidentified flying object," was coined in 1953 by the United States Air Force to serve as a catch-all for describing aerial phenomena that didn't match natural explanations. Even though well over a hundred thousand people claim to have seen UFOs in the past hundred years,[350] most of the observations can be explained as natural physical occurrences. Some even claim that a number of these sightings are simply secret military advancements and that "aliens" and "flying saucers" are merely the government's cover story.

However, there are still a substantial number of sightings that defy any of these explanations. Those left over from the scientifically and rationally explainable occurrences are often referred to as "residual UFOs" (RUFOs).

In 2019, the Gallup polling organization reported that more than a third of Americans believe these objects are physically real and are inhabited by extraterrestrial aliens, intelligent beings from other planets. More than two-thirds believe the US government is withholding information regarding RUFOs.[351]

The fascination with RUFOs is not just the stuff of back-channel conspiracy sites. The topic has been the intense focus of official national security concerns, government research projects, and military investigations, as well as exhaustive scientific studies, numerous books, serious-minded television documentaries, and the like.

A 2018 History.com report catalogued the 1961 alien abduction event that sparked the first official government investigation of the phenomenon. The incident involved the account of Barney and Betty Hill.

Gray beings with large eyes had walked them into a metallic disc as wide, Betty said, as her house was long. Once inside, the beings examined the couple and erased their memories.

Their experience would kick off an Air Force inquiry, part of the secretive initiative Project Blue Book that investigated UFO sightings across the country. The incident would also become the first-ever widely publicized alien-abduction account.... The Air Force's Project Blue Book would ultimately dismiss the story.... The Hills stuck by their story, despite years of skeptics and detractors.[352]

# US NAVY MEETS ET

Even the United States Navy has reported close encounters with other-worldly phenomena that have thus far defied explanation. In September 2019, *Popular Mechanics* ran a headline reading "The Navy Says Those UFO Videos Are Real. And they were never meant to be released to the public."

But released to the public *they were,* And in dramatic fashion! Here's an excerpt from the article:

> **The U.S. Navy has confirmed** that three online videos purportedly showing UFOs **are genuine.** The service says the videos, taken by Navy pilots, show "unexplained aerial phenomena," but also states that *the clips should have never been released to the public in the first place.*
>
> The three videos in question…show two separate encounters between Navy aircraft and UFOs. In the videos, *air crews loudly debate what the objects are and where they came from.*[353] (Emphasis added)

The distinguishing characteristic of the Navy-spotted UFOs were that they appeared to possess otherworldly technological capabilities.

> In each case, the objects in the videos undertook aerial *maneuvers that aren't possible with current aviation technology.* In the 2004 incident, according to the *New York Times,* the objects "*appeared suddenly at 80,000 feet,* and then hurtled toward the sea, eventually stopping at 20,000 feet and hovering. Then they either dropped out of radar range or *shot straight back up.*"[354] (Emphasis added)

LiveScience.com added even more info to the Navy's most recent admission—namely, that the US Navy still doesn't have a clue whether they are alien craft:

In December 2017 and March 2018, *The New York Times* released three allegedly declassified videos showing U.S. Navy pilots trailing some unidentified flying objects. The mystery crafts *moved at hypersonic speeds*, flying tens of thousands of feet above the Earth with **no distinct wings, engines or visible signs of propulsion whatsoever.** Were they flying saucers? Incredibly high-tech drones? **The pilots had no idea**—and, according to a recent statement from Navy intelligence officials, *neither does the U.S. government.*

The objects, which were *detected in restricted military training airspaces* in 2004 and 2015, were *not supposed to be there.* The objects **still** *have not been* successfully identified as any known type of aircraft.[355] (Emphasis added)

In May 2019, the *New York Times* offered additional details to the seemingly supernatural nature of the Navy's unintentionally leaked encounters:

The strange objects, one of them like a spinning top moving against the wind, **appeared** *almost daily* **from the summer of 2014 to March 2015,** high in the skies over the East Coast. **Navy pilots reported to their superiors** that the objects had *no visible engine or infrared exhaust plumes*, but that they could reach 30,000 feet and hypersonic speeds.[356] (Emphasis added)

Then, in late December, as 2019 was coming to a close, Slate.com ran an article titled "The Year UFOs Became a Little More Legit." However, the subtitle was even more intriguing: "We didn't find ETs in 2019, but the U.S. government did become a little chattier about flying saucers."

The Slate.com article documented that not only was President Trump apprised of the latest information regarding supposed UFO sightings by the US military, but also a select group of US senators had been gathered for "classified" disclosures and discussions of the phenomenon.

Lt. Cmdr. Daniel Day said the meeting centered "on efforts to understand and identify these threats to the safety and security of our aviators." Later, Sen. Mark Walker accused the Navy of withholding UFO info, saying, "There is frustration with the lack of answers to specific questions about the threat that superior aircraft flying in United States airspace may pose."[357]

As sensational as these accounts have proven to be, they're not the end of the matter. As of this writing, the Navy reports, these objects are still drawing international attention and scientific scrutiny.

# WHY? WHERE? WHAT?

## 50

*There has been a tremendous rise in overall reported UFO sightings among the general population.*

**R**ight after the May 2019 report by the *New York Times*, Fox News offered additional disturbing information:

> Former Deputy Assistant Secretary of Defense for Intelligence Christopher Mellon said, "*We know that UFOs exist. This is no longer an issue,*" he said. "The issue is *why are they here? Where are they coming from* and *what is the technology behind these devices* that we are observing?"
>
> There are indications, Mellon said, that the objects reported by Navy pilots in 2014 and 2015 were **doing things that aren't possible in this physical realm.**
>
> The speeds being reported (about 5,000 miles per hour, according to Mellon) were **only sustainable for about an hour** by an aircraft in the air, and **these objects would be flying around all day long**, the pilots said.[358] (Emphasis added)

## THE EVIDENCE DISAPPEARS

In November of 2019, *Popular Mechanics* ran yet another alarming piece on the story, titled "The Witnesses," detailing the accounts of an additional five Navy officers: Gary Voorhis, Jason Turner, P. J. Hughes, Ryan

Weigelt, and Kevin Day. In that article, the officers speak of unprecedented "radar tracks" regarding the objects that were chased by the flight
crews of the USS Nimitz. They also claimed the grainy one-minute clip
that was eventually leaked to the press of the Navy's UFO encounter was
actually much longer in its original format. They claimed the original
was eight to ten minutes in length, and much clearer.

But the most shocking assertion revolves around their account of
how those recordings of the encounter eventually "disappeared:"

[On the *Nimitz*] Shortly after securing the data bricks, Hughes
said he was **visited by his commanding officer and two unknown
individuals**…. According to Hughes, his commanding officer
told him to **turn over the recently secured harddrives.** "We put
them in the bags, he took them, then he and the two anonymous officers left," Hughes said.

Inside the *Princeton*, Voorhis had a similar encounter. "These
**two guys show up on a helicopter**, which wasn't uncommon,
but shortly after they arrived, maybe 20 minutes, I was told by
my chain of command to **turn over all the data recording**s for
the AEGIS system," says Voorhis.

In addition to **turning over his data tapes**, Voorhis says he
was told by this chain of command he needed to **reload the
recorders** for the ship's advanced Combat Engagement Center
(CEC) because it **had also been wiped clean**, along with the
optical drives with all the radio communications. "They even
told me to **erase everything that's in the shop—even the blank
tapes.**"[359] (Emphasis and brackets added)


## INCREASED NUMBERS OF SIGHTINGS

Regardless of what the Navy UFO sightings might prove to be, the fact
remains that there has been a tremendous rise in the number of reported

UFO sightings among the general population. This is true not only over the last hundred, years but even in the last few years. In fact, a Fox News article reported that the phenomenon was currently being registered at an "all-time high." The majority of the sightings were being reported in the United States.[360]

Sam Monfort, a doctoral student in Human Factors and Applied Cognition at George Mason University, authored a report on the topic, gleaning his information from the National UFO Reporting Center (NUFORC), an organization that documents such sightings. Monfort stated that UFOs have been increasingly manifesting, adding to the total of the 104,947 reported sightings over the past one hundred-plus years.[361]

After that report, the *New York Times* published another tantalizing piece about Project Blue Book,[362] the official U.S. Air Force inquiry into the UFO phenomenon. One of that article's most sensational revelations is related in the following excerpt:

In 1967, a glowing red oval-shaped object hovered over Malmstrom Air Force Base in Montana, and **all 10 of the facility's underground nuclear missiles *became disabled almost simultaneously* while the U.F.O. was present**, according to interviews with witnesses and official government reports.[363] (Emphasis added)

## LITTLE GREEN MEN

It seems the world is thoroughly infatuated with the idea of a "visitation," of one kind or another, from some type of cosmic intelligent input. Collectively, if the planet appears desirous of such an experience, Satan would surely seek to grant it, especially if the ruse would help him pull off his final grand delusion concerning setting up his Antichrist kingdom.

Could something like this be a part of the demonic outpouring and delusion of the last days? Could we be witnessing the world being sucked into the grips of a massive demonic "setup?" Considering the biblical signs of the last days that we've already uncovered and the fact that we're the first generation to be experiencing them, it's not too far-fetched to consider the possibility.

A growing number of biblical researchers set forth the very real likelihood that fallen *elohim* from the demonic realm might make a public appearance relatively soon. Most likely, they would present themselves as visitors from other planets, even, perhaps, from other dimensions.[364]

Most who see this satanic deception as a legitimate possibility think the domain of the demonic might very well display itself through the vehicle of interdimensional travel.[365]

Certainly Satan operates within that realm, even now.

# THE VISITING GODS

*He insisted that he believed the UFO phenomenon is some sort of anciently existing "mind-control" technology.*

**51**

**D**r. Hugh Ross, who holds an undergraduate degree in physics and a PhD in astronomy, is the director of Reasons to Believe.[366] In 2002, Dr. Ross coauthored a book with Dr. Mark Clark, a professor of political science and director of the National Security Studies program at California State University. That book was also coauthored with Kenneth Samples, the vice president of Philosophical and Theological Apologetics at Reasons to Believe.

The name of their book is *Lights in the Sky & Little Green Men: A Rational Christian Look at UFOs and Extraterrestrials.* Following is a brief excerpt written by Dr. Ross:

> **The authors of this book *are fully convinced* that both science and Scripture point to the *supradimensional* beings *known as demons* as *the malevolent sources* of RUFO [residual unidentified flying object] phenomena...**
>
> Yet amid a host of diverse and often confusing facts and opinions about UFO phenomena, *at least one point of agreement stands out* among **physical scientists, social scientists, behavioral scientists, and students of the Bible**: pursue truth where it may be found and tested, and *beware of any pursuit*

*that links, directly or indirectly, with occult power or "secret" knowledge.*[367] (Emphasis and brackets added)

In a CBN article that recounted a television interview concerning his book, Dr. Ross made it clear that he also thinks *interdimensional demonic travel* is the most likely explanation for the RUFO phenomenon:

> **Most people think UFOs are physical. "But *they can't be* physical,"** says Hugh, **"because *they defy gravity*."**...
>
> What [the] evidence suggests is that **RUFOs are capable of producing physical effects**, such as burnt grass, *but are not physical themselves.*
>
> Hugh says the **Bible proclaims the existence of a personal** *Creator who can act independently outside the cosmos* **and who is** *not restricted by the four, large space-time dimensions* (length, width, height, or time). **The Bible also describes the spirit realm (the realm** *beyond matter, energy, and space-time dimensions*) and declares the existence of God and two or more distinct creatures: humans and angels. **Hugh explains that humans remain physically restricted to the dimensions** of the cosmos and cannot account for the unexplained phenomena. *Angels, or fallen angels,* remain *as possible links*...and are *an identifiable source of explanation.*[368] (Emphasis and brackets added)

Through this interview, and long before the US Navy inadvertently released the videos of the RUFOs, Dr. Ross described those Navy-identified objects *to a tee.* They appear to be physical, yet are manifestly "defying gravity."

Based upon Dr. Ross' analysis as related in the CBN interview, we can only assume he would deduce that these law-defying craft are therefore "not physical" after all. And, if that is the case, the best evidence would suggest that they are interdimensional—therefore demonic in origin.

## UFOLOGISTS SEE DEMONS

However, really shocking is that several globally renowned experts In ufology have arrived at basically the same conclusions as those of a number of Christian scholars and research scientists. What's more, these secular ufologists aren't known as being deeply spiritual people at all. Following are a few prominent examples.

### John Keel

Even the famed UFO researcher John Keel[369] wrote of a potential demonic connection:

> The UFOs *do not seem to exist as tangible*, manufactured objects. They *do not conform to the natural laws* of our environment. **They seem to be nothing more than** *transmogrifications* **tailoring themselves to our abilities to understand.**
>
> The thousands of contacts with the entities indicate that *they are liars and put-on artists*.
>
> **The UFO manifestations seem to be,** by and large, merely **minor variations of the age-old** *demonological* **phenomenon.**[370] (Emphasis added)

Keel eventually hypothesized that these so-called alien entities are more along the lines of manifestations from the demonic realm. He says they are basically morphing into whatever it is we need them to be. And here's the real giveaway: Keel says they are "liars" and "put-on artists"— *two of the most distinct fingerprints of Nachash*.

### Jacques Vallée

Cited as one of the most famous UFO researchers of all time is the PhD computer scientist and astronomer Jacques Vallée. As far back as 1977, he was insisting that he believed the UFO phenomenon to be some sort of ancient "mind-control" technology:

I propose the hypothesis that *there is a control system for human consciousness....* I am suggesting that **what takes place through close encounters with UFOs** *is control of human beliefs*, control of **the relationship between our consciousness and physical reality**, that this control **has been** *in force throughout history* and that it is of secondary importance that it should *now assume the form of sightings of space visitors.*[371] (Emphasis added)

Again, perhaps without realizing it, Vallée is actually describing demonic entities. Not only that, but he describes their mode of operation and overall purpose in a way that lines up almost identically with biblical teaching concerning the prophesied last-days demonic outpouring.

## David Michael Jacobs

Equally as shocking is the conclusion that Dr. David Michael Jacobs has reached. Dr. Jacobs holds a PhD from the University of Wisconsin at Madison in the field of intellectual history. He wrote his dissertation on the myriad topics of controversy surrounding unidentified flying objects in America, and for more than twenty-five years has taught a course on "UFOs in American Society" at Temple University in Philadelphia, Pennsylvania.[372]

Internationally renowned in the field of ufology, Jacobs has lectured widely, been interviewed frequently, and participated in numerous television and radio shows to address the subject of alien abductions. Further, he has written five books on the topic of UFOs.[373]

Dr. Jacobs hypothesizes that the evidence from his mammoth amount of detailed research suggests that alien-human hybrids were engaged in a covert program of infiltration into human society with possibly *the final goal of taking over earth*. He further claims that some of his research subjects are teaching these hybrids how to blend into human society so they cannot be differentiated from humans, and that this activity is occurring worldwide.[374]

Regardless of how far-fetched Dr. Jacobs' findings might initially sound, we cannot discount the obvious connections to the biblically stated truths of a last-days demonic outpouring. This event will result in a global takeover by the prophesied and coming Antichrist figure, the one who is empowered by Satan himself.

## Nick Redfern

There's still more. Famed ufologist Nick Redfern, who has written over a dozen books, as well as numerous articles for various publications, and has appeared as a regular guest on the History Channel's *UFO Hunters*, made the following stunning admission. Observe the progression of his self-professed views that have transpired over the years and where he has finally arrived in his understanding of the matter:

> **My views on the nature of the UFO phenomenon have radically changed** over the years. Back when I was in my twenties, I was of the opinion that UFOs (the truly unknown ones) were extraterrestrial.... As I slid into my thirties, however, **my thoughts slowly began to change** (something which *also happened for a few friends of mine* in the field, too).
>
> And as many people will also know, **my views—today—are far closer to those suggested by John Keel.** Namely, that **we're dealing with something that** *co-exists with us* and *which masquerades* as ET.[375] (Emphasis added)

Yes, Mr. Redfern used the word "masquerade."

Again, whether or not he knows it, Redfern is describing something much more akin to the demonic realm. Notice that he speaks of their "coexistence" with us. The idea that there are other intelligent entities that have and/or continue to coexist with us is yet another biblical concept that goes all the way back to Genesis 3–6.

So, why should we be surprised by any of this?

# LOOK AT US!

52

*The demonic are more than happy to show themselves.*

To a growing number of serious-minded researchers, the rash of reported UFO sightings, especially in the last decade or so, might be some sort of a message. This fact, coupled with the various manifestations and abduction scenarios that have also been well-documented, appears to indicate that the "visiting entities" are declaring: *We're here!*

To quote Nick Redfern:

> There's the nature of the entities themselves: **they practically** *overemphasize* who, or *what, they claim to be.* We only have to take a careful look at such cases…to see that these **"incidents"** are *clearly stage-managed.* It's a game, a scenario that has everything to do with *trying to emphasize the ET meme….*
>
> **Of course, they could easily avoid us! But, here's the deal:** *they want to be seen.* It's not an accident. *It's carefully planned.* And it's *designed to plant an image* of "ET scientists" in the mind(s) of the witness(es).[376] (Emphasis added)

The context of the following statement from Dr. Michael Heiser is from a book review he wrote about a 2005 book titled, *Alien Intrusion: UFOs and the Evolution Connection,* by Gary Bates, a former hardcore evolutionist who is now CEO of Creation Ministries International, US. Dr. Heiser wrote:

I have to give Gary [Bates] kudos for his view that **the current alien** *abduction phenomenon* **has** *nothing to do with an actual breeding program*—by true aliens or demonic beings. Gary's position is that **it's all about** *erecting a paradigm in front of people* to embrace the idea of alien-human "advancement" or "merging." *I agree.*[377] (Emphasis and brackets added)

Gary Bates also wrote an article, titled "UFOs Are Not Extraterrestrial! Modern Secular Researchers Are Getting Closer to the Truth," in which he declared:

Vallée and even Keel showed that ETs were...some kind of **"psychic" force** that **would alter** [their] appearance **depending upon [their] audience's ability to understand.**

**In the past they were elves, fairies and even spirit beings manifesting** themselves *to third-world cultures*. However, to the "true believer" [in alien beings] *who really desires* there to be **benevolent aliens visiting us** from different star systems, then perhaps *they are interdimensional and not really from our own physical universe*. Speculative ideas [from the scientific realm of quantum physics research] about the evolution of the cosmos such as *string theory and multiverse have only accelerated this idea.*[378] (Emphasis and brackets added)

The writers at Gotquestions.org, a decidedly conservative Christian question-and-answer site,[379] also address the topic in an article titled, "Could an Alien Deception Be Part of the End Times?"

We know that the events surrounding the end times, as described in the Bible, *will include a powerful deception* (Matthew 24:24). Recently, interest has been rising in the theory that *this deception will include alien* beings from another planet. Odd as it may seem, *this theory is entirely plausible from a Christian perspective.*

Another **notable instance of their interaction with us is found in Genesis 6:4 with the arrival of the** *"sons of God."* The Genesis account states that these powerful beings had sexual intercourse with women and produced a super race of beings known as the Nephilim. This sounds like the stuff of science fiction, yet it is right there in the Bible.[380] (Emphasis added)

## PHYSICAL TRACE EVIDENCE

How do we respond to mockers who claim there is no physical evidence of UFO existence? Again, Dr. Michael Heiser offers a salient answer to the question.

> Peter Sturrock's book *The UFO Enigma: A New Review of the Physical Evidence* (2000) **demonstrates quite well that there is an abundance of physical evidence for UFOs….** Sturrock, **a scientist with a PhD** who knows what the scientific method is, **documents a wide range of evidence**, including radar, vehicle interference, aircraft malfunction, ground traces, injuries to plants (e.g., radiation), and actual debris analysis.[381] (Emphasis added)

Please don't miss the similarities of what we are discovering about the connections between demonic manifestations of "alien beings" with that of necromancy and familiar spirits. In both cases, the demonic are more than happy to show themselves. They can even leave "physical evidence" of their nonphysical appearances, if that is what's necessary to make people become "believers."

The demonic entities are apparently more than capable of "appearing" in any form that one wishes to see, such as a deceased relative or friend, a little green man, an alien grey, or an angel of light.

As long as one is willing to deny the truth of Jesus Christ and the Word of God, the unseen and dark realm of Nachash is quite anxious to show humanity whatever it is they wish to experience. In fact, they seem to relish the thought, and seek out the opportunities.

That is what makes this last-days demonic masquerading phenomenon so dangerous, and so overwhelmingly convincing to those who "could be deceived."

# THE FINAL TERROR

*Men's hearts failing them for fear, and for looking after those things which are coming on the earth: for the powers of heaven shall be shaken.*

—Luke 21:26, KJV

# 53

The Word of God is clear. One final, terrifying, demonic masquerade is yet on its way.

Whatever the phenomenon ultimately proves to be, Jesus appears to be hinting that it will be something the world's population has never before witnessed and, perhaps, has never imagined. It will be spectacular. It will involve the "powers of the heavens."[382] But, what could something of that magnitude prove to be?

Although the immediate context of Jesus' words in Luke 21:26 refers to the single day of His literal return, a number of scholars—from classical to modern—agree that the "powers of the heavens" that cause men's hearts to "fail" will begin manifesting during those days (or years) just *prior* to Christ's coming. Some even put it in the period just before the global manifestation of the Antichrist.[383]

This ominous warning indicates that something is going to happen that eventually brings the entire planet to a state of panicked frenzy. The terror and dread will be so great that it will even cause widespread death[384] among those who are horror-struck by the event(s).

*Bengel's Gnomen*:

Luke 21:26. Fear and expectation ["looking after"]) fear, viz. **of things present; expectation, viz.** *of things future. Not even the*

287

*saints* shall be altogether *exempt from some degree of terror.*[385]
(Emphasis added; brackets in original)

*Pulpit Commentary:*

*At the end* of this violent but short distress, [*then*] *the world* **shall
see [Jesus] appear.**[386] (Brackets and emphasis added)

*Benson Commentary:*

What follows **appears to have a more extensive object**, and to
relate to the nations and **the inhabitable earth in general**. There
we hear of distress, or anguish of nations, and of **the things coming upon the habitable world**; not to mention *what immediately follows,* **to wit, that the Son of man shall be seen** coming
in a cloud, with great glory and power.[387] (Emphasis added)

*Peter Pett's Commentary on the Bible* is another scholarly work that
presents Jesus' words as meaning some type of global phenomenon that
creates an atmosphere of deadly dread among all the nations. Pett even
explores the possibility of these spectacles as being demonically driven:

And there can be no doubt **that such fear and distress** and perplexity *has been present in all centuries, and never more so than
now* as we see the rise of *militant Islam,* the fear of *nuclear weapons* reaching uncontrolled hands, the approach of *the unknown
effects of global warming,* the possibility of the cessation of the
gulf stream, the thinning of the ozone layer, the rising of sea levels, and the effects of *other phenomena that could bring disaster
on our world, and about which we can do very little.*
    *If "the powers of the heavens"* are seen as shaken, then times
are really bad. **That is not to deny that behind the words** is the
fact that *unearthly influences might also be at work.* If we con-

sider Romans 8:38; Ephesians 1:21 (compare also Daniel 10) these may indicate that *more is involved than just the physical.*[388] (Emphasis added)

Leslie M. Grant, the author of *L. M. Grant's Commentary on the Bible,* also understood Jesus' ominous warning to mean of a general global calamity of some sort, a spectacular event that would *precede* the literal return of the Lord:

Verse 25 [of Luke 21] now **goes on** *to the time of the end.* The supreme light of **the knowledge of God will be darkened** *through widespread apostasy*—a complete turning away from the Lord. *Nations on earth will be torn by distress*, with perplexity, and *the evidence of this has already begun in our day.* The hearts *of many are failing them for fear now*, seen for example in the great fright over the *possibility of a nuclear holocaust and terrorism, and the alarm over certain nations becoming militarily strong and bold.*[389] (Emphasis and brackets added)

## WHAT IN THE WORLD?

Think about this scenario for just a moment. Today's world is already filled with the *science fiction-type* wonders of quantum computing, vast Internet networks, space weapons, human-like robotics, killer military robots, brain-chip implants, biometric identification technologies, AI that learns, genetic-editing tech, dramatic lifespan-increasing technologies, holographic imagery, high-tech killer drones, deepfake video and audio technologies, almost total immersion *virtual reality* tech, and so much more.

What in the world could so thoroughly impress today's global population—especially the most youthful among us who have grown up with all these technological wonders—that those duped ones would collectively experience something that would cause their "hearts to fail" (Luke 21:26)? And how could the delusion be so plausible that even a number of God's own people could come close to being fooled by it?

Also consider that these marvels will occur in the midst of the days just *before* the return of the Lord. What illusion could be so powerful that whoever is still here at the time would gladly worship a singular man as some sort of *God* (Revelation 13), in order to be delivered from the perceived calamity that is about to befall them? Given the world we're already living in, how could that even be possible?

Of course, we can't say with certainty until it finally happens. Scholars have debated for almost two millennia what that final terror might prove to be. However, Jesus revealed several facts about those days that might line up with the subject we're now exploring.

## THE GREAT DECEPTION

Jesus warned that the last-days delusion would be so powerful that even some of those who are deeply devoted to Him would still be tempted to cave in to the demonic aberration.

In the light of our current topic, have another look at Jesus' well-known words in Matthew 24:24. Admittedly, many scholars understand these words to simply mean that the garden variety of "false messiahs" and "false prophets" will increase as the return of Jesus draws closer. But we might be overlooking something here. The ones Jesus speaks of in this passage—words that are directly related to the very last days—are exhibiting relatively uninhibited demonic powers, proving to be the most deceptive displays of trickery in humanity's existence:

> For *false messiahs* [representing themselves to be saviors] and *false prophets* [heralds of the arrival of these saviors] **will appear** and perform **great signs and wonders** *to deceive, if possible,*

*even the elect* [because they are demonic in origin (2 Thessalonians 2:9)]. See, I have told you ahead of time. (Matthew 24:24; emphasis and brackets with commentary added)

Truly, a genuine display of this kind of power, wrought at the hands of numerous "messiah figures," would have to be supernaturally unprecedented—that is, at least since the time of the days *after* Noah's Flood.

Consider this scripturally revealed fact. The supernatural "visitation" of the fallen unseen realm upon humanity was one of the most prominently portentous features of the days of Noah (see Genesis 6:4). Jesus said the very last days before His return will follow suit.

[Jesus said to them] *Just as it was* in the days of Noah, *so also will it be* in the days of the Son of Man. *It will be just like this* on the day the Son of Man is revealed. (Luke 17:26, 30; emphasis added)

Note that Jesus did not say those days would be "kind of like," "similar to," or "almost the same as" the days of Noah. He said they will be "just as it was" and "just like this." He couldn't have been much clearer.

## THE SCHOLARS

Jesus didn't disclose the details of what will happen in the last days—a time that was still thousands of years into the future of His original audience. How could He have unveiled the particulars to people who were still riding donkeys or walking everywhere they went? So, instead, Jesus spoke in general terms, yet while still describing a literal and unthinkable reality still to come upon the earth in the very last days.

Look at what various renowned scholars have had to say regarding Jesus' words in Matthew 24:24.

*Matthew Henry's Concise Commentary:*

**What Christ here said** to his disciples, **tended more to** *promote caution than to satisfy their curiosity;* more to *prepare them* for the events that *should happen,* than to give *a distinct idea of the events.*[390] (Emphasis added)

These cataclysmic events would be accomplished by supernatural manifestations that were emanating from the demonic realm. They would be *illusions.* They would be lies. But, they would appear in the form of "wonders." These wonders would usher in the rule of Antichrist. In his global rule, the illusions and deceit will finally be embodied *in a man.* *Ellicott's Commentary for English Readers:*

So "signs and **lying wonders**" are **the notes of** *the coming* [before he takes his throne] **of the Wicked One,** in whom *the mystery of iniquity* shall [finally] receive its *full development* (2 Thessalonians 2:9).[391] (Emphasis and brackets added)

Jesus also warned His audience that the unparalleled supernatural crisis emerging in the last days would fuel the necessary opportunity for the Antichrist to reveal himself. *Expositor's Greek Testament:*

**What would one not give** for *a Deliverer,* a Messiah at such a *dire crisis!* The *demand would create the supply*…and **assuring a despairing people** of *deliverance at the last hour.*[392] (Emphasis added)

In Jesus' words, there was also something of a warning concerning the demonic realm's ability to tailor its "appearances" and "manifestations" to the audiences of each generation. The last-days generation, already immersed in futuristic technological wonders and expectations, would then be victims of the most spectacular of custom-made demonic illusions that Satan's power could produce.

*Vincent's Word Studies*:

The words **do not denote different classes** of supernatural man ifestations, **but these manifestations regarded from** *different points of view*. The same miracle may be a mighty work, or a glorious work, *regarded with reference* to its power and grandeur; or a sign of **the doer's supernatural power**; or a wonder, *as it appeals to the spectator*.[393] (Emphasis added)

And, Jesus told them, in no uncertain terms, that these lying wonders would be wrought by the words and actions of mere *pretenders*. Liars. Con artists. Cosmic play actors.

*Pulpit Commentary*:

Many of these wonders…[were] therefore considered as… *derived from the spiritual world,* but necessarily from that realm thereof which is **under** *the control of evil demons*. **Whatever may have been their source, they were** *displayed in support of lies and errors*.…

[Jesus] **foretells the** *appearance of pretenders* who shall *assume the part of Christ*.[394] (Emphasis and brackets added)

Without even knowing it, these classical scholars were shown things in their spirits about the last days that even they could not have fully imagined.

# IGNITING THE UNITER

## 54

*The final and climactic ruse will be utterly overwhelming, and decidedly demonic in its origin.*

Think of what you've read in the last several chapters. The physical manifestations of lying interdimensional spirits? Entities pretending to be our saviors? Adjusting manifest wonders and signs for a specific audience and generation? Preparing the way for the global worship of Antichrist?

Surely the writers of the commentaries we've looked at most likely wouldn't have had UFO manifestations and alien contacts on their minds when they wrote these things. Yet, consider the distinctive terminology we've seen employed by various Christian writers and even secular ufologists: *transmogrifications*,[395] technologies that *defy the laws of physics* and *appear to be physical*, but are not.

Furthermore, we've seen these "aliens" described as liars and put-on artists, beings that masquerade to be something they are not; they are said to possess a "control system" that allows them to manipulate the human consciousness.

We also saw these additional vivid descriptions: They are a force that has coexisted with us throughout history, they assume whatever form is necessary for any generation, and their appearances are "stage-managed" and carefully planned. They *want* to be seen. The entire ruse is about *erecting a paradigm* in front of people. They are *interdimensional* and not really from our own physical universe. Most important, they are *demonic in origin*.

Since we're now quite certain these alien-poser-appearances are demonic in nature, we can ask yet another important question: *What is the ultimate end-game of all their hard work and play-acting?*

## COULD IT BE?

Because we know Jesus' description of those days, as revealed in Matthew 24:24, involves the days just prior to the arrival of Antichrist, then we once again have to consider what the Apostle Paul said about those very same days. Paul's warning is found in his second letter to the church at Thessalonica:

> **The coming** [the days of his pre-arrival] **of the lawless one** [Antichrist] will be *in accordance with how Satan works*. He will use all sorts of *displays of power* through **signs and wonders** *that serve the lie*, and all the ways that wickedness deceives those who are perishing. They perish because *they refused to love the truth* and so be saved. **For this reason** *God sends them* [allows][396] a *powerful delusion* so that they will believe the lie. (2 Thessalonians 2:9–11; emphasis and brackets added)

Notice the shared elements between the prophecies of Matthew 24 and 2 Thessalonians 2. Those commonalities include grand deceptions, powerful delusions, unearthly signs and wonders, and a promise of deliverance through a "savior," as well as the unleashed powers of the demonic forces. All of it is designed to serve the greatest "lie" of the last days. The schemes will be used to prepare humanity for the global worship of the Antichrist, the one who, by that time, will have already "set himself up in the temple of God." Now, however, he can actually demand to be worshipped *as God*. And they *will* worship him.

Again, Gotquestions.org offers an interesting hypothesis concerning the potential connection to these passages:

In order to achieve an agreement between all the world's religions, it would make sense for the "uniter" to come from an entirely new source—an extraterrestrial source.

**It is hard to imagine one religion becoming head of all the others, unless new, unearthly knowledge were the source** of the appeal and power of the new "religion."

This would be in keeping with past deceptions and would be a very **effective way to deceive a large number** of people.

**If alien beings arrived and gave us an extraterrestrial explanation for life on earth**, the origins of the world religions, and **even the origins of our planet**, it would be **very persuasive.**[397] (Emphasis added)

## PERSPECTIVE

Please understand that I'm not categorically insisting the great deception of the last days will prove to be some sort of a literal UFO/demonic deception. It could well be that the demonic con job still on the horizon will far surpass even that likelihood. Regardless, the final deception will be awe-inspiring and decidedly demonic in its origin.

Because the inhabitants of the earth will refuse to believe the truth of God's Word, Yahweh will "send" or "allow" the delusion, so that rebellious humanity will be given over to the lie they have yearned to believe.

Is the world even now being "prepped" for this great delusion? Of course it is. Exactly *how* is still a matter of discussion and debate. But in light of what we've put together in the last few chapters, things appear to be looking a little clearer.

It makes you think, *doesn't it?*

## PART X

# THE WAY IT ENDS

The Lord confides in those who fear him; he makes his covenant known to them.

~Psalm 25:14

# THE STARRY SKY

## 55

*Your young men will have visions.*
*Your old men will dream dreams.*
~Joel 2:28; Acts 2:17

What you will read next is so unbelievable you might be tempted to close the book after you've read a few pages. *Please don't!*

I assure you that as you keep reading, the saga will make much more sense. Plus, as you go forward, you'll see the logical confirmation of the account—observed by *two or three* witnesses.[398]

## THE REVERIE

Years ago, I had a dream. Not just any dream; it was much closer to a biblical vision.

Please believe me; I do not base my life and ministry upon visions and dreams, nor do I attach literal interpretations to various elements of dreams. But, I do know fully well that our heavenly Father *can* speak to us through these vehicles of delivery. Even though I've never been prone to seek them, the Bible is replete with such occurrences, and it includes the promise that the very last days will be marked by an outpouring of dreams and visions among God's people.

Because of my many years of law enforcement experience, I'm always skeptical of so-called *experiences* until I've thoroughly searched them out and squared them with the Word of God. That rule applies to my own experiences, as well as to the experiences of those to whom I minister.

However, my recent public retelling of this dream has since burst forth into a global outpouring of an utterly unexpected response. I'll get to that in a moment, but that response is why you're reading about the dream now.

That dream is the only one I've ever had about which I can still remember *every single* detail in living color. Even as I'm writing this, I can smell the air, hear the sounds, and see the colors I saw that night. I can even feel the deep-seated emotions I felt. To this day, they well up inside of me when I think about that night. There was a reality to it, a *physicality* that I cannot describe.

I pray the Lord will use my retelling of the dream in your life, in a similar way that He is already using it among many others around the world.

## NIGHT

As I entered the depth of the dream, I found myself standing in a vast field. It was night. I was looking up into the starry sky. The heavens stretched before me as far as the eye could see in every direction. The sky was crystal clear, more so than anything I had ever seen before.

I could hear the sounds of life behind me: Children laughing. People talking. Horns honking. Traffic whirring down what sounded like multiple and vast interstate highway systems. An occasional siren. People laughing. People crying. Many engaged in normal conversation. Others screaming at each other in anger. I can only interpret this to mean that *life* was merely going on as usual just behind me, yet it was unseen to me.

I felt as though I had complete freedom to turn around and look behind me to see what was back there and find out where in the world I might have been standing. *But, I didn't want to.* I was glued to the activity of gazing up into the heavens. *Why?* Because the heavens were beginning to come alive! I was mesmerized by what I saw.

The stars took on dazzling countenances, bursting with vivid colors. I recognized certain constellations; I remember correctly calling out some of their astronomical names. I watched *them* especially, because they were beginning to move!

They were almost dancing as they moved in slow, graceful circles and across long, undulating paths, shifting places at will throughout the heavenly realms. It was as though the stars and their collective constellations had become living entities, relocating themselves in the heavens to whatever positions they chose.

I remember thinking that what was occurring certainly was not normal. I knew something had happened to the natural elements of life itself. The laws of physics appeared to have been thrown out the window. But I wasn't frightened. Instead, I was fascinated, and I was almost in a state of worship. I knew something supernatural was going on right before my eyes, but it wasn't an *unholy* event. In fact, it felt *ultra-holy*.

A sudden, energizing breeze arose, bathing my face in freshness. I could smell its cleanness. Yet, at the same time I was in that state of ecstatic delight, the sounds behind me grew more ominous.

It was in the moment of the moving and shifting of the stars that I began to hear panicked screaming. Cars were starting to screech to a halt. Horns started honking. There was intensified screaming from the throngs. Louder and louder. With cursing. Threats. Children crying. Panicked searching.

Then I heard people in apparent anguish, as they spoke about what was happening in the sky. I could tell that the spectacle, which had actually been transporting me into a state of delight, was causing the world behind me to slip into a condition of unmitigated horror. Pandemonium exploded. Multiple sirens blared. Loud, booming noises began to erupt behind me. I could feel their shockwaves on my back.

Warning sirens, like old fashioned air-raid horns, echoed across the field. It felt as though the earth was coming apart at its seams. Now I *wanted* to turn around. *I wanted to see.* But this time I was prevented from doing so by means of an unseen, gentle hand.

Then the pandemonium I'd been hearing escalated into what sounded like the groaning of countless millions of anguished souls. It was eerie, yet I still was not panicked. I wasn't in any state of undue distress at all, I was just sad. Heartbroken for what I knew was occurring behind me. I was a bit anxious, yet I had no real fear. Somehow I knew I would be okay.

## UP

Then it happened!

What I had first thought were stars seemed to be coming unglued from their heavenly perches. They appeared to be falling from the sky! They were streaking across the heavens, then whistling earthward. That's when hell on earth sounded as if it had just unleashed behind me. The screaming and crashing noises became almost unbearable.

Then one of the "stars," looking as if it were about to hit the ground in front of me, became a life form. I wasn't allowed to see it clearly. Again, not only did I have no fear, but I realized it was an angel. At once I was lifted up by this "star."

In the next instant, I felt myself seated in a container of sorts, open in the top, open to the sights of the heavens. I turned to my left. My wife was seated beside me. My hand was held tightly in hers. I turned to my right and was only allowed to know that I was in the hands of the "star" that had whisked me up from the earth. I could not see his face, but there was no fear. No pain. No anxiety. Only an indescribable joy. My wife and I didn't even have to speak. We just *knew.*

The heavens began to whiz past our eyes at what appeared to be the speed of light. The pinpoints of light became blurry streaks. It was like something out of a science-fiction movie, as if I were aboard the *Starship Enterprise* traveling at warp speed! I can still feel the exhilaration of the moment even as I'm typing these words.

Then, no more than an instant later, our "container" came into view of a literal paradise. I don't really know how to describe it. I've never before seen such beauty. We gently touched down into the most luscious grassy field one could imagine. I turned to my right and spoke to the living entity that I still was not allowed to see. "Is this Heaven?" I asked.

The only answer I received was, "This is your new home. Enjoy it! Forever!"

I sucked in an invigorating breath. The fragrance of the air was like luxurious potpourri, only *better* than that! I saw picturesque villages stretched across the lavish landscape as far as one could see. It was as if I could smell and taste the colors. Everything having to do with my natural senses had been sharpened to infinite levels.

I looked at my wife. We were both weeping with joy. I stepped out, my hand in hers. My foot hit the ground.

Then I woke up…

I was actually angry that I was awake. I wanted to go back! I closed my eyes as I lay upon my bed. I tried to "will" the ethereal experience back into life, but I couldn't make it happen. I've never had that dream again, nor any others that have even come close.

But now I *know* what it was, *where* I was taken, and *what* really happened to me. I also know *what* I had been allowed to see.

But wait. This story isn't even close to being over!

I would soon find out *why* I had the vision.

And that's where the saga gets really interesting!

# OUT OF THE MOUTHS
# OF BABES

*Through the praise of children and infants you have
established a stronghold against your enemies, to
silence the foe and the avenger.*

~Psalm 8:2

**56**

I had that dream about a dozen years before I started writing this book. It would be years after having the dream before I shared it with my wife.

I can hear you screaming at me now: "Why didn't you tell your wife about the dream, You idiot?"

I know. I know.

It does seem rather silly now. However, for the longest time, I was afraid to say anything to *anyone*. But I understand that reaction now. I've since ministered to several people who have had similar experiences, or even near-death experiences.

I have spoken to a number of trusting church members who have "died" and come back to life on the operating table. They, too, were afraid, or at least hesitant, to share the details of what they saw, heard, and experienced. For some, it also took years before they shared the experience with me, their own pastor. Some hadn't even told their family members yet. *Why?* Because those experiences are just too otherworldly. They're not really describable—not with earthly words, anyway. And when they are described, the words still don't do justice to the experience.

Plus, there is always the fear that people won't believe you or will think you're trying to be "more spiritual" than they are. Sadly, a lot of people are like that.

Worse, they may think you made up the story just to get some kind of sick attention. Still worse, they might think you've lost your mind! I can't really describe all the emotions that attend something like this. But I do, now, understand others who have had similar experiences.

## FINALLY REVEALED

I remember when I finally told my wife. We were having coffee one afternoon in our living room. Years after having that dream, I still couldn't get it off my mind. I had even tried to "make it go away" during the ensuing years.

I was hoping it had just been a reaction to some bad pizza I'd eaten. It wasn't that I was ungrateful for having had the experience; I just felt that if it had been a genuine dimensional transference, I simply wasn't worthy of such a thing. Why me? And if it had been genuine, how in the world could I share its reality? And *with whom?* Was I even *supposed* to share it?

But it wouldn't go away. All those years later, the unearthly experience was as real as ever, and I could still recall every detail without ever having described the dream to anyone else before.

So, on that afternoon, as we shared a moment of fellowship with each other, I sipped my coffee and told my wife everything. She listened without emotion. I couldn't quite read her expression. I desperately wanted to know that she didn't think I had lost my mind.

She waited until I was finished before she spoke.

"What do you think?" I asked.

"Well," she said. "I have something to tell you."

I thought: *Okay, here it comes. I'm off to the nuthouse.*

But that's not what she said.

"You need to ask your grandson about his *Rapture* dream." She smiled, yet she was absolutely serious.

"*What* Rapture dream?" I asked. "When did he have this *Rapture* dream?"

"I'm not telling you anything about it," she said. "I want you to hear it from him, in his words, with no prompting from me."

I took another sip of coffee, and gulped. This was getting surreal.

"He's coming over, later this evening. When he comes in, I won't coach him in any way. I'm just going to tell him to share his Rapture dream with you."

"Okay," I said. "But please, at least tell me *when* he had it."

"Years ago," my wife answered. "He was only about five. But, he still has told no one else but me. He swore me to secrecy. I'm sure he won't mind telling you, though. Not now. Especially after what I've heard you tell me about yours."

I swallowed again and nodded in agreement.

## REDUX

My grandson came over that evening.

We sat down to chat and, after a few moments of small talk, my wife said to him, "Tell Paw-Paw about your Rapture dream." He snapped his head around at her as if to say, "You *told* him?"

"It's okay. I promise." she assured. "You're going to be glad you told him, and you're going to want to hear about *his* dream as well. I assure you, I've told your Paw-Paw nothing about your dream. Go on. Tell him…"

My grandson opened his mouth to speak.

"I was standing in a field," he began. "There were people behind me screaming. I could hear cars, and what sounded like a big city. And I was looking up into the sky. I saw the stars turn into all kinds of colors and they were moving around in the sky!"

I could barely breathe. *This could not be happening*, I thought. I didn't believe I could really be hearing this. *This was absolutely impossible.*

"Paw-Paw, suddenly the stars were falling from the sky. They were rushing towards the earth. The people went nuts! They screamed louder and louder! Then, all of a sudden, I was taken up. Up and up and up. I was in a chariot. I realized that the *stars* were not really stars, they were angels! I saw an angel that was in charge of the chariot. You and Giggy (that's what he calls my wife) were there. Mom and Dad were there."

I was trying to swallow the lump in my throat that was about to strangle me as I fought back my welling emotions.

He continued. "We went to Heaven, Paw-Paw. It was a beautiful place filled with amazing colors. It was indescribable. But it was real. It was physical. I didn't want to leave. But that's when I woke up."

I looked at my wife. "Is this the same description he gave you when he first had the dream, years ago?"

"Yes," she assured me. "It's the very same account he gave me. He was just a little boy when he had it."

I asked my grandson's permission to share this with his parents. I told him I thought it was time that others knew. It couldn't be a mere coincidence. He agreed.

I related the entire account with my son, Brandon, and my daughter-in-law, Hannah, my grandson's parents. They, too, were overwhelmed by the story. Yet, none of us really knew what to *do* with it. Were we supposed to tell it? If so, to whom? When? Where? And, to what end?

It seemed the Lord was up to something. I couldn't quite put my finger on it, but I just knew this revelation was unfurling before us for a reason. I had no idea ...

# A WORD FROM GOD

**57**

*In the last days, God says, I will pour out my Spirit
on all people. Your sons and daughters will prophesy.*
-ACTS 2:17

We all went on with our lives.

Bills had to be paid. Grass had to be mowed. Plans for the future had to be laid. *You know.* The *stuff* of life. It has to go on. One's life and ministry cannot daily exist on top of the mountain of *visions and dreams.*

None of us had yet to share our family's identical dream experiences with anyone. We still didn't know how we should do it, or even *if* we should.

Years later (yes…*years later,* again), I was asked to preach at a prophecy conference on the outskirts of Minneapolis, Minnesota. It was my first invitation to such an event.

Not long before that conference, I had been on the ground at our church's mission field in Comas-Lima, Peru. We had become deeply committed to the life and ministry of a Christian school there. That school also services a number of the very poor of the area, and our church was helping ensure that children there were able to experience the finest Christian education possible. We were consistently sending missionary teams to the school and the area.

The name of the school is the Jack Goldfarb Christian School, named for a former associate pastor and a dear friend who had started the school. He had been raised there as a small child. His Jewish parents had fled there during the days of World War I, escaping the pogroms of Europe.

In a few moments, you'll understand why I related this back-story.

## MINNEAPOLIS

Back to the Minneapolis prophecy conference…

The event was held in a large, evangelical church. After my preaching session was completed, I made my way out to the huge foyer where the guest speakers had their tables set up so they could meet with the attendees.

My son had come with me, and we stood talking to people as they flooded to our table. I was signing books and spending a few moments with those who wanted some personal ministry.

In the midst of the very crowded foyer, I noticed a young woman trying to make her way to my table. She had a look of mild desperation on her face, and when her eyes met mine, I knew something was wrong.

As she came nearer, she began to ease through the remaining people who stood between us. She was kind of breaking in line, but she wasn't being rude about it. She continued to push through, seeming more anxious than ever.

I was still talking with someone when she approached my right side. I tried to wrap up that lengthy conversation so I could speak to her when she apparently gave up. She abruptly turned and walked away. She didn't appear angry; she just left, in a hurry. She walked back through the foyer and straight out the front doors. Gone.

I looked at my son. "Did you see that?"

"I saw her trying to get to you," he said. "I guess she just got tired of waiting. I nodded in agreement and we kept greeting people at our table.

After about ten more minutes of signing books and chatting with the remaining small crowd, my son grabbed my arm and motioned toward the front door with his head. I looked up. Way across the foyer, just entering the doors, was the same young lady. She was headed straight for us again. This was getting interesting. This woman had a purpose, and it looked as if she wasn't giving up.

## THE MESSAGE

I had just finished talking with someone when she came right up to me and started a conversation.

"Pastor Gallups, can I please see you for a moment?"

"Of course you can," I assured her. "I'm sorry we missed each other a little while ago. I was trying to wrap up that conversation, but you left before I could get to you." Her eyes welled up with tears.

"I know," she said. "It wasn't your fault. I just got scared. I was afraid you were going to think I was crazy, so I left." She hung her head in embarrassment for just a moment. I asked her name. She told me it was Veronica.

"Veronica, why would I think you're crazy?" I asked.

"Well…. the Lord spoke to me when you were preaching. He told me that I had to talk to you—*only you*. He told me you would know the answer to my question, and only you would understand it. He was very clear about this. I've never heard the voice of the Lord like this before. I thought maybe I was going crazy."

She went on. "When I left a few minutes ago, I went straight out to my car. My husband and two children are there waiting on me. I was crying. My husband told me to come back in and talk to you. He kinda *made* me do it. He knows what I'm getting ready to ask you." She slightly smiled as she finished her explanation.

"What was it you were supposed to ask me?"

"Please don't think I'm crazy," she begged, "but I need you to explain a dream that I had. The Lord told me you would know what it was about."

Before I continue, I need to tell you a couple of important things. First, my son was standing right beside me at the time. Second, it had now been about five years since our family had discussed the dreams my grandson and I had. The thought of that particular dream never crossed my mind when Veronica asked me to interpret a dream for her.

I remember feeling very uneasy about where this conversation was going because the woman appeared to be so distraught, and I had never before been asked to "interpret" a dream for someone.

"Well, I've never done this before," I said. "I can't promise you anything profound, but why don't you tell me your dream, and I'll ask the Lord to tell me what to say to you?"

She looked at me and somberly declared, "You'll know what to say. The Lord told me you would."

I smiled. "Okay then, tell me about your dream."

So she did.

And my life has never been the same …

# DAMSEL IN DISTRESS

## 58

*I will show wonders in the heavens above and signs on the earth below, blood and fire and billows of smoke.*
                                                        ~ACTS 2:19

With tears streaming down her cheeks, Veronica continued her story. My son grabbed up a handful of tissues for her. She dabbed her eyes as she spoke.

"The dream was real. *Too real.* It was like a nightmare. I can't even describe everything that I saw and felt. But here's how it happened..."

Brandon and I listened intently. He was paying especially close attention, trying to size up Veronica. Was she sincere? Was she telling the truth? Did she have something else up her sleeve? Was this a ruse of some sort?

Please don't think poorly of my son. That's what he was there for. We come from a family of cops. On top of that, as mentioned earlier, I had served in Florida law enforcement for a little over ten years, with most of those spent as a deputy sheriff. We're just naturally suspicious—especially when we meet someone with an unusual request, and with such emotion attached to it.

She continued. "In my dream, I was standing in a field. It was night-time and the stars were doing strange things."

My son, standing to my left, let out an audible gasp and grabbed my arm. I turned to look at him. "It's the same dream!" he mouthed.

I was dumbfounded. The woman now had my full attention. She continued to relate her experience, even describing it as a "vision" rather than a dream. She told about the screaming. The sounds of a huge city. The terror of the humanity behind her.

She said she hadn't been allowed to turn around and look. She had seen the colors change in the heavens and the "stars" moving. And she had seen them fall from the sky and hurtle themselves toward the earth.

The difference between her dream and mine and my grandson's was that she was not at peace during the vision. She was horrified. She was now crying as she told the story.

"Keep going, Veronica," I told her gently. "I know exactly what this dream is about."

As I spoke those last words, she began to sob. "So God *did* speak to me?"

"Yes," I assured her, "He certainly did."

"It was so clear," she said. "His voice! But I thought you would think I was crazy."

"*No.* Far from it. You're not crazy. Tell me about the rest of your dream."

Veronica went on. Her vision had come to an abrupt ending when the "stars" were plunging towards earth. Just as they were about to arrive, she woke up. The dream had disturbed her, and she knew it was meant to be some kind of warning.

"Pastor," she asked through teary eyes, "what *was* it? What did I see? What was happening?"

"My grandson and I have had the exact same dream!" I told her.

Veronica was now certain the Lord had spoken to her and had led her directly to me. I assured her that my son knew all about my dream and could testify that I wasn't exaggerating when I said her dream was practically identical.

I explained that our dreams went even farther than hers, though. I told her this was why I felt I could tell her what the dream was supposed to mean.

I also said the dreams were obviously about some point in the very last days. Some would say it was the very moment just before the Rapture. Others might say it was just before the return of Jesus Christ.

Regardless of which eschatological formula the dream most properly fits, I said, it appeared the Lord was giving us a heavenly heads-up. Then, I explained how my dream and my grandson's had ended—with "touchdowns" in paradise. She was astounded.

I asked her if her fear was related to her relationship with Jesus Christ, or a lack thereof. She related that she indeed had wandered far from the Lord, and only recently had returned to Him in sincerity. She had her dream just before returning to the Lord with her life's commitment of faithfulness.

"Maybe I was getting ready to be left behind?" she asked.

"I'm not certain of that point as it applies to your life," I responded. "I only know how the dream is *supposed* to end."

She smiled. "Me too! *Now!*" she exclaimed, "I know what I need to do. The Lord has been calling me to be much more involved in direct evangelism. So that's what I'm going to do!"

The three of us grabbed each other's hands and prayed.

However, believe it or not, this still isn't the end of this amazing account.


## CONNECTIONS

When we finished praying, I had a question for Veronica. "It's obvious that you are Hispanic—where are you from, if you don't mind me asking?"

"Peru," she responded with a smile.

Again, I was stunned. What could be the chances?

"Well, that's pretty amazing," I said. "My church has ministered in Peru for many years. We have a Christian school down there for very poor children. We've led tons of children and their families to the Lord through that ministry, and we've met a lot of personal human needs by working in the school and the community it serves."

"That's awesome!" she responded. "Where is this school?"

"Are you familiar with the district of Comas?" I asked. "It's just outside of Lima."

"*That's where I'm from!* All my family lives there now!" Veronica became emotional again as she asked, "What school do you minister through?"

"It's the Jack Goldfarb Christian School."

She clasped her hand over her mouth. "I live just down from there! I knew people there! I knew families that went there, and families that went to the church right next door to the school!"

We were speechless for a moment. This story was getting increasingly farther-fetched the more we delved into it. I was almost afraid to ask her any more questions.

When I gathered my thoughts enough to speak again, I asked for her permission to share the dream story, and even to use her name. I told her that I thought all of this was too important not to share. She assured me it was okay; she even encouraged me to share it. "You certainly can use my name, Pastor Carl," she said. "This is a story directly from the Lord!"

We hugged each other and I said another quick prayer over her, with my son by my side, before she turned and went to the front doors to go back to her family. She stopped at the doors and waved, then walked outside.

As of this writing, I've never seen her again.

Veronica, if you're reading this now, the Lord has used you in the field of evangelism in a bigger way than you might have ever imagined! Your message is now going around the world! Thank you so much for coming back to my table that second time. And thank you for encouraging me to put your story in a book. Sorry it took so long.

> Then will appear the sign of the Son of Man in heaven. And then all the peoples of the earth will mourn when they see the Son of Man coming on the clouds of heaven, with power and great glory. And he will send his angels with a loud trumpet call, and they will gather his elect from the four winds, from one end of the heavens to the other. (Matthew 24:30–31)[399]

# THE AFTERMATH

**59**

*To everything there is a season, and a time
to every purpose under the heaven.*
~Ecclesiastes 3:1, KJV

In a large prophecy conference setting in Dallas, Texas, in early 2019, I shared the story of that Rapture vision, including Veronica's part, in a public session.

If you're doing the math, that's *five more years after* Veronica's 2014 revelation to me! Why wait so long, *yet again*? Simple. I was waiting on the Lord. But, I knew I would one day share it on the right platform and in the Lord's timing.

However, after that day in 2014, I knew I finally had Heaven's divine permission and biblical justification to share the experience with the world.

Until that moment, however, the whole matter had been only a family affair, because it would have been far too easy for someone to cry "foul" and try to claim we had concocted the whole tale. I certainly didn't want to be perceived as "one of those guys who's always talking about his fantastical 'dreams and visions.'"

However, all those years later, at the Minneapolis prophecy conference, of all places, Veronica had appeared. She had the same dream my grandson and I had experienced. And, she had been given instructions from the Lord to seek me out, *and only me*.

On top of all that, her account was witnessed by my son. Veronica also had direct connections to Comas, Peru, and to the school in Peru I had been attached to in ministry for a number of years.

The chance that all of these elements would converge during a highly unlikely prophecy conference connection was just too remote to dismiss everything as mere coincidence. The matter had now been biblically confirmed by "two or three witnesses," so I was finally free to share it.

I arrived at the 2019 Dallas prophecy conference with no inkling that I would reveal the dream there. However, while I was on the stage, in front of the live audience, with my message being streamed to the world, the words were in my spirit as if I heard them being spoken aloud: "Tell it now!" I tried to push the thought to the back of my mind, but I couldn't shake it.

If you watch the video of that conference, you can see it happen for yourself.[400] As I began to recount the saga, I still had to build up courage. I even sort of apologized for sharing the story, assuring the crowd that I knew it would be a bit unbelievable for some.

## THE OUTPOURING

After I shared the story, however, the response was astounding—not only at that conference, but it still is!

As I'm writing this, almost a year after the Dallas event, my church office, my home office, and our social media sites are still getting slammed with many thousands of responses from God's people around the globe. The vast majority of the communications are very positive. People are coming to the Lord Jesus Christ in salvation. Others, like Veronica, are coming back to the Lord. Many others are being emboldened and encouraged. All express in one way or the other that they, too, feel *the time* is near.

I suppose most stunning of all is the sheer number of respondents who say they've had the *same* dream or something similar to it. Still others have revealed that they've not had that particular dream, but that they, too, *have had* very real and moving dreams unmistakably indicating that the coming of the Lord is going to be very soon.

I am not a date-setter. I never have been, in the entirety of my years in ministry. I simply know that we are living in the most prophetic times since the First Coming of Jesus Christ. I am certain.

If you've read all the chapters of this book before these last several "dream" chapters, then you'll know why I can make this claim with such biblical conviction. And if we truly are in the midst of unprecedentedly prophetic times, then it might be a genuine biblical phenomenon that these "catching-up" visions are occurring on a global level.

The prophet Joel actually foresaw just such a time:

Blow the trumpet in Zion; **sound the alarm on my holy hill.** Let all who live in the land tremble, for **the day of the Lord is coming.** It is close at hand...

And afterward, **I will pour out my Spirit on all people.** Your **sons and daughters** will prophesy, your **old men** will *dream dreams*, your **young men** will see visions. Even on my servants, both men and women, I will pour out my Spirit in those days. (Joel 2:1, 27–29; emphasis added)

## LAST THINGS

# 60

*I have a feeling we're not in Kansas anymore.*

**W**hat we have accomplished in our journey is what I call the *Toto Effect.*

Hopefully, this book has played the part of something like Dorothy's tenacious little dog. Toto knew that behind the thick, black curtain was a scam artist, one pulling off a monumental masquerade. The so-called wizard was a first-class shyster possessing great power, to be sure, but he certainly was not the "All-Powerful Oz" that he wanted everyone to think he was. He only knew how to keep people fooled with his otherworldly wizardry, spell-binding illusions, cutting-edge technological wonders, and fiendishly deceptive manifestations.

But Toto knew better. He could smell the man's presence from a mile away, even when no one else could. When the time was right, the pup pitter-patted right up to the curtains and snatched them back with his teeth, snarling as he tugged. Right in front of everyone, the ruse was up. The "All-Powerful Fraud" was exposed.

Maybe this book has been used by the Lord to pull back the foreboding curtains in the dimly lit room of demonic mind games and exposed the ultimate frailty of the one who has been pulling the levers of deceit all along. All this time, he has been masquerading as something much bigger and much more powerful than he really is.

Oh, we know Satan is terrifyingly formidable—supernaturally, and wickedly so. He is much more powerful than we are. And, he is not to be trifled with. He certainly is not to be unduly mocked and taunted.[401]

But the final truth is that the curtains *will* be pulled back, and the "man" lurking behind them will be exposed before the nations. God's judgment against Nachash will fall. His grip on God's people will be relinquished. His thieving claims on God's original Paradise will ultimately be annihilated.

God's Word assures us of all this. The promise is found in Isaiah 14.

## IS THIS THE MAN?

Right after Satan's five arrogant statements of "I will!" there is also a dreadful pronouncement leveled upon him. The final indictment is straight from the mouth of Yahweh Himself.

The following excerpt picks up at Isaiah 14:14, just as Satan is winding down his prideful proclamations, exalting his own will above that of Heaven's throne. Read what Yahweh says next:

> [Satan said] I will ascend above the tops of the clouds; *I will make myself like the Most High*.
>
> [The LORD says] "But [instead] *you are brought down* to the realm of the dead, *to the depths of the pit*."
>
> **Those who see you stare at you,** *they ponder your fate*: **"Is this *the man* who shook the earth *and made kingdoms tremble*, the *man* who made the world a wilderness,** who overthrew its cities and would not let his captives go home?" (Isaiah 14:14–17; emphasis and brackets added)

*Ironsides' Notes on Isaiah 14* is one of several sources[402] affirming that, in the final analysis, the dreadful sentence pronounced in Isaiah 14:16–17 is not actually about the king of Babylon, it is ultimately about Satan himself:

*These words cannot apply to any mere mortal man.* [Satan] is a created angel of the very highest order, *identical with the covering cherub of Ezekiel 28.*

Therefore we need not be surprised to find in the [verses after v 15] of our chapter that **the king of Babylon seems to be, as it were, confounded** *with Lucifer.* The actual meaning, of course, is that [the king] was controlled or dominated by [Satan]. This passage is highly poetical, but **describes in no uncertain terms the utter destruction of the last great enemy of Israel in the Day of the Lord.** See also Ezekiel 31:16-18. *All the glory of the warrior* and the pride of world conquest *end in utter destruction.*[403] (Emphasis and brackets added)

On the Day of the Lord, when the final curtain is pulled back to expose the vileness of our accuser, the whole world will see Satan for what he really is. The *Great Masquerader* will finally come to his inglorious end. His stolen kingdom will be no more. Forever.

For the Lord God, He is the Lord, and beside Him there is no other![404]

## IN THE MEANTIME

What should be our perspective until then? How do we conduct ourselves as we go about our daily routines of mowing the grass, paying the bills, raising our children, preparing for the future, and endeavoring to thrive while meandering in the midst of this thing called *life*?

The words of Jude summarize the answer:

But, dear friends, remember what the apostles of our Lord Jesus Christ foretold. They said to you, "In the last times there will be scoffers who will follow their own ungodly desires." These are the people who divide you, who follow mere natural instincts and do not have the Spirit.

But you, dear friends, by building yourselves up in your most holy faith and praying in the Holy Spirit, keep yourselves in God's love as you wait for the mercy of our Lord Jesus Christ to bring you to eternal life.

Be merciful to those who doubt; save others by snatching them from the fire; to others show mercy, mixed with fear—hating even the clothing stained by corrupted flesh.

To him who is able to keep you from stumbling and to present you before his glorious presence without fault and with great joy—to the only God our Savior be glory, majesty, power and authority, through Jesus Christ our Lord, before all ages, now and forevermore! Amen. (Jude 1:17–25)

There is also this great biblical truth, delivered by Peter and eventually circulated to all the early churches of the first century:

*We also have the prophetic message* as something *completely reliable*, and you will do well to pay attention to it, as to a *light shining in a dark place, until the day dawns and the morning star rises in your hearts.*
Above all, you must understand that **no prophecy of Scripture came about** by the **prophet's own interpretation** of things. For *prophecy never had its origin in the human will, but prophets, though human, spoke from God* as they were carried along **by the Holy Spirit.** (1 Peter 1:19–22; emphasis added)

Peter affirms the truth. As we witness the detailed words and warnings of prophetic Scripture bursting forth upon our world—only in our own generation—then we can be even more certain that everything is in His hands, and that the Word of the Lord stands forever!

And…so does His kingdom.

The kingdoms of men rise and fall. They always have. They always will.

But the eternal kingdom of Jesus Christ will never end.

For *His* is the genuine kingdom. And the power. And the glory. *Forever.*

It *always* has been.

His kingdom will soon be upon the earth, as it is now, in Heaven. He has promised it. He even taught us to pray that way. *It will happen.* It's been decreed.

In that glorious day, there will be no more pain, crying, mourning, or death. No more lies, deceit, fakery, or masquerades. All things will be made new. Everything that is fallen will be banished forever. The *King of Kings and Lord of Lords* will reign—and we will reign with Him.[405]

And *that's* the way the story really ends.

Because of the grace and mercy of our Lord Jesus Christ, and His shed blood of salvation's plan, I hope to see you there soon…

Somewhere around the throne of Yeshua.

In His kingdom…

And ours.

# ADDENDUM

# DELIVERANCE

*Your healing can actually commence*
*before you close the pages of this chapter.*

If the statistics concerning the number of people on the planet caught in the web of horrific addictions are even close to accurate, a sizable number of people reading this book are also directly affected by demonic entry points, in one way or another. In fact, you may be struggling with bondage, or perhaps you might have family members and/or friends and other loved ones wrapped up in the oppression of these areas of darkness.

You might be asking: *What can I do?* How can I or others I'm concerned about escape these debilitating burdens of addiction and dead-end lifestyles?

*Following are biblical steps to the beginning of recovery and spiritual freedom.* Not only do these steps apply to any form of addiction, they also apply to any other form of demonic oppression, even attachments to occult activity and/or secret societies.

Let's get started.

## NEW BEGINNINGS

**Stop right this moment and pray.** In the name of Jesus, you have the power to affect your own deliverance, beginning right now. Your healing can actually commence before you close the pages of this chapter. The Bible assures us of this truth.

The weapons we fight with are not the weapons of the world. On the contrary, *they have divine power to demolish strongholds*. We demolish arguments and every pretension that sets itself up against the knowledge of God, and we take captive *every thought* to make it obedient to Christ. (2 Corinthians 10:4–5; emphasis added)

**In your praying, admit your sin** to the Lord. *Call it by name.* Say it aloud and ask the Lord to release you from its bondage. *Repent* of that sin or sins (i.e., drugs, alcohol, pornography, sexual perversion, lying, deception, stealing, occult activities, affiliations with secret societies, etc.).

Acknowledge your willingness to completely turn from these areas of debilitating iniquity. Ask the Lord to infuse you with His strength, enabling you to leave them behind. Ask the Holy Spirit to take captive your addictive thoughts and activities and place them under the blood of Jesus. Be fervent in your prayers. Speak the words of 2 Corinthians 10:4–5. Meditate upon them. Memorize them. Claim those promises as absolute truth, in Jesus' name.

**In your praying, *do not* speak to Satan!** Don't speak to demons. Don't speak to the realm of darkness at all. Speak *against* it, and in so doing, speak only to the Lord of Glory, your heavenly Father. Speak to the Savior of your soul, Jesus Christ. Call upon the power of the realm of light, through the Holy Spirit of God, to deliver you from the realm of darkness.

**For example:** "I ask you, my Heavenly Father, in the name of Jesus Christ, to break the chains of my bondage in the area of _____. I renounce this domain of darkness and any demonic grip that has captured me, and I willingly place it under the blood of Jesus and under the power of your Holy Spirit and your eternal Word."

**In your praying, acknowledge that the Word of God** is the genuine truth, and that Satan is the ultimate liar and father of all lies. Confess

that the greatest power in the universe is found within the Word of God
and your relationship with Jesus Christ, not within the realm of Satan's
darkness. Speak this acknowledgement aloud. Speak it in the name of
Jesus.

In your praying, speak these spiritual weapons of truth *back to
the Lord.* Claim them as your own. Claim them aloud. That's why they
were given to us. Speak them into the darkness. Give your thought life,
your physical temptations, and the lying allurements of Satan's deception to Jesus Christ. Give them to the Lord from the depths of your soul
and heart. Cry out to your Creator, the One who loves you more than
you could ever imagine.

**In your praying, pray to the Lord of Glory** something like this, putting these words into your own:

> Lord Jesus, I am turning my thought life over to your domain.
> Deliver me from the domain of the darkness of pornography
> and bring me into the Light of your Word and truth.
>
> Wash me. Cleanse me. Fill my brain and soul with pure
> thoughts. Godly thoughts. I acknowledge that this evil has set
> itself up against *you!* And, it is using *me!*
>
> In the name of Jesus Christ, I relinquish this wickedness and
> repent of it, and place it under the blood of Jesus—in obedience
> to Him alone.

**Speak the words of your testimony aloud,** before the Lord. Then,
eventually, do it before other people. Acknowledge without shame that
you belong to Jesus by His grace and by His blood alone. Where ever
possible, ask forgiveness from those you have wronged.

> They [the people of God] triumphed over [Satan] *by the blood
> of the Lamb* and by *the word of their testimony.* (Revelation
> 12:11; emphasis and brackets added)

# HEALING SCRIPTURE

**Wash yourself in the Word of God.**  In the endnotes section of this book, I have supplied over two dozen passages of Scripture that you can begin using now. They are verses of promise, hope, and healing. They are not mere references; the actual passages themselves are there. You can read them *now* if you desire. **They are at** *this endnote*.[406]

Pore over them daily and *whenever* you feel the demonic temptation tugging at your soul. This is the very same power that Jesus Himself used during His own wilderness temptation (Matthew 4).  He merely spoke the truth of the Word *aloud*. Read these passages. Meditate upon them. *Pray the words back* to the Lord, in your own words, one by one. Healing will come. Temptation will fade.

> [Jesus said to them] "If you **abide in my word**, you are truly my disciples, and **you will know the truth**, and *the truth will set you free*." (John 8:31–32; emphasis added)

Even after all this, there's still work to be done. But it will be worth it.

# WORSHIP MUSIC

Immerse your environs with worshipful Christian music. Play that music continuously, when you can. Play it in your home, office, car, and in the course of enjoying your hobbies. Satan cannot inhabit the depths of our heartfelt praise of Jesus. In fact, the very opposite is true. God Himself promises to intimately honor the praise of His people![407] Praise Him. Worship Him. Sing to Jesus Christ. Satan will have to flee.

# REWIRING YOUR BRAIN

Please remember the vital portion of Romans 12:2 that we read in the last chapter:

Do not conform to the pattern of this world, but **be transformed** *by the renewing of your mind.* (Emphasis added)

The words in the original Greek language of the New Testament indicate a *continual motion* of progress, as in "always be *in the state of being* transformed. Always be in the state of renewing your mind."

This is especially important to remember after one has ultimately placed their demonic entry-point portals, whatever they might be, under the blood of Jesus Christ, through repentance and prayer. From that point on, with the Lord's help, the recovery process becomes a matter of daily renewal and recommitment until the brain is finally rewired *and healed.*

But you must be prepared. Satan is not going to like that he's losing you from the grips of one of his diabolical deceptions. So, you must persist through prayer and a committed attachment to a consistently godly support group.

The following words of warning, from the *Expositor's Greek Testament,* are stunningly accurate:

"**This world**" or "**age**" **is opposed to that which is to come.** [The Kingdom of Heaven and the restitution of all things!] **We live in an evil world** (Galatians 1:4) of which *Satan is the God* (2 Corinthians 4:4). *Even apparent* or *superficial conformity* **to a system controlled by such a spirit,** much more *an actual accommodation* to its ways, *would be fatal* to the Christian life.[408] (Emphasis and brackets added)

Those are sobering, but accurate, admonitions. Read them again. Meditate upon their truth.

## OVERCOMING

Once again we discover that science is only recently catching up to what the Bible has asserted all along. Through addiction, Satan hijacks our brain. We have to willfully take it back, *seize it back*, and then intentionally hand it back over to our Creator.

## CHANGING PATHS

To overcome addiction, the brain must "unlearn" the obsessive craving and wipe it from its "memory." Recovery is the process in which the influence of those diabolical brain memories slowly diminish and eventually disappear.

The process is akin to the "muscle memory" developed by a weightlifter. Once that weightlifter starts working out, the muscles begin to learn a new reality. They adapt and conform to that reality. Muscle is built. Fat is burned. The body begins to take a new shape. The old is gone, and the new is continually bursting forth in strength and vitality. This is what has to happen in the brain of someone who is addicted.

Clearing a new neural pathway involving your memory process is accomplished by consistently making "new neural memories." This happens by making healthy and godly choices every single day. Cleaning out the old pathways and clearing the way for the new neural pathways requires effort, but eventually causes the old pathways to atrophy, or fade away.

Addiction recovery is literally a brain-healing process. It'll take some time, so be patient. Be prayerful. Be faithful. The healing and deliverance will come. That's God's promise to you.

# A HELPFUL ILLUSTRATION

Imagine that, for years, you've been using the same trail to explore the thousands of acres of forest behind your house. By now, it is well-worn and thoroughly beaten down. You know every nuance of the long path you've trekked over the years and feel comfortable while you're on it. Your pleasant little walkway ultimately leads to a place that you have enjoyed for a very long time.

However, you've recently discovered that this path has become prone to instantaneous sinkholes that, without warning, open up and swallow anything in its reach—into a black hole of a horrible and suffocating death.

You now understand that by continuing down this trail, there's a real chance that your life and the lives of any who might follow, will be in grave danger. Obviously, a radical path change is in order.

So, you begin to hack out another trail, starting from an entirely different part of your large piece of property. Over time, your new path is opened up and you grow increasingly comfortable on it.

Not only that, but by faithfully beating down this new path, you discovered a previously unknown serene lake surrounded by a gorgeous meadow! The lake is filled with fish, and the meadow is teeming with beautiful wildlife. You find yourself wondering, "Why haven't I come down this path before? Look what I've been missing!"

Then, one day, you go back to where the old path used to be. You see where it started, but you can no longer find the trail. The entrance has grown over, tangled with briars and poisonous weeds, and the path itself has disappeared. Whatever dangers were along that way are no longer a hazard to you or anyone else. The old threat is gone. The new path is now wide open, and it's safe. You're finally free from the once life-threatening danger.[409]

That is, admittedly, a very simple illustration of how our brain works, but it *is* an adequate illustration of how God designed us and how genuine healing is finally accomplished. New *paths* have to be built. The old ones have to *heal over*.

The problem is that we live in an unregenerate world ruled by the fallen *Mighty One*.[410] He knows an awful lot about how we're made. He was there when it happened in the beginning, and he's been studying humanity ever since. Satan knows what makes us tick, and he knows exactly how to pervert our "ticker."[411]

Consequently, he's the one who put on the *mask of allurement* and started you down the path of rewiring your brain. He actively seduced you and *beguiled* you, appealing to your fallen sin nature. He did this so that the sure-to-come cerebral rewiring process would eventually accommodate that addictive behavior into which you were spiritually lured.

## LET IT BEGIN!

It's time to do battle.

Let's get started undoing what Satan has done. It's like burning down a house and then rebuilding it—brand new. Or, it's like recovering from a major surgical procedure. It's slow at first. It's not easy. There's work involved—even a little pain. But every bit of the process of your complete recovery can be accomplished, especially with supernatural help from your Creator, Jesus Christ. And every successful day, taken one step and one day at a time, is a day of healing. And every day of healing piles upon all the other days of healing—until you are whole again, and free.

Please hear my heart. I'm not trying to oversimplify the matter of addiction. Deliverance from addiction always involves immersion in a renewed structure of one's life. That transformed life will seek to eliminate every avenue of Satan's inroads into one's thought life and portals of temptation.

This process obviously involves focused planning and strategy. It takes time. It takes patience. It takes encouragement from other godly people and often it requires the addicted one to get involved in a dedicated support structure or recovery-group environment. It might also require accountability partners and continued counseling with a trusted pastor or other trained professionals in the areas of addiction recovery for Christians.

## ADDICTION RECOVERY RESOURCES

**I've listed several resources** that might help you or a loved one begin the biblical recovery process. These can get you started. **Please have a look at them.**[412]

I pray that God's deliverance for you or your loved one will be accomplished in a powerfully supernatural way, regardless of how long the brain-rewiring/healing process might take. It's worth it. We're talking about life. We're talking about eternity.

Don't let Satan pervert it or steal it. He's a liar and a con artist.

For He who is in you is greater than he who is in the world. (1 John 4:4)

# ABOUT THE AUTHOR

Carl Gallups has been the senior pastor of Hickory Hammock Baptist Church in Milton, Florida, since 1987. He is a graduate of the Florida Law Enforcement Officer Academy, Florida State University (BSc Criminology) and New Orleans Baptist Theological Seminary (MDiv), and has served on the board of regents at the University of Mobile in Mobile, Alabama, since 2000.

Carl is a former decorated Florida law-enforcement officer, having served under three sheriffs with two different sheriff's offices, as well as working in an administrative capacity in the Central Office of the Florida Department of Corrections. He was also appointed as a special deputy, in January 2016, under former Sheriff Joe Arpaio, Maricopa County, Arizona.

Pastor Gallups is a critically acclaimed Amazon Top 60 bestselling author, an internationally known talk-radio host since 2002, and a regular guest pundit on numerous television and radio programs. He is also a frequent guest preacher at national prophecy and Bible conferences. He has preached the gospel of Jesus Christ on three continents, in four nations, including Peru and Israel, and all over the United States, including Hawaii and Alaska. He has also preached in the Canadian provinces of British Colombia, Alberta, and Ontario.

Carl was featured on Fox News Business Report in 2016 as an "influential evangelical leader," publicly endorsing candidate Donald Trump for the office of president. Carl was asked by the Trump campaign to open the internationally broadcast Trump for President Rally in Pensacola, Florida, in January 2016. More than twelve thousand people attended that rally.

Pastor Carl Gallups lives in Milton, Florida, with his wife, Pam. You can find more information about him at www.carlgallups.com.

# NOTES

1. "2 Corinthians 11:14," *Matthew Poole's Commentary*, Biblehub.com, https://biblehub.com/commentaries/2_corinthians/11-14.htm.

2. Masquerade Quotes, "Dietrich Bonhoeffer," AZQuotes.com, accessed 9-2-19, https://www.azquotes.com/quotes/topics/masquerade.html.

3. This narrative is based upon the accounts of Matthew 12–13 and their counterparts found in Mark 2–3 and Luke 6. Names of characters that are not specifically mentioned in Scripture are fictional names assigned by the author.

4. The Pharisees were a social and religious Jewish movement originating in the Holy Land during the time of Second Temple Judaism. After the destruction of the Second Temple in 70 CE, Pharisaic beliefs became the foundational, liturgical, and ritualistic basis for rabbinic Judaism. See https://en.wikipedia.org/wiki/Pharisees.

5. "Matthew 12:4," *Ellicott's Commentary for English Readers*, Biblehub.com.

   In the position in which the narrative stands in the other two Gospels, the Pharisees would appear as belonging to the company that had come down from Jerusalem to watch and accuse the new Teacher (Luke 5:17). https://biblehub.com/commentaries/matthew/12-4.htm.

6. See Matthew 4 and Luke 4.

7. Matthew 4.

8. Kinneret, in Hebrew, means "a harp." The lake is so named because of its harp-like shape. Also called "the Sea" and Lake Galilee.

9. Matthew 4.

10. Herod Antipas was the son of Herod the Great. It was Herod the Great who had launched the massacre of the male children in Bethlehem upon the departure of the wise men's visit to the child, Jesus, in Bethlehem.

11. Matthew 4, 14:3–5.

12. Isaiah 9:1–2.

13. "Matthew 12:2," *Cambridge Bible for Schools and Colleges*, Biblehub.com. This prohibition is a Pharisaic rule not found in the Mosaic Law. It was a principle with the Pharisees to extend the provisions of the Law and make minute regulations over and beyond what Moses commanded, in order to avoid the possibility of transgression. (https://biblehub.com/commentaries/matthew/12-2.htm)

14. "Matthew 12:2," Benson Commentary, Biblehub.com. It was into the house or chamber of the high-priest that he entered, situated beside the tabernacle, and called the house of God on that account. See note on 1 Samuel 21:3-6. Thus the apartment in which the High-priest Eli and his servant Samuel slept, is called the house of the Lord, 1 Samuel 3:15. (https://biblehub.com/commentaries/matthew/12-2.htm)

15. With this declaration, Jesus declared that from now on, His "body"—and the "church" that would come from it—would be the true and greatest earthly "temple" of God. Within two decades of Jesus speaking these words, the temple in Jerusalem was destroyed. As of this date, it has not been rebuilt. Yet, Paul wrote profusely about the Church itself as being the new and "rebuilt" temple of God in the last days. The vast majority of the scholars all the way back to the first several centuries understood that this is exactly what Jesus and Paul meant. This topic will be explored more fully in later chapters of this book.

16. Hosea 6:6.

17. "Matthew 12:9," *Ellicott's Commentary for English Readers*, Biblehub.com. He went into their synagogue—i.e., that of the Pharisees whom He had just reproved, probably, therefore, the synagogue of Capernaum. The narratives in St. Matthew and St. Mark convey the impression that it was on the same Sabbath. St. Luke, however, as if he had made more careful

inquiry, states definitely that it was on another, and this the others do not directly contradict. (https://biblehub.com/commentaries/matthew/12-9.htm)

18. *Shaliach Tzibbur*—a Jewish prayer leader in the synagogue. Also known as a cantor.

19. The full prayer consists of Deuteronomy 6:4, 11:13–21, and Numbers 15:37–41.

20. Torah (or the Law)—the first five books of the Old Testament. The Nevi'im—the Prophets.

21. Concerning Jesus' challenging question to the Pharisee:

*Meyer's New Testament Commentary:*

> There must have been no doubt as to whether such a thing was allowable, for Jesus argues ex concesso. [An argument based on a prior admission or confession of one's opponent.]          The Talmud (Gemara) contains no such concession, but answers the question partly in a negative way, and partly by making casuistical stipulations. (Brackets added; seehttps://biblehub.com/commentaries/matthew/12-11.htm)

22. A small leather box, containing Hebrew texts, worn by Jewish men, especially the orthodox Jewish leaders, as a reminder to keep the law.

23. Herodians:

> The Herodians derived their name as followers of King Herod. The Herodians were a political party that wanted to restore a Herod to the throne in Judea as well as other areas ruled by Herod the Great. They were political foes of the Pharisees who wished to restore the kingdom of David. (https://www.blueletterbible.org/faq/don_stewart/don_stewart)

24. Trees, Fruit, Vipers:

*Dictionary of Scripture and Ethics:*

> Biblical metaphors highlight the personal and social degradation associated with vice. One image involves the tree and its fruit, which calls to mind the story in which Adam and Eve eat of the forbidden fruit in the Garden of Eden. [In the same way] Jesus warns that bad trees can be expected to bear bad fruit (Matthew 12:33).

See Joel Green, *Dictionary of Scripture and Ethics*, Baker Academic; New edition (November 1, 2011) 807. (Joel B. Green is professor of New Testament Interpretation and associate dean for the Center for Advanced Theological Studies, Fuller Theological Seminary.)

*MacLaren's Expositions*:

> "Take the bitter tree," as I remember an old Jewish saying has it, "take the bitter tree and plant it in Eden, and water it with the rivers there; and let the angel Gabriel be the gardener, and the tree will still bear bitter fruit."

See https://biblehub.com/commentaries/matthew/12-33.htm.

*Lange's Commentary on the Holy Scriptures: Critical, Doctrinal, and Homiletical*:

> Poisonous plants, and a generation of vipers, were the noxious remnants of pre-Adamic times, and hence served as allegorical figures of satanic evil. Hence the first symbol of coming salvation was, that the seed of the woman should bruise the head of the serpent.—How can ye? etc.—The physical impossibility that a generation of vipers could give forth what was salutary, served as an emblem of the moral impossibility of this moral generation of vipers speaking good things.

See https://www.studylight.org/commentaries/lcc/matthew-12.html.

25. Ibid.

26. Matthew 12:14. "But the Pharisees went out and plotted how they might kill Jesus." (Also see Mark 3:6. Here the Pharisees join forces with the Herodians to kill Jesus).

27. See Matthew 12:36 and Matthew 13:1. The "house" was most likely that of Peter.

*Pulpit Commentary*:

> Went Jesus out of the house. Where he had been when his mother came (Matthew 12:46, note), and presumably the one to which he returned in ver. 36. Possibly it was St. Peter's house at Capernaum (Matthew 8:14).

See https://biblehub.com/commentaries/matthew/13-1.htm.

28. *Gill's Exposition of the Entire Bible*:

> This parable fitly suited them, the Scribes and Pharisees, and

the men of that generation, from whom in some measure the
unclean spirit might be said to depart through the doctrine,
and miracles of Christ, to go into the Gentile world; but
being followed there with the preaching of the Gospel by
the apostles, returns to the Jews, and fills them with more
malice, blasphemy, and blindness, than ever, which issued in
their utter ruin and destruction; of which this parable may
be justly thought to be prophetical. https://biblehub.com/
commentaries/matthew/12-45.htm.

29. See Mark 3:20–21.

30. *MacLaren's Expositions*:

Members of His own family-sad to say, as would appear
from the context, including His mother-came with a kindly
design to rescue their misguided kinsman from danger,
and laying hands upon Him, to carry Him off to some safe
restraint in Nazareth, where He might indulge His delusions
without doing any harm to Himself. (https://biblehub.com/
commentaries/mark/3-21.htm)

31. John 7:4–5: "For no one who wants to be known publicly acts in secret.
Since you are doing these things, show yourself to the world. For even His
own brothers did not believe in Him." (Berean Study Bible).

32. Mark 3:8: "When they heard about all [Jesus] was doing, many people came
to him from Judea, Jerusalem, Idumea, and the regions across the Jordan
and around Tyre and Sidon."

33. See my previous book, *Gods of the Final Kingdom* (Crane, MO: Defender
Publishing, 2019), for the biblical and scientific understanding of this
certain spiritual truth.

34. See examples of first-century Pharisee garments at Bible History Online:
https://www.bible-history.com/pharisees/PHARISEESDress.htm.
Watch Tower Online: https://wol.jw.org/en/wol/d/r1/lp-e/1001072005.

35. Tallit—The Jewish prayer shawl, often worn to this day by the very
orthodox. Rabbi Abraham Millgram, "The Tallit: Spiritual Significance,"
My Jewish Learning, accessed July 12, 2019, https://www.myjewishlearning.
com/article/the-tallit-spiritual-significance.

36. Ephesians 6:10–13:

Finally, be strong in the Lord and in his mighty power. Put on the full armor of God, so that you can take your stand against the devil's schemes. For our struggle is not against flesh and blood, but against the rulers, against the authorities, against the powers of this dark world and against the spiritual forces of evil in the heavenly realms. Therefore put on the full armor of God, so that when the day of evil comes, you may be able to stand your ground, and after you have done everything, to stand.

37. John 9:39–41:

Jesus said, "For judgment I have come into this world, so that the blind will see and those who see will become blind." Some Pharisees who were with him heard him say this and asked, "What? Are we blind too?" Jesus said, "If you were blind, you would not be guilty of sin; but now that you claim you can see, your guilt remains."

38. Jesus twice called Satan the prince of this world (John 12:31; Matthew 27:46). Paul called him the god of this age (2 Corinthians 4:4).

39. Various English translations represent the words as "temple of God," "God's temple," "God's sanctuary," or the "sanctuary of God." "Temple of God" is by far the most popular English representation, with "God's temple" being the second most frequently used translation. See https://biblehub.com/2_thessalonians/2-4.htm.

40. Messianic Rabbi Zev Porat (Tel Aviv, Israel) is a dear friend and ministry partner. Together we authored the internationally bestselling book, *The Rabbi, The Secret Message, and the Identity of Messiah* (Crane, MO: Defender Publishing, 2019).

Rabbi Zev grew up in an immersive Israeli orthodox rabbinical family in Israel's most orthodox community, B'nai Brak. His father, grandfather, and great-grandfather were highly respected and important Israeli rabbis. Zev studied to be a Sanhedrin rabbi and was officially certified to serve as such. In the midst of those studies, he came to faith in Yeshua as the true Messiah and Lord. Rabbi Zev Porat is the one who first told me of these well-known statistics concerning the Jews in Israel and the lack of desire for a rebuilt Temple on the Temple Mount by the vast majority of Israel's current population. See his ministry website here—www.messiahofisraelministries.com.

41. Joshua Gerstein, "Dr. Theodor Herzl & Building the 3rd
    Temple," *Times of Israel*, 7-2-18, https://blogs.timesofisrael.com/
    dr-theodor-herzl-building-the-3rd-temple.
    Michael S. Arnold, "Faithful to the Bitter End?" *Jerusalem Post*, 8-18-2000
    (Reprint) Accessed July 20, 2019, http://www.templemount.org/bitterend.
    html.

    > (Yisrael Medad, founder of El Har Hashem says: **There has
    > been no mainstream Temple Mount activist group that has
    > succeeded in talking to the majority of the people**, because
    > they have refused to adopt legitimate messages that could be
    > understood by the majority of the population. **When they
    > hear people talking about mikva'ot [ritual baths] and ritual
    > purity, it sounds like mumbo-jumbo.**).

42. Giles Fraser, "An Israeli Claim to Temple Mount Would Trigger
    Unimaginable Violence," *The Guardian*, 9-13-13 ("The orthodox
    position has long been that the Temple can only be rebuilt and sacrifices
    resumed when the Jewish messiah returns. But since the foundation of
    the state of Israel, the idea of Jews returning to Temple Mount prior to
    *the arrival of the messiah has been the obsession of a tiny minority*."),
    https://www.theguardian.com/commentisfree/belief/2013/sep/13/
    israeli-temple-mount-trigger-unimaginable-violence.

43. Daniel J. Elazar, "How Religious Are Israeli Jews?" Jerusalem Center for
    Public Affairs, accessed July 22, 2019, http://www.jcpa.org/dje/articles2/
    howrelisr.htm.

    > Israel's Jews are…divided into four [groups]: ultra-Orthodox,
    > religious Zionists, traditional Jews, and secular. Some 8 percent
    > are ultra-Orthodox. Another 17 percent are religious Zionists.
    > The third group consists of the vast majority of Israeli Jews,
    > some 55 percent, who define themselves as "traditional." The
    > fourth and second smallest group consists of those who define
    > themselves as secular, some 20 percent of the Jewish population.

44. Rick Gladstone, "Historical Certainty Proves Elusive at Jerusalem's Holiest
    Place," *New York Times*, 10-8-15, https://www.nytimes.com/2015/10/09/
    world/middleeast/historical-certainty-proves-elusive-at-jerusalems-holiest-
    place.html.

45. Frank Turek, "The Jewish Temple That May Prevent World War III," *Christian Post*, 7-2-14, https://www.christianpost.com/news/the-jewish-temple-that-may-prevent-world-war-iii.html.

46. www.messiahofisraelministries.com.

47. See Rabbi Zev Porat's full testimony in the book, *The Rabbi, The Secret Message, and the Identity of Messiah*. Zev and I coauthored this book about the amazing true story of the late acclaimed Israeli Rabbi Yitzhak Kaduri. The book was published by Defender Publishing in February 2019.

48. http://templeinstitute.org.

49. Gilad, Moshe. "Visiting the Holy Temple in Jerusalem, No Time Machine Necessary," *Haaretz*, 10-25-16, https://www.haaretz.com/israel-news/.premium.MAGAZINE-dazzling-visit-to-the-holy-temple-before-its-destruction-1.5452077.
From the article: "The director, Yitzhak Aloni, told me the institute exhibit attracts around 70,000 visitors a year, half of them Israelis."

50. Yeshiva—A rabbinical training school similar to a seminary.

51. These are Rabbi Zev Porat's approved words, to be used in this book. He sent them to me in an email.

52. The Jerusalem Center for Public Affairs is a leading independent research institute specializing in public diplomacy and foreign policy. Founded in 1976, the Center has produced hundreds of studies and initiatives by leading experts on a wide range of strategic topics. The Center is headed by Ambassador Dore Gold, former Israeli ambassador to the UN and director-general of the Israel Ministry of Foreign Affairs. See the website: http://jcpa.org/about.

53. *Halakha* is the collective body of Jewish religious laws derived from the written and Oral Torah. See https://en.wikipedia.org/wiki/Halakha.

54. Jerusalem Center for Public Affairs, "Israel Relinquishes the Temple Mount," accessed July 20, 2019, http://jcpa.org/al-aksa-is-in-danger-libel-temple-mount.

55. The Amidah Prayer—The central prayer of the Jewish liturgy. Observant Jews recite the Amidah at each of three prayer services in a typical weekday: morning, afternoon, and evening. See https://en.wikipedia.org/wiki/Amidah.

56. Ben Sales, "Laying the Groundwork for a Third Temple in

Jerusalem," *Times of Israel,* 7-16-13, https://www.timesofisrael.com/laying-the-groundwork-for-a-third-temple-in-jerusalem.

57. Dr. Randall Price, "Update on the Building of the Temple," *Jewish Voice* (2019), accessed Aug. 25, 2019, https://www.jewishvoice.org/read/article/update-building-third-temple.

58. As we have referenced in previous quotes, this right-wing flank is only a tiny minority of all the orthodox Jews, who themselves are a small minority of the total of Jews living in Israel.

59. Sharon, Jeremy. "Jewish Prayer Has Returned to the Temple Mount—Exclusive," *Jerusalem Post,* December 12, 2019, https://www.jpost.com/Arab-Israeli-Conflict/Jewish-prayer-has-returned-to-the-Temple-Mount-exclusive-610781.

60. Revelation 11:1, Matthew 24:15, and 2 Thessalonians 2:4 are the only three verses in the New Testament that come anywhere near suggesting that the "temple" of the Antichrist might be a literal, rebuilt third temple in Jerusalem. The entirety of that study is much too detailed to include in this book. However, for your own further study, Rabbi Zev Porat and I have written about this topic, examining each verse in its original language and context. You may read that study at the following web link: "Does a Third Temple Have To Be Constructed for Jesus to Return?" By Pastor Carl Gallups and Messianic Rabbi Zev Porat (Tel Aviv, Israel), https://ppsimmons.blogspot.com/2019/06/does-third-temple-have-to-be.html.

61. By "classical scholars," I am including those who are the most popularly quoted, and who wrote from about one hundred years ago all the way back to the first several centuries of church history.

62. I emphasize the commentaries of the ***classical scholars and biblical encyclopedias*** to demonstrate that a large portion of what today's Western evangelical church hears is a relatively "new interpretation" of end-time events. While the newer interpretations may prove to be correct, the more modernistic line of thinking certainly was not the prevailing interpretation from the first to the nineteenth centuries.

63. Contextual excerpts from the twelve mentioned classical scholars, with emphasis added:
    *Cambridge Bible for Schools and Colleges*:
    [The] Temple was the type and **representative of all places**

consecrated to the worship of the true God. The great
Usurper who claims for himself that he "is God," **appropriates
consequently the sanctuaries of religion** and prostitutes them
to his own worship. **"Within the temple of God—not in
Jerusalem alone,"** says Chrysostom, **"but in every church."**

*Ellicott's Commentary for English Readers*:

We may say with some confidence that St. Paul *did not* expect
the Antichrist as a prose fact to take his seat in that edifice.
[The Jewish Temple]...The Man of Sin will make formal
claim to occupy *that central seat in men's* [Christian people]
*minds and aspirations*. (Brackets added to express the proper
context of *Ellicott's* entire thesis)

*Gill's Exposition of the Entire Bible*:

**The temple of God; not in the temple of Jerusalem**, which
was to be destroyed and never to be rebuilt more, and was
destroyed before this man of sin was revealed; **but in the
church of God, so called, 1 Corinthians 3:16.**

*Geneva Study Bible*:

He foretells that the antichrist (that is, whoever he is that will
occupy that seat that falls away from God) **will not reign
outside of the Church, but in the very bosom of the Church.**

*Matthew Poole's Commentary*:

The temple of God: 2 Corinthians 6:16 Revelation 3:12,
etc. **But it is a spiritual temple, as the church is called,**
1 Corinthians 3:16, 17. So Augustine, Jerome, Hilary,
Chrysostom, understand it. **And he is said here to sit, to have
here his cathedral.**

*Barnes' Notes on the Bible*:

**[The idea] denotes the church as a society,** and the idea is, that the
Antichrist here referred to would present himself **in the midst of that
church** as claiming the honors due to God alone....
That is, in the Christian church. It is by no means necessary to
understand this of the temple at Jerusalem.... In the Christian church
he would usurp the place which God had occupied in the temple.

*Matthew Henry's Concise Commentary*:

As God was in the temple of old, and worshipped there, and is in and with his church now; so the antichrist here mentioned, **is a usurper of God's authority in the Christian church, who claims Divine honors**

*Jamieson-Fausset-Brown Bible Commentary:*

It is likely that, as Messiah was revealed among the Jews at Jerusalem, so Antimessiah shall appear among them when restored to their own land, and after they have rebuilt their temple at Jerusalem.

*Bengel's Gnomen:*

**In the temple of God**—in **that temple of God** which is mentioned, Revelation 11:1.

*Meyer's New Testament Commentary:*

[This passage] **cannot be otherwise understood than in its proper sense.** But on account of the repetition of the article can only one definite temple of one definite true God—**that is, the temple of Jerusalem**—**be meant.**

64. "2 Thessalonians 2:4," *Pulpit Commentary*, Biblehub.com, https://biblehub.com/commentaries/2_thessalonians/2-4.htm.

65. "2 Thessalonians 2:4," *Vincent's Word Studies*, Biblehub.com, https://biblehub.com/commentaries/2_thessalonians/2-4.htm.

66. Following are excerpts from each of the listed commentaries, both majority and minority views:

*People's Commentary:*

"[The "temple of God" means that the apostasy] arose in the church." ("2 Thessalonians 2:4," *Peoples' Commentary*, Bible Study Tools, https://www.biblestudytools.com/commentaries/peoples-new-testament/2-thessalonians/2.html)

*Cyclopedia of Biblical, Theological and Ecclesiastical Literature:*

This passage must be understood as employing the conventional Scriptural language symbolically to indicate a then (and perhaps still) future effort on the part of some hostile power to overthrow Christianity [the church] and induce its professors to renounce it. (*Cyclopedia of Biblical, Theological and Ecclesiastical Literature.* "Man of Sin," Study

Light [Published in the nineteenth century, begun in 1853, coauthored by John McClintock, academic and minister, and Dr. James Strong, professor of exegetical theology), accessed July 18, 2019, https://www.studylight.org/encyclopedias/ mse/m/man-of-sin.html?hilite=Man%20of%20Sin.)

*Calvin's Commentaries*:

As, however, interpreters have twisted this passage in various ways, we must first of all endeavor to ascertain Paul's true meaning. He says that the day of Christ will not come, until the world has fallen into apostasy, and the reign of Antichrist has obtained a footing in the Church. ("2 Thessalonians 2," *Calvin's Commentaries*, Biblehub.com, https://biblehub.com/ commentaries/calvin/2_thessalonians/2.htm.)

*The Biblical Illustrator*:

Universal headship and supremacy over *all the Churches* of Christ. This is Christ's right, and whoever challenges it sits as God in His temple. ("2 Thessalonians 2:4," *The Biblical Illustrator*, Studylight.org, https://www.studylight.org/ commentary/2-thessalonians/2-4.html.)

*Clarke's Commentary*:

He stands against and exalts himself above all Divine authority…so that sitting in the temple of God [means] having the highest place and authority in the Christian Church. ("2 Thessalonians 2," *Clarke's Commentary*, Biblehub.com, https:// biblehub.com/commentaries/clarke/2_thessalonians/2.htm.)

*Expositor's Bible Commentary*:

The temple of God is, therefore, *the temple at Jerusalem*; it was standing when Paul wrote; and he expected it to stand till all this was fulfilled. ("2 Thessalonians 2," *Expositor's Bible Commentary*, Biblehub.com, https://biblehub.com/ commentaries/expositors/2_thessalonians/2.htm.)

Irenaeus (c. AD 130–202, a bishop of the early Roman Catholic Church):

But when this Antichrist shall have devastated all things in this world, he will reign for three years and six months, and sit in the temple at Jerusalem. ("2 Thessalonians 2—the Coming

of that Day," *Enduring Word*, Enduringword.com, https://
enduringword.com/bible-commentary/2-thessalonians-2/.)

*Arno Gaebelein's Annotated Bible*:

The temple of God does not mean the Church. It is a Jewish
temple. When the true Church is gone [in the Rapture] the
Jewish people, restored once more to their own land, [that
has now happened. Gaebelein was writing before 1948] was
established there as a nation, though still in unbelief, will erect
another temple and institute once more the temple worship.
(Brackets added; Arno Clemens Gaebelein, "Commentary
on 2 Thessalonians 2:4," *Gaebelein's Annotated Bible*, https://
www.studylight.org/commentaries/gab/2-thessalonians-2.html.
1913-1922.)

*International Critical Commentary*:

The second epistle [of Thessalonians] is not a doctrinal treatise
on the Anti-Christ, as if 2:1–12 were the sole point of the
letter, but a practical exhortation, written by request and
designed to encourage the faint-hearted and to admonish the
idlers. [Paul's descriptions here] are manifestly intended not to
convey new information but to encourage the faint-hearted by
reminding them of his oral instructions. ("Epistles of St. Paul
to the Thessalonians," *The International Critical Commentary*,
(1912), Dr. James Everett Frame, accessed July 18, 2019,
https://archive.org/details/criticalexegetic00framuoft/page/20.)

*Robertson's Word Pictures*:

The whole subject is left by Paul in such a vague form that
we can hardly hope to clear it up. It is possible that his own
preaching while with them gave his readers a clue that we do
not possess. ("2 Thessalonians 2:4," Bible Study Tools, https://
www.biblestudytools.com/commentaries/robertsons-word-
pictures/2-thessalonians/2-thessalonians-2-4.html.)

67. "2 Thessalonians 2:4," *Whedon's Commentary on the Bible*, Studylight,
https://www.studylight.org/commentaries/whe/2-thessalonians-2.html.

68. "2 Thessalonians 2," *Joseph Benson's Commentary of the Old and New Testaments*,
https://www.studylight.org/commentaries/rbc/2-thessalonians-2.html.

69. "Antichrist," *International Standard Bible Encyclopedia* (1915), accessed July 18, 2019, https://www.internationalstandardbible.com/A/antichrist.html.

70. "2 Thessalonians 2:4," *The International Critical Commentary*, accessed July 12, 2019, https://archive.org/details/criticalexegetic00framuoft/page/256.

71. "Commentary on 2 Thessalonians 2" (Views of the early church fathers), accessed August 21, 2019, https://sites.google.com/site/aquinasstudybible/home/2-thessalonians/2-thess-q/2-thess-2.
    Only the Church (or Antichrist "becomes" the counterfeit "temple"-church.
    (St. Andrew of Caesarea) [This passage] *referred to the churches*, in which he will arrogate to himself pride of place, striving to declare himself God. Theodore of Mopsuestia, Theodoret of Cyrus and Oecumenius include **only the Christian Churches** and **not the Temple of Jerusalem**. St. Augustine, Thietland and Lyra propose that the text may mean that the *Antichrist becomes the counterfeit temple in comparison to Christ* as the Temple.
    The Church *and* the Jewish Temple
    (Theodoret of Cyrus) St. John Chrysostom and Theophylact include *both the Jewish Temple and the Christian Churches*. St. Andrew and Haimo give an *either/or,* as well as St. Augustine and Thietland.
    Only the Jewish Temple
    St. Irenaeus, St. Hippolytus, St. Cyril of Jerusalem, Ambrosiaster, St. John of Damascus, Apollinarius of Laodicea and Origen include *only the Temple* of Solomon.

72. At this site—https://www.studylight.org/commentaries/—over sixty classical commentaries (some already referenced in this chapter) that address 2 Thessalonians 2:4 are indexed on a single page. The overwhelming majority indicate that the "temple of God" is the church, based upon the context of all of Paul's other writings that use that phrase.

73. Paul claimed to have learned from Jesus personally. See Galatians 1:12.

74. "2 Thessalonians 2:4," *Coffman's Commentary on the Bible*, Studylight.org, https://www.studylight.org/commentary/2-thessalonians/2-4.html.

75. "2 Thessalonians 2:4," *Robertson's Word Pictures*, Studylight.org, https://www.studylight.org/commentary/2-thessalonians/2-4.html#rwp.
    But the whole subject is left by Paul in such a vague form that

we can hardly hope to clear it up. It is possible that his own preaching while with them gave his readers a clue that we do not possess."

76. "2 Thessalonians," *Lange's Commentary on the Holy Scriptures: Critical, Doctrinal, and Homiletical,* Studylight, https://www.studylight.org/commentaries/lcc/2-thessalonians-2.html.

77. Ibid.

78. "2 Thessalonians 2:2–3," *Ellicott's Commentary for English Readers,* Biblehub. com, https://biblehub.com/commentaries/2_thessalonians/2-3.htm.

79. "Matthew 12:6, *Ellicott's Commentary for English Readers,* Biblehub.com, https://biblehub.com/commentaries/matthew/12-6.htm.

80. "Matthew 12:6," *Matthew Poole's Commentary,* Biblehub.com, https://biblehub.com/commentaries/matthew/12-6.htm.

81. Dean R. Ulrich (PhD, Westminster Theological Seminary) has been associate professor of Old Testament at Trinity Episcopal School for Ministry in Ambridge, Pennsylvania. He also served on the Faculty of Humanities, Subject Group Theology, Northwest University, Vaal Campus, in South Africa. His articles have been included in the *Journal of Biblical Counseling, Journal of the Evangelical Theological So*ciety, and *Westminster Theological Journal.*

82. D. R. Ulrich, 2015, "Jesus and the Six Objectives of Daniel 9:24," *In die Skriflig* 49(1), Art. #1934, 9 pages. http:// dx.doi.org/10.4102/ids. v49i1.1934.
PDF download here: https://www.indieskriflig.org.za/index.php/skriflig/article/download/1934/3488.

83. "Romans 12," *Pulpit Commentary,* Biblehub.com, https://biblehub.com/commentaries/romans/12-2.htm.

84. "NT:2411. *Hieron* (hee-er-on')" "neuter of NT:2413; a sacred place, i.e. the entire precincts (whereas NT:3485 denotes the central sanctuary itself) of the Temple (at Jerusalem or elsewhere)." (*Biblesoft's New Exhaustive Strong's Numbers and Concordance with Expanded Greek-Hebrew Dictionary* [1994, 2003, 2006, Biblesoft, Inc. and International Bible Translators, Inc.]).

85. It is disputed among scholars which author penned the book of Hebrews. Some believe Paul wrote it. If this is so, then Paul would have written fourteen of the twenty-seven New Testament books. If he wrote Hebrews,

he never uses the word "temple" in it. The words "sanctuary" and "tabernacle" are used instead.

86. Some translations of Romans 9:4 put the word "temple" in Paul's mouth. However, the word is not there in the Greek texts. The translators are inserting the word for what they think is greater clarity. However, scholars dispute whether the word "temple" was what Paul was even talking about in the first place. Regardless of what the apostle meant, he did not include the words *heiron* or *naos* in the actual text there. See https://biblehub.com/romans/9-4.htm.

87. "GK. 3485, *Naos*," *Thayer's Greek Lexicon*, Biblehub.com, https://biblehub.com/greek/3485.htm.

88. **Author's no**te: Some Bible students insist that to interpret Paul's "temple of God" in any way other than a literal temple on the Temple Mount is "spiritualizing" the apostle's clear meaning. Following is an example of how that argument is stated. This example is found in its complete context at the following website. I defend the writer's privilege to hold any view he desires. However, as you will see, I believe his view is exegetically flawed from the outset.

Precept Austin, "2 Thessalonians 2:4 Commentary," 8-29-26, accessed 8-21-19, https://www.preceptaustin.org/2_thessalonians_24_commentary. The bracketed and bold words contained in the quoted text below **are mine alone**. I have included them to demonstrate article's drift away from the proper interpretation process:

"Temple" is *naos* which refers to the inner sanctuary of the Temple. [True. But it can—*and does*—often represent the *metaphor of the church*, or the Christian's body, as well. This is the *only* way in which Paul *ever* uses naos in *all* his other writings. Either the writer is unfamiliar with this GK word, or he is familiar with its metaphorical use and is purposely excluding that use in his treatise.]

The definite article before naos signifies not just any temple but the specific Temple. [That is not necessarily so. Since every other time Paul uses *naos* he also uses the definitive article to indicate *the church*].

The simplest reading of the plain text is to interpret Paul as referring to a literal Temple of God. [Yes. That is normally correct. But only if one does not take into consideration any of the other of Paul's writings, and how he uses that phrase within them. *Every* time Paul uses that phrase, he is clearly referencing *the church*. When that fact is considered, then 2 Thessalonians 2:4 "temple of God" is certainly not the "simplest reading of the plain text." Not by any stretch of the imagination].

And yet many try to spiritualize "Temple of God." [However, now we have seen that this is not "spiritualizing" at all. Rather, what we have done is to put all of Paul's writings and his use of *naos,* in context. This is the opposite of spiritualization. If anyone "spiritualized" the phrase, it would have been Paul himself, and we are simply following his lead in equating "temple of God" with the church. And, as we have already catalogued, this is exactly the way the majority of scholars for the last 1,900 years have interpreted Paul's usage of this phrase.]

89. See John Piper, "Destroy This Temple, and in Three Days I Will Raise It Up," Desiring God, 12-21-2008, https://www.desiringgod.org/messages/destroy-this-temple-and-in-three-days-i-will-raise-it-up.

> This church building is not the temple of God. Jesus is. When Jesus died for us and rose from the dead, *he replaced the temple with himself.* He is the universal Immanuel, God with us.

See Ligonier Ministries, "The Temple of Jesus' Body," Accessed August 3-2019, https://www.ligonier.org/learn/devotionals/temple-of-jesus-body.

> Many Christians are eagerly expecting the day in which the physical temple in Jerusalem will be rebuilt. Today's passage, however, tells us that the only temple we should be looking forward to is the temple that is Christ's body, which we will see in the new heaven and earth. The temple pointed to Christ and *it is fulfilled in Christ and His church*, so let us love Christ and His people.

90. Revelation 11:1, Matthew 24:15, and 2 Thessalonians 2:4 are the only three verses in the New Testament that come anywhere near suggesting that the "temple" of the Antichrist might be a literal rebuilt third temple in Jerusalem. That entire study is much too detailed to include in this book. However, for your own further study, in this matter, Rabbi Zev Porat and I have written about this topic, examining each verse in its original language and context. You may read that study at the following web link: "Does a Third Temple Have to Be Constructed for Jesus to Return?" Pastor

Carl Gallups and Messianic Rabbi Zev Porat (Tel Aviv, Israel), https://
ppsimmons.blogspot.com/2019/06/does-third-temple-have-to-be.html.

91. As an example of this assertion, note the commentary entries of the fourteen
    classical scholars located on a single page at Biblehub.com. They are
    commenting on Matthew 24:15, wherein Jesus speaks of "the abomination
    that causes desolation standing in the holy place, as spoken of by the
    prophet Daniel." Not one of those fourteen scholars even suggests that Jesus,
    or Daniel, was referring to a rebuilt third temple in Jerusalem when He
    spoke those words. Again, that concept was largely a foreign one for a full
    eighteen hundred years after the Church was born. https://biblehub.com/
    commentaries/matthew/24-15.htm.

92. Revelation 12:9 and 20:2.

93. The concept of Heaven's divine council is thoroughly revealed in my book,
    *Gods and Thrones* (Crane, MO: Defender Publishing, 2017).

94. "2 Thessalonians 2:9," *Matthew Poole's Commentary*, Biblehub.com, https://
    biblehub.com/commentaries/2_thessalonians/2-9.htm.

95. "Matthew 13," *Arno Gaebelein's Annotated Bible*, Studylight.org, https://
    www.studylight.org/commentaries/gab/matthew-13.html.

96. "Matthew 13:31," *Coffman's Commentary on the Bible*, Studylight.org,
    https://www.studylight.org/commentary/matthew/13-31.html.

        Matthew gives us here seven parables—the usual number
        indicating completeness. In some sense, surely, they are
        designed to give us a perfect picture of the Kingdom, but in
        what sense we are not entitled to decide without examination
        of the whole series; which is divided by difference of place
        and audience into four and three, the usual division of a seven
        -part series. Four are spoken to the multitude upon the sea-
        shore; the last three to the disciples in the house. The numbers
        concur with the circumstances to lead us to expect in the first
        four a more external, in the last three a more internal and
        spiritual view. The explanation of the second parable has its
        place also with the three.

97. The parable of the treasure and the parable of the pearl, Matthew 13:44–45.

98. The parable of the net (Matthew 13:47–50).

99. John MacArthur, "The Kingdom of God," Grace to You, accessed

July 14, 2019, https://www.gty.org/library/bibleqnas-library/QA0158/ what-is-the-kingdom-of-heaven.

100. "Matthew 13:38," *Barnes' Notes on the Bible*, Biblehub.com, https:// biblehub.com/commentaries/matthew/13 38.htm.

101. There are a total of ten kingdom parables in the book of Matthew. The first seven are found in Matthew 13, as we are studying here. The last three are found in Matthew 18:23, 20:1, and 22:2. The last three clearly speak to the very last days and the coming judgment as well. They also speak to the enemy's constant attacks used against the Kingdom work, right up until the very end. There is simply no denying the deeply prophetic nature of these parables. They were designed to warn the Church of all ages, and especially the church of the very last days, just before the return of Jesus.

102. "Ephesians 2:2," *Cambridge Bible for Schools and Colleges*, Biblehub.com, https://biblehub.com/commentaries/ephesians/2-2.htm.

103. "Luke 13:19," *The Wiersbe Bible Commentary: New Testament*, (David C. Cook, New edition; November 1, 2007) 182, referenced at https:// godspeakyouth.files.wordpress.com/2017/09/wiersbe-nt.pdf (182).

104. Dr. Martin G. Collins, "Bible Verses about Bird as Symbol of Demon (*Forerunner Commentary*)," "Parables of Matthew 13 (Part Four): The Parable of the Mustard Seed," https://www.bibletools.org/index.cfm/ fuseaction/Topical.show/RTD/CGG/ID/3600/Bird-as-Symbol-of-Demon-.htm.

105. "Matthew 13:31," *Coffman's Commentary on the Bible*, Studylight.org, https://www.studylight.org/commentary/matthew/13-31.html.

106. F. W. Grant, "The Gospels" (The Kingdom in the Hands of Men), STEM Publishing, accessed July 18, 2019, https://www.stempublishing.com/ authors/FW_Grant/Numerical_Bible/FWG_Numerical_Bible21d.html.

107. Arno Clemens Gaebelein, "Commentary on Matthew 13:4," *Gaebelein's Annotated Bible*, https://www.studylight.org/commentaries/gab/ matthew-13.html. 1913-1922.

108. A sizeable number of the classical scholars believed that visible apostate church would most conspicuously be represented by the Roman Catholic Church and its long history of violence, bloodshed, and sexual perversion, as well as its deep and loathsome attachments to a multitude of governments of the world. One will find this idea throughout the

writings of the classical scholars of the Protestant as well as the evangelical persuasions.

I happen to believe they are most likely correct in their assessment, with one caveat: I also believe that, in the very last days, it is very likely that the apostasy will be rampant throughout *the entire visible church*, whether it is represented as Catholic, Protestant, or evangelical. Actually, we are already witnessing that phenomenon begin to converge within our own lifetime. See a sampling of commentary entries for this verse at: https://biblehub. com/commentaries/revelation/18-2.htm.

109. See the commentary entries at https://biblehub.com/commentaries/1_ corinthians/10-21.htm.

110. See the commentary entries at https://biblehub.com/commentaries/2_ corinthians/6-15.htm.

111. Some argue that the two leavened loaves used as wave-offerings at the feast of Pentecost, as prescribed in Leviticus 23, were loaves that contained "good leaven." But the Bible presents no such thing. See the following explanation at Jews for Jesus website:

> Thus, the inclusion of the Gentiles completed the symbolism of the wave offering, where the High Priest offered two loaves of fine wheat flour baked with leaven. Centuries before it came to pass, the two loaves of the wave offering symbolized the Body of Messiah made up of both Jewish and Gentile believers. Though the loaves were made of fine wheat flour, **they contained leaven, a symbol of sin.** That speaks of the fact that the Church, though refined (cleansed by the blood of Yeshua's sacrifice), still retains the human sin nature until that day when she will be presented as the Bride of Christ, without spot or wrinkle. (Jews for Jesus, "From Passover to Pentecost," jewsforjesus.org/pulications/newsletter/newletter-j-1995/ from-passover-to-pentecost-newletter-jun-1995.)

112. F. W. Grant, F. W., "The Gospels" (The Kingdom in the Hands of Men), STEM Publishing, accessed July 18, 2019, https://www.stempublishing. com/authors/FW_Grant/Numerical_Bible/FWG_Numerical_Bible21d. html.

113. "Matthew 13," *Arno Gaebelein's Annotated Bible*, Studylight.org, https://www.studylight.org/commentaries/gab/matthew-13.html.

114. "Matthew 13:33," *Cambridge Bible for Schools and Colleges*, Biblehub.com, http://biblehub.com/commentaries/matthew/13-33.htm.

115. "Matthew 13:33," *John Gill's Exposition of the Whole Bible*, Studylight.org, https://www.studylight.org/commentary/matthew/13-33.html.

116. "2 Thessalonians 2:7," *Benson Commentary*, Biblehub.com, https://biblehub.com/commentaries/2_thessalonians/2-7.htm.

117. "2 Thessalonians 2:7, *Pulpit Commentary*, Biblehub.com, https://biblehub.com/commentaries/2_thessalonians/2-7.htm.

118. "2 Thessalonians 2:7," *Barnes' Notes*, Studylight.org, https://www.studylight.org/commentary/2-thessalonians/2-7.html.

119. "2 Thessalonians 2:7," *Biblical Illustrator*, Studylight.org, https://www.studylight.org/commentary/2-thessalonians/2-7.html.

120. "2 Thessalonians 2:7," *John Gill's Exposition of the Whole Bible*, Studylight.org, https://www.studylight.org/commentary/2-thessalonians/2-7.html.

121. "2 Thessalonians 2:7," "*Robertson's Word Pictures*," Studylight.org, https://www.studylight.org/commentary/2-thessalonians/2-7.html.

122. "2 Thessalonians 2:7," *Wesley's Notes*, Studylight.org, https://www.studylight.org/commentary/2-thessalonians/2-7.html.

123. "NT 458, *Anomia*," Biblehub.com, https://biblehub.com/greek/458.htm.

124. **Apostasy** (A proper understanding of the word)—There has arisen a false notion in modern Christian teaching that the word "apostasy," especially as it is used in 2 Thessalonians 2:3, means "a departure." Usually this notion is proffered so that the word can be forced into meaning "the Rapture" of the church. While it is not the purpose of this book to defend any particular view of the Rapture and/or its timing, it must be pointed out that the Greek word *apostasia* (NT 646) simply does not properly mean "a departure," as in the Rapture.

Rather, *apostasia* always means a "departure *from a stance*," a "falling away," or "defection *from the truth*." (See all Greek dictionary references at https://biblehub.com/greek/646.htm.) This word is used *only one other time* in the New Testament: Acts 21:21. In that verse, *apostasia* clearly speaks of a departure from biblical truth, not a simple "departure" as from the earth, in the Rapture.

As the *HELPS Word-studies* tells us, *apostasia* is made of two distinct Greek words. One means "to depart away from"; the other means "a stand, or position."

> apostasía (from 868 /aphístēmi, "leave, depart," which is derived from 575 /apó, "away from" and 2476 /histémi, "stand")—properly, departure (implying desertion); apostasy— literally, "a leaving, from a previous standing."

125. Dr. Thomas D. Williams, "Pew: U.S. Christian Population in Freefall, 12% Drop in Ten Years," Breitbart, October 18, 2019, https://www.breitbart.com/faith/2019/10/18/pew-u-s-christian-population-in-freefall-12-drop-in-ten-years.

126. Avery Foley, "Study Shows Only 10% of Americans Have a Biblical Worldview," Answers in Genesis, May 2, 2017, https://answersingenesis.org/culture/study-shows-only-10-percent-americans-have-biblical-worldview.

127. George Barna, "Groundbreaking ACFI survey Reveals How Many Adults Have a Biblical Worldview," 2027-17, http://www.georgebarna.com/research-flow/2017/4/5/groundbreaking-acfi-survey-reveals-how-many-adults-have-a-biblical-worldview.

128. See Matthew 7:21 and John 8:31ff.

129. Sun T'zu's Art of War. "3. Attack by Stratagem," accessed August 5, 2019, https://suntzusaid.com/book/3/18.

130. *Satan* is a Hebrew word. It means "one who accuses" or "adversary." O.T. 7854.
    Bodie Hodge, "Who Is Satan and Was He Always Called "Satan"? Answers in Genesis, March 16, 2010, https://answersingenesis.org/angels-and-demons/satan/who-is-satan-and-was-he-always-called-satan/. From the article:

> Even though Satan is first mentioned by name in Job, other historical accounts record his actions (see Genesis 3–4; 1 John 3:12; and Revelation 12:9). Devil (diabolos) means "false accuser, Satan, and slanderer" in Greek, and is the word from which the English word diabolical is formed.
> Satan is called "dragon" in Revelation 12:9 and 20:2, as well as "the evil one" in several places. Other names for Satan include

"ancient serpent" and "serpent of old" (Revelation 12:9), "Beelzebub" and "Beelzebul" (Matthew 12:27), "Belial" (2 Corinthians 6:15), and "tempter" (Matthew 4:3). Satan is also referred to as the "god of this world/age" (2 Corinthians 4:4), "prince of this world" (John 12:31), and "father of lies" (John 8:44).

[Isaiah 14] is the only passage that uses the name Lucifer to refer to Satan. In Latin, Lucifer means "light bringer." The Hebrew is heylel and means "light bearer, shining one, or morning star." Many modern translations translate this as "star of the morning" or "morning star."

131. Author's note: This is not to say that, in God's absolute sovereignty and grand omniscience, He did not ultimately know what Satan would do. It does mean that God did not create Satan as an evil being. The Bible emphatically declares that Satan was created in perfection (Ezekiel 28). However, in his freedom to choose, Satan rebelled and thus became God's enemy—and the tormentor of humanity.

See Bodie Hodge, "What about Satan and the Origin of Evil?" Answers in Genesis, July 29, 2010, https://answersingenesis.org/angels-and-demons/satan/what-about-satan-and-the-origin-of-evil.

Also see my books *Gods and Thrones* and *Gods of Ground Zero* (Defender Publishers) for a much more thorough study of these biblical truths.

Also see Chuck Lawless, "God's Mission Has an Enemy: 10 Facts about Spiritual Warfare," May 17, 2017, https://www.imb.org/2017/05/17/mission-enemy-10-facts-spiritual-warfare.

132. Some biblical researchers have surmised that the actual fall of Satan could have occurred as many as a hundred years or more after the creation of the first human couple.

See Eric Hovind, "When Did Satan Fall from Heaven? May 6, 2010, http://creationtoday.org/when-did-satan-fall-from-heaven.

See also Bodie Hodge, "What about Satan and the Origin of Evil?" July 20, 2010, https://answersingenesis.org/angels-and-demons/satan/what-about-satan-and-the-origin-of-evil/.

See also: Got Questions? "How, Why, and When Did Satan Fall from Heaven?" accessed January 8, 2018, https://www.gotquestions.org/Satan-fall.html.

133. All of these metaphors are used in the Book of Revelation for either Jesus or Satan, respectively. Revelation 12 and 20 plainly tell us that the "serpent" and the "dragon" are obvious metaphors for the person of Satan. He never was a literal snake or a literal dragon.

134. "Genesis 3:1," *Benson Commentary*, Biblehub.com, https://biblehub.com/commentaries/genesis/3-1.htm.

135. "Genesis 3:1," *Matthew Henry's Concise Commentary*, Biblehub.com, https://biblehub.com/commentaries/genesis/3-1.htm.

136. "Genesis 3," *Coffman's Commentaries on the Bible*, Studylight.org, https://www.studylight.org/commentaries/bcc/genesis-3.html.

137. See my book *Gods of Ground Zero: The Truth of Eden's Iniquity* (Crane, MO: Defender Publishing, Oct. 2018) for an exhaustive biblical study of this fact. The word studies, commentary attestations, and contextual connections offer amazing insight.

138. *Ellicott's Commentary for English Readers*:

   **The imagery is taken from the Temple upon Mount Zion.** Upon the holy mountain of God.—the prophet still has his mind upon Mount Zion (comp. Isaiah 11:9; Isaiah 56:7).

   *Benson Commentary*:

   Fixed on the holy mountain **where the temple of God** stands.

   *Jamieson-Fausset-Brown Bible Commentary*:

   Upon the holy mountain of God—Zion. The imagery employed by Ezekiel as a priest is **from the Jewish temple**.

   *The Pulpit Commentary*:

   The splendor-of the King of Tyre had suggested the idea of Eden the garden of God. This, in its turn, led on to that of the cherub that was the warder of that garden (Genesis 3:24). **The Paradise of God is pictured as still existing.**

   (Also see my book *Gods of Ground Zero* for a thorough study of Jerusalem and the Temple Mount as the original location of the Garden of Eden)

   *Cambridge Bible for Schools and Colleges*:

   **The mountain here is the same as the garden** of Ezekiel 28:13, cf. Ezekiel 28:16. It is the abode of God, where the cherub was and where the prince was placed on the day when he was created.

For all the above commentary entries for this verse see https://biblehub.com/commentaries/ezekiel/28-14.htm.

139. Dr. Lehman Strauss, "Bible Prophecy (A Principle of Prophetic Interpretation; Isaiah's Prophecies; Micah's Prophecies)," Bible.org, accessed November 4, 2017, https://bible.org/article/bible-prophecy. Author's Note: A compound prophecy, or a compound reference, is one that either contains several layers of meaning and context or one that begins as a reference to one thing or person, but then shifts to a symbolic reference to something or someone else. See several examples of this well-known biblical phenomenon in the above-listed reference material by Dr. Strauss.

140. Robert Jamieson, A. R. Fausset, and David Brown, *Commentary Critical and Explanatory on the Whole Bible* (Ezekiel 28), 1871, http://www.biblestudytools.com/commentaries/jamieson-fausset-brown/ezekiel/ezekiel-28.html.

141. "Ezekiel 28:11–19," *The Bible Exposition Commentary: Old Testament*, Biblesoft PC Study Bible, copyright from 1988–2008 *Bible Exposition Commentary: Old Testament* © 2001–2004 by Warren W. Wiersbe. All rights reserved. Accessed on December 14, 2017.

142. "Ezekiel 28," *Coffman's Commentaries on the Bible*, Studylight.org, https://www.studylight.org/commentaries/bcc/ezekiel-28.html.

143. "Ezekiel 28:18," *Coffman's Commentaries on the Bible* (See reference to FF Bruce, *New Layman's Bible Commentary*, p.886), https://www.studylight.org/commentaries/bcc/ezekiel-28.html.

144. "Ezekiel 28," *Guzik Bible Commentary—Enduring Word* (Against Satan—King of Tyre), Enduring Word, https://enduringword.com/bible-commentary/ezekiel-28.

145. "Ezekiel 28," *Wells of Living Water*, Studylight.org, https://www.studylight.org/commentaries/lwc/ezekiel-28.html.

146. See my book *Gods of Ground Zero* (Crane, MO: Defender Publishing, 2018) for an in-depth study on the entirety of the Genesis 3 account and how it relates to the rest of Scripture.

147. See Luke 22:3 and John 13:27. Also see Matthew 26:45–46.

148. Some translations have this "title" as Lucifer. We will see that neither of these designations are "names" for Satan. In a later chapter, we will completely uncover this enigmatic description of the evil one.

149. "Isaiah 14," *Lange's Commentary on the Holy Scriptures: Critical, Doctrinal, and Homiletical,* Studylight.org, https://www.studylight.org/commentaries/lcc/isaiah-14.html#_ftnref21.

150. "Isaiah 14," *Arno Gaebelein's Annotated B*ible, Studylight.org, https://www.studylight.org/commentaries/gab/isaiah-14.html.

151. "Isaiah 14:13," *E. W. Bullinger's Companion Bible Notes,* Studylight.org, https://www.studylight.org/commentaries/bul/isaiah-14.html.

152. "Isaiah 14," *Ironside's Notes on Selected Books,* Studylight.org, https://www.studylight.org/commentaries/isn/isaiah-14.html.

153. "Isaiah 14," *The Bible Exposition Commentary: Old Testament,* Biblesoft PC Study Bible,1988–2008, *Bible Exposition Commentary: Old Testament,* 2001–2004 by Warren W. Wiersbe. All rights reserved. Accessed on December 14, 2017.

154. Isaiah 14:13. "Commentaries," Biblehub.com, https://biblehub.com/commentaries/isaiah/14-13.htm.

155. See my book *Gods and Thrones* (Crane, MO: Defender Publishing, 2017) for an in-depth study of the term "gods" (Heb. *elohim*) as it is used in the Bible, particularly in relation to the angelic beings of Yahweh's domain.

156. **Eat dust and crawl on your belly.** The metaphor continues. This phrase is used throughout Scripture to mean that a person or nation has been utterly debased. See Isaiah 14:12, 15; Ezekiel 28:17–18. These two passages are also about Satan himself, where the illusions of the Genesis 3:15 curses are repeated.

    Nations will see and be ashamed, deprived of all their power.
    They will put their hands over their mouths and their ears will
    become deaf. **They will lick dust like a snake, like creatures
    that crawl on the ground.** (Micah 7:16–17)

    Also, Satan, in Revelation 12:12, is said to have been "thrown down" to the earth.

157. Dr. Deffinbaugh, Bob, "The Anticipation of Israel's Messiah," Bible.org, June 22, 2004, https://bible.org/article/anticipation-israels-messiah#P24_5301.

158. "Genesis 3:14," *Keil and Delitzsch Biblical Commentary on the Old Testament,* Biblehub.com, http://biblehub.com/commentaries/genesis/3-14.htm.

159. "Genesis 3," *Gill's Exposition of the Entire Bible*, Biblehub.com, http://biblehub.com/commentaries/gill/genesis/3.htm.

160. Please see my book *Gods of Ground Zero* (Crane, MO: Defender Publishing, 2018) for a detailed study of the Hebrew words that make up this passage. It becomes clear, through that study, that Coffman is exactly right. Satan is not called an animal, but a "created being." As he is declared to be craftier than "any created being," he is then placed at the top of the creative order. He was not in the form of a snake, and the tempter was not an actual snake.

161. "Genesis 3," "*Coffman's Commentary on the Bible*," Studylight.org, https://www.studylight.org/commentaries/bcc/genesis-3.html.

162. "Genesis 3," *Expositor's Dictionaries of Texts*, (The Gospel of Genesis) Dinsdale T. Young, Studylight.org. https://www.studylight.org/commentaries/edt/genesis-3.html.

163. Lewis. C. S., *The Screwtape Letters* (The Existence of the Devil), (From Chapter/Letter VII), accessed 8-22-19, http://www.ourladyofkirkstall.org.uk/Talk%20Of%20The%20Devil/DEVIL%20-%20QUOTES%20FROM%20SCREWTAPE.pdf.

164. Here are a few examples of the extremes to which otherwise astute scholars have gone in trying to explain a literal, walking and talking snake in the garden. These commentary entries can be found at https://biblehub.com/commentaries/genesis/3-1.htm.

*Jamieson-Fausset-Brown Bible Commentary*:
The serpent—the fall of man was effected by the seductions of a serpent. That it was a real serpent is evident from the plain and artless style of the history.

*Gill's Exposition of the Entire Bible*:
Many instances are given of the subtlety of serpents ... not naturally, but through Satan being in it, and using it in a very subtle manner, to answer his purposes, and gain his point: for though a real serpent, and not the mere form or appearance of one, is here meant.

*Keil and Delitzsch Biblical Commentary on the Old Testament*:
The serpent is here described not only as a beast, but also as a creature of God; it must therefore have been good, like everything else that He had

made. Subtilty was a natural characteristic of the serpent (Matthew 10:16), which led the evil one to select it as his instrument.

165. "OT 3742, *Kerub* (Cherub)," https://biblehub.com/hebrew/3742.htm.

166. Abarim-Publications, "Cherubim Meaning." (The name Cherubim: Summary), accessed August 22, 2019, http://www.abarim-publications. com/Meaning/Cherubim.html#.XV7RROhKgdU.
Also see Delitzch (*Assyrisches Handwörterbuch*) connects the name with Assyrian *kirubu* (a name of the *shedu*) and *karabu* ("great, mighty"). Karppe (1897).
"Cherub," *Jewish Encyclopedia*. 2002–2011 (1906), http:// jewishencyclopedia.com/articles/4311-cherub.

167. "Ezekiel 28," *Benson Commentary*, Biblehub.org, https://biblehub.com/ commentaries/ezekiel/28-14.htm.

168. Whitney Hopler, "The Differences Between Cherubs, Cupids, and Other Angels in Art," Learn Religions, April 17, 2018, https://www. learnreligions.com/cherubs-and-cupids-angels-of-love-124005.

169. See my book *Gods and Thrones* (Crane, MO: Defender Publishing, 2017) for an in-depth study of the biblical concept of the divine council and God's holy mountain.

170. "Ezekiel 28," *Expositor's Bible Commentary*, Biblehub.com, http:// biblehub.com/commentaries/expositors/ezekiel/28.htm.

171. "Ezekiel 28," *Pulpit Commentary*, Biblehub.com, http://biblehub.com/ commentaries/pulpit/ezekiel/28.htm.

172. "OT 1966. *Helel*," Biblehub.com, https://biblehub.com/hebrew/1966. htm.

173. *Strong's Exhaustive Concordance*:
Lucifer—*From halal* (in the sense of brightness); the morning-star—lucifer. see HEBREW halal." https://biblehub.com/ hebrew/1966.htm.

174. "Isaiah 14:12," *Keil & Delitzsch Commentary on the Old Testament*, Studylight.org, https://www.studylight.org/commentaries/kdo/isaiah-14. html.

175. "Isaiah 14:12," *Barnes' Notes on the Bible*, Biblehub.com, https://biblehub. com/commentaries/isaiah/14-12.htm.

176. "Isaiah 14:12," *Clarke's Commentary on the Bible*, Biblehub.com, https:// biblehub.com/niv/isaiah/14-12.htm.

177. "OT 1984, *Halal,*" See the *Brown-Driver-Briggs* definitions of word usage. II. [הָלַל] verb be boastful, Qal Imperfect 2masculine plural Psalm 75:5; Participle Psalm 5:6 2t.; —be boastful Psalm 75:5 Participle boastful ones, boasters Psalm 5:6); Psalm 73:3; Psalm 75:5. https://biblehub.com/hebrew/1984.htm.

178. "OT 3314. *Yiphah,*" Biblehub.com, https://biblehub.com/hebrew/3314.htm.

179. "OT 3313, *Yapha,*" Biblehub.com, https://biblehub.com/hebrew/3313.htm.

180. See this reference for eighteen examples of Scripture proclaiming that there is worship in Heaven among the angelic realm: https://bible.knowing-jesus.com/topics/Heaven,-Worshiping-God.

181. "OT 8596, *Toph,*" Biblehub.com, https://biblehub.com/hebrew/8596.htm.

182. "Ezekiel 28:13," *Parallel Versions,* Biblehub.com, https://biblehub.com/ezekiel/28-13.htm.

183. Additional commentary entries on Revelation 5:8:

    *Barnes' Notes on the Bible*:

    > Tabrets—(or, drums) and "pipes" were a common expression for festivity and triumph. (https://biblehub.com/commentaries/ezekiel/28-13.htm)

    *Matthew Poole's Commentary*:

    > Now the prophet notes their joys, music and songs; both to wind or loud music, and to softer music, as the lute and tabret, in the day of their king's coronation, and all this music on instruments. (https://biblehub.com/commentaries/ezekiel/28-13.htm)

    *Gill's Exposition of the Entire Bible*:

    > Of thy tabrets and of thy pipes was prepared in thee in the day that thou wast created…drums, and pipes, and such like instruments of music, were…made use of by way of rejoicing. (https://biblehub.com/commentaries/ezekiel/28 13.htm).

    *Pulpit Commentary*:

    > Furst takes the words as meaning musical instruments that were of gold set with jewels. (https://biblehub.com/commentaries/ezekiel/28-13.htm).

*Matthew Henry Commentary on the Whole Bible*:
> Another thing that made him think his palace a paradise was the curious music he had, the tabrets and pipes, hand-instruments and wind-instruments. The workmanship of these was extraordinary, and they were prepared for him on purpose. (https://www.biblestudytools.com/commentaries/matthew-henry-complete/ezekiel/28.html)

*Joseph Benson's Commentary of the Old and New Testaments*:
> The highest expressions of joy, such as are the sounding of all sorts of musical instruments, ushered thee into the world. (https://www.studylight.org/commentaries/rbc/ezekiel-28.html)

*Thru the Bible with Dr. J. Vernon McGee*:
> The workmanship of your timbrels and flutes were prepared for you on the day you were created. He could not only sing! He was a band! He was music itself! (Audio recording, chapters 13–16, starting at about the 50-second mark; https://www.studylight.org/commentaries/ttb/ezekiel-28.html)

*Dr. Peter Pett's Commentary on the Bible*, Professor London Bible College:
> The workings of your tabrets and pipes in you. The idea of splendour continues. The meaning of the word for "pipes" (nekeb) is unknown. Its only other use is in Joshua 19:33 where a "pass" or "hollow" has been suggested, but tabrets or timbrels were musical instruments, thus the suggestion of a musical instrument as a translation for nekeb. (https://www.studylight.org/commentaries/pet.html)

*Whedon's Commentary on the Bible*:
> These are the jeweled musical instruments used at the king's coronation in the day when he was created king (Ezekiel 26:13; Isaiah 5:12; Daniel 3:5). (ttps://www.studylight.org/commentaries/whe/ezekiel-28.html)

184. John MacArthur, "The Fall of Satan," Grace to You, 2-27-2000, https://www.gty.org/library/sermons-library/90-237/the-fall-of-satan.

185. "Ezekiel 28," *Guzik Bible Commentary—Enduring Word*, (Against Satan—King of Tyre), Enduring Word, https://enduringword.com/bible-commentary/ezekiel-28.

186. Matt Slick, "Was Lucifer Originally an Angel of Worship?" CARM, accessed August 11, 2019, https://carm.org/questions/about-demons/was-lucifer-originally-angel-worship.

187. "Ezekiel 28:13," *Jamieson, Fausset, and Brown Commentary* (from *Jamieson, Fausset, and Brown Commentary*, Electronic Database. Copyright © 1997, 2003, 2005, 2006 by Biblesoft, Inc. All rights reserved.).

188. "Ezekiel 28," *Keil & Delitzsch Commentary on the Old Testament*, Studylight. org, https://www.studylight.org/commentaries/kdo/ezekiel-28.html.

189. "Ezekiel 28," *Guzik Bible Commentary—Enduring Word*, (Against Satan—King of Tyre), Enduring Word, https://enduringword.com/bible-commentary/ezekiel-28.

190. *"Revelation 5:8," Greek* Testament Critical Exegetical Commentary, Studylight.org, https://www.studylight.org/commentaries/hac/revelation-5.html.

191. "Revelation 5:8," *Cambridge Greek Testament for Schools and Colleges*, Studylight.org, https://www.studylight.org/commentaries/cgt/revelation-5.html.

192. "Revelation 5:8," *Ironside's Notes on Selected Books*, Studylight.org, https://www.studylight.org/commentaries/isn/revelation-5.html.

193. Brandon Specktor, "Human Civilization Will Crumble by 2050 If We Don't Stop Climate Change Now, New Paper Claims," *Live Science*, June 4, 2019, https://www.livescience.com/65633-climate-change-dooms-humans-by-2050.html.

194. Tom O'Conner, "World War III: How Likely Is It U.S. Will Fight in Iran, North Korea, Ukraine or Venezuela?" *Newsweek*, June 12, 2019, https://www.newsweek.com/world-war-3-ww3-iii-start-us-iran-russia-china-venezuela-ukraine-syria-1395020.

195. Youssef Gingihey, "World War 3 Is Coming," *Independent*, March 10, 2017, https://www.independent.co.uk/news/long_reads/world-war-3-is-coming-a7622296.html.

196. CBInsights. "How AI Will Go Out of Control According to 52 Experts," February 19, 2019, https://www.cbinsights.com/research/ai-threatens-humanity-expert-quotes.

197. Ed Yong, "The Next Plague Is Coming. Is America Ready?" *Atlantic*, July/August 2018, https://www.theatlantic.com/magazine/archive/2018/07/when-the-next-plague-hits/561734.

198. World Watch Institute, "Global Population Reduction: Confronting the Inevitable," Updated September 23, 2019, http://www.worldwatch.org/node/563.
For the board of directors, etc. see http://www.worldwatch.org/node/991. For global corporate partners see http://www.worldwatch.org/organizations-partner-us-and-support-our-work.

199. Tom Hanks, Fake World Quote. Full Quote: https://www.azquotes.com/quote/1179702?ref=fake-world.

200. u/bringmedamuffin, "Why do I feel like everything is fake during day to day life and feel more in touch with 'reality' when I am dreaming? Am I alone?" Posted 2015, accessed September 2, 2019, https://www.reddit.com/r/askphilosophy/comments/354uxg/why_do_i_feel_like_everything_is_fake_during_day.

201. Samuel Sigal, "Robot Priests Can Bless you, Advise You, and Even Perform Your funeral," VOX, Sept. 9, 2019, https://www.vox.com/future-perfect/2019/9/9/20851753/ai-religion-robot-priest-mindar-buddhism-christianity.

202. Pseudoscience: "A collection of beliefs or practices mistakenly regarded as being based on scientific method." https://www.coursehero.com/file/p7vpu7r/Pseudoscience-A-collection-of-beliefs-or-practices-mistakenly-regarded-as-being.
Science: "Empirical science entails a systematic approach to epistemology that uses observable, testable, repeatable, and falsifiable experimentation," https://www.allaboutscience.org/scientific-method.htm.

203. Erika Hayasaki, "Better Living Through Crispr: Growing Human Organs in Pigs: Scientist Juan Carlos Izpisua Belmonte wants to use gene editing to create human-animal hybrids that we can harvest for parts. What could go wrong?" *Wired* (Science), March 19, 2019, https://www.wired.com/story/belmonte-crispr-human-animal-hybrid-organs/.

204. Maayan Jaffe-Hoffman, "Israeli Team Makes Embryo Stem Cells Out of Skin," *Jerusalem Post*, May 9, 2019, https://www.jpost.com/OMG/A-baby-from-skin-cells-Israeli-team-makes-embryo-stem-cells-out-of-skin-588531. "What we actually did is convert skin cells into three types of stem cells that can produce embryos," explained Dr. Yossi Buganim of HU's Department of Developmental Biology and Cancer Research.

205. Henry Holloway, "Genetically Engineered Babies 'within two years' as Scientists Make Breakthrough," *Star*, November 19, 2019, https://www.dailystar.co.uk/news/world-news/genetically-engineered-babies-within-two-20907651.

206. Kristina Libby, "This Bill Hader Deepfake Video Is Amazing. It's Also Terrifying for Our Future. Everything you need to know about the technology that poses real dangers to our democracy," *Popular Mechanics*, August 13, 2019, https://www.popularmechanics.com/technology/security/a28691128/deepfake-technology.

207. Simon Elegant, "Now Its Fake Water," Time, 7-10-7, http://world.time.com/2007/07/10/now_its_fake_water.

208. Caroline Miller, "Does Social Media Cause Depression?" Child Mind Institute, accessed September 22, 2019, https://childmind.org/article/is-social-media-use-causing-depression.

209. Daniel Benjamin and Steven Simon, "How Fake News Could Lead to Real War," *Politico*, July 5, 2019, https://www.politico.com/magazine/story/2019/07/05/fake-news-real-war-227272.

210. Robert Lawrence Kuhn, "Is Our Universe a Fake?" Science.com (Science and Astronomy), July 31, 2015, https://www.space.com/30124-is-our-universe-a-fake.html.

211. Clara Moskowitz, "Are We Living in a Computer Simulation?" *Scientific American*, April 7, 2016, https://www.scientificamerican.com/article/are-we-living-in-a-computer-simulation.

212. Dan Falk, "Are We Living in a Simulated Universe? Here's What Scientists Say," NBC News, July 6, 2019, https://www.nbcnews.com/mach/science/are-we-living-simulated-universe-here-s-what-scientists-say-ncna1026916.

213. Olivia Solon, "Is Our World a Simulation? Why Some Scientists Say It's More Likely Than Not," *Guardian*, 10-11-16, https://www.theguardian.com/technology/2016/oct/11/simulated-world-elon-musk-the-matrix.

214. John Tierney, "Even if Life Is a Computer Simulation…" *New York Times*, August 13, 2007, https://tierneylab.blogs.nytimes.com/2007/08/13/even-if-life-is-but-a-computer-simulation.

215. Phillip Ball, Phillip, "We Might Live in a Computer Program, But It May Not Matter," BBC, 9-5-16, http://www.bbc.com/earth/story/20160901-we-might-live-in-a-computer-program-but-it-may-not-matter.

216. Dr. Preston Greene, "Are We Really Living in a Computer Simulation? Let's Not Find Out," *New York Times*, August 10, 2019, https://www.nytimes.com/2019/08/10/opinion/sunday/are-we-living-in-a-computer-simulation-lets-not-find-out.html.

217. Aylin Woodward, "20 Years after 'The Matrix' Hit Theaters, Another Sequel Is in the Works. Many Scientists and Philosophers Still Think We're Living in a Simulation," *Business Insider*, August 21, 2019, https://www.businessinsider.com/the-matrix-do-we-live-in-a-simulation-2019-4.

218. Andrew Masterson, "Physicists Find We're Not Living in a Computer Simulation," *Cosmos Magazine*, October 2, 2017, https://cosmosmagazine.com/physics/physicists-find-we-re-not-living-in-a-computer-simulation.

219. *The Truman Show* is a 1998 American satirical science fiction film. The film stars Jim Carrey as Truman Burbank, adopted and raised by a corporation inside a simulated television show revolving around his life, until he discovers it and decides to escape. https://en.wikipedia.org/wiki/The_Truman_Show.

220. *The Matrix* is a 1999 science fiction action film. It depicts a dystopian future in which humanity is unknowingly trapped inside a simulated reality, the Matrix, created by thought-capable machines (artificial beings) to distract humans while using their bodies as an energy source. See https://en.wikipedia.org/wiki/The_Matrix.

221. Robert Lawrence Kuhn, "Is Our Universe a Fake?" Science.com (Science and Astronomy), July 31, 2015, https://www.space.com/30124-is-our-universe-a-fake.html.

222. Jean Hopfensperger, "Exorcisms Make a 21st Century Comeback in Minnesota, U.S." *Star Tribune*, November 11, 2019, http://www.startribune.com/exorcisms-make-a-21st-century-comeback/564708901.

223. John Blake, "When Exorcists Need Help, They Call Him," CNN, August 4, 2017, https://www.cnn.com/2017/08/04/health/exorcism-doctor/index.html.

224. Ibid.

225. For example, see Brian Prowse-Gany and Joyzel Acevedo, "Unfiltered: 'She was completely demonically possessed,'" Yahoo News, 5-24-18, https://www.yahoo.com/news/unfiltered-completely-demonically-possessed-193926407.html.

226. "Deuteronomy 32:17," *Matthew Poole's Commentary*, Biblehub.com, http://biblehub.com/commentaries/deuteronomy/32-17.htm.

227. Don Stewart, "What Are Demons?" Blue Letter Bible (Commentary), https://www.blueletterbible.org/faq/don_stewart/don_stewart_50.cfm. Also see my book *Gods of the Final Kingdom* (Crane, MO: Defender Publishing, July 2019) for an in-depth biblical and scientific exploration of multiple dimensions of physical reality, especially as presented in the Word of God.
Also see Dr. Roger Barrier, "Demons in the Bible," Biblestudytools.org, https://www.biblestudytools.com/topical-verses/demons-in-the-bible.

228. "Hebrews 1:14," *Barnes' Notes on the Bible*, Biblehub.com, https://biblehub.com/commentaries/hebrews/1-14.htm.

229. "Hebrews 13:2," *Barnes' Notes on the Bible*, Biblehub.com, https://biblehub.com/commentaries/hebrews/13-2.htm.

230. "Hebrews 13:2," *Meyer's New Testament Commentary*, Biblehub.com, https://biblehub.com/commentaries/hebrews/13-2.htm.

231. "Hebrews 13:2," *Gill's Exposition of the Entire Bible*, Biblehub.com, https://biblehub.com/commentaries/hebrews/13-2.htm.

232. Scholars are divided over the issue of whether demons can appear in human form and literally walk among us, as the unfallen ones are sometimes allowed to do. However, there simply is no direct biblical evidence of a demon appearing in human flesh, looking like a human, in the same manner in which good angels have been known to manifest.

233. "Colossians 2:18," *Vincent's Word Studies*, Biblehub.com, https://biblehub.com/commentaries/colossians/2-18.htm.

234. "2 Corinthians 11:14," *Ellicott's Commentary for English Readers*, Biblehub.com, https://biblehub.com/commentaries/2_corinthians/11-14.htm.

235. Webster's Dictionary definition of "familiar spirit": 1) a spirit or demon that serves or prompts an individual; 2): the spirit of a dead person invoked by a medium to advise or prophesy, https://www.merriam-webster.com/dictionary/familiar%20spirit?src=search-dict-box. Biblical examples of the use of "familiar spirit":

> So Saul died for his transgression which he committed against the LORD, [even] against the word of the LORD, which he kept not, and also for asking [counsel] of [one that had] a familiar

spirit, to enquire [of it]; And enquired not of the Lord:
therefore he slew him, and turned the kingdom unto David
the son of Jesse. (1 Chronicles 10:13–24, KJV; see also KJV of
Leviticus 20:27; 1 Samuel 28; 2 Chronicles 33:6; Isaiah 29:4).
What is a familiar spirit?

A familiar spirit is a demon that is summoned by a medium
with the intention that the spirit summoned will obey his
or her commands. Often, familiar spirits are believed to be
the spirits of people who have died (Deut. 18:11). However,
biblically this is not the case. Such appearances are in actuality
demonic forces imitating people in order to deceive. https://
carm.org/what-is-a-familiar-spirit.

236. Ron Rhodes, "Are There Ghosts?" Evidence and Answers, April 25, 2014
(Apologetics), https://evidenceandanswers.org/article/ghosts.

237. "1 Samuel 28," *Expository Notes of Dr. Thomas Constable*, Studylight.org,
https://www.studylight.org/commentaries/dcc/1-samuel-28.html.

238. See 1 Samuel 28.

239. See the commentaries on this page as examples of some who try to make
Samuel's "appearance" to be a genuine exception to God's otherwise
explicit commands against such a practice.
"1 Samuel 28:15," *Commentaries*, Biblehub.com, https://biblehub.com/
commentaries/1_samuel/28-15.htm.

240. "1 Samuel 28:15," *Matthew Poole's Commentary*, Biblehub.com, https://
biblehub.com/commentaries/1_samuel/28-15.htm.

241. "1 Samuel 28:15," *Gill's Exposition of the Entire Bible*, Biblehub.com,
https://biblehub.com/commentaries/1_samuel/28-15.htm.

242. "1 Samuel 28," *Lange's Commentary on the Holy Scriptures: Critical,
Doctrinal, and Homiletical*, Studylight.org, https://www.studylight.org/
commentaries/lcc/1-samuel-28.html.

243. "2 Corinthians 11:15," *Meyer's New Testament Commentary*, Biblehub.
com, https://biblehub.com/commentaries/2_corinthians/11-15.htm.

244. "2 Corinthians 11:15," *Barnes' Notes on the Bible*, Biblehub.com, https://
biblehub.com/commentaries/2_corinthians/11-15.htm.

245. See Ezekiel 39:27–28 as an example of this truth.

246. "Jude 1:6," *Parallel Translations*, Biblehub.com, https://biblehub.com/
jude/1-6.htm.

247. NT 316. *oikétérion*. "Greek" Biblehub.com, https://biblehub.com/greek/3613.htm.

248. Here is a commentary example of this truth:
*Ellicott's Commentary for English Readers*:
> The comparison of the body to the house or dwelling-place of the Spirit was, of course, natural, and common enough, and, it may be noted, was common among the Greek medical writers (as, e.g., in Hippocrates, with whom St. Luke must have been familiar). The modification introduced by the idea of the "tent" emphasizes the transitory character of the habitation. (https://biblehub.com/commentaries/2_corinthians/5-1.htm)

249. The "doctrine" of which *Meyer's* speaks is the Book of Enoch's postulation that the divine beings (sons of God) of Genesis 6 descended to the earthly regions and had actual physical relations with earthly women—producing the Nephilim giants of the pre-Flood age.

250. *The Book of Enoch*:
> While the book of Enoch (Noah's great-grandson) is non-canonical, it is an influential ancient Jewish work, with parts of it dating to around 300 BC. Eleven fragments of the book were found among the Dead Sea Scrolls, proving its impact upon at least some within the earliest Jewish community. There is a particular passage in the book of Enoch that is very similar to the reference in Jude 1:6–7.
> Enoch is mentioned by name in the New Testament in three different places (Luke 3:37, Hebrews 11:5, Jude 1:14). It is also alleged that there are a number of allusions (paraphrased quotes, etc.) to the Book of Enoch throughout the New Testament as well. The identification of those particular passages as having Enochian influence is disputed, and hold varying degrees of interpretation among Bible students. However, the greater point is the indisputable fact that a good portion of early Jewish thought that the sons of God were fallen elohim. This understanding apparently came from biblical, as well as non-biblical, sources and was prevalent among early orthodox Jews as well as the early church."

Wayne, Jackson, "Did Jude Quote from the Book of Enoch?" *Christian Courier*, accessed March 11, 2017, https://www.christiancourier.com/articles/562-did-jude-quote-from-the-book-of-enoch.

251. "Jude 1:6," *Meyer's New Testament Commentary*, Biblehub.com, https://biblehub.com/commentaries/jude/1-6.htm.

252. "Jude 1:6," *Pulpit Commentary*, Biblehub.com, https://biblehub.com/commentaries/jude/1-6.htm.

253. "Jude 1:6," *Lange's Commentary on the Holy Scriptures: Critical, Doctrinal, and Homiletical*, Studylight.org, https://www.studylight.org/commentaries/lcc/jude-1.html.

254. "2 Peter 2:4," *Cambridge Bible for Schools and Colleges*, Biblehub.com, https://biblehub.com/commentaries/2_peter/2-4.htm.

255. "2 Corinthians 11:14," *Gill's Exposition of the Entire Bible*, Biblehub.com, https://biblehub.com/commentaries/2_corinthians/11-14.htm.

256. "2 Corinthians 11:14," *Barnes' Notes on the Bible*, Biblehub.com, https://biblehub.com/commentaries/2_corinthians/11-14.htm.

257. "2 Corinthians 11:14," *Ellicott's Commentary for English Readers*, Biblehub.com, https://biblehub.com/commentaries/2_corinthians/11-14.htm.

258. "NT 3345, *Metaschématizó*," *Greek*, Biblehub.com, https://biblehub.com/greek/3345.htm.

259. Ibid.

260. For a much more in-depth look at the ramifications of the Genesis 6 account, please see my books *Gods and Thrones* and *Gods of Ground Zero*. (Defender Publishing).

261. "Genesis 6:4," *Parallel Translations*, Biblehub.com, https://biblehub.com/genesis/6-4.htm.

262. The Septuagint is a Greek version of the Hebrew Old Testament, including the Apocrypha. It was translated specifically for the Greek-speaking Jews in the third and second centuries BC. It was widely read and used by the early Christian churches. Since that version was translated by a group of seventy to seventy-two Hebrew scholars, and it translated "sons of God" (Heb. *bene elohim*) in Genesis 6:4 as "angels," it is fairly safe to assume this translation is contextually accurate.

263. "Genesis 6," *Guzik Bible Commentary*, Biblehub.com, http://biblehub.com/commentaries/guzik/genesis/6.htm.

264. "Job 1:6," *Commentaries*, Biblehub.com, http://biblehub.com/commentaries/job/1-6.htm.

265. C. Fred Dickason, ThD, "Sons of God," *Names of Angels*, (Chicago: Moody Press, August 1, 1997, copyright by C. Fred Dickason.

266. Michael S. Heiser, PhD, *The Unseen Realm: Recovering the Supernatural World View of the Bible*, (Lexham Press, September 1, 2015) 101.

267. "Job 38:7," *Barnes' Notes on the Bible*, Biblehub.com, http://biblehub.com/commentaries/job/38-7.htm.

268. "Job 38:7," *Matthew Poole's Commentary*, Biblehub.com, http://biblehub.com/commentaries/job/38-7.htm.

269. "Genesis 6:1–2," *Biblical Commentary on the Old Testament*, by Carl Friedrich Keil and Franz Delitzsch, accessed March 11, 2017, https://www.studylight.org/commentaries/kdo/genesis-6.html9.

270. "2 Peter 2:5," *Ellicott's Commentary for English Readers*, Biblehub.com, https://biblehub.com/commentaries/2_peter/2-5.htm.

271. "2 Peter 2:4," *Meyer's New Testament Commentary*, Biblehub.com, https://biblehub.com/commentaries/2_peter/2-5.htm.

272. "2 Peter 2:5," *Meyer's New Testament Commentary*, Biblehub.com, https://biblehub.com/commentaries/2_peter/2-5.htm.

273. Mark 6:3.

274. See Colossians 1.

275. "Genesis 3," *J. Vaughan, Fifty Sermons*, Studylight.org, https://www.studylight.org/commentaries/edt/genesis-3.html.

276. "NT Greek 5333," *Pharmakos. Helps Word Studies*, Biblehub.com, https://biblehub.com/greek/5333.htm.

277. "NT Greek 5333. *Pharmakos*," *NAS Exhaustive Concordance*, Biblehub.com, https://biblehub.com/greek/5333.htm.

278. "Sorcery/Witchcraft/*Pharmakeia*," *International Standard Bible Encyclopedia*, James Orr, Ed., Vol. 5, p. 3097.

279. Spiros Zodhiates, *Complete Word Study Dictionary: New Testament*, (AMG Publishers; Reissue edition, June 1, 1991) 1437, 1438.

280. Philippus Aureolus Paracelsus (1493–1541), Wolfram Research, accessed September 2, 2019, http://scienceworld.wolfram.com/biography/Paracelsus.html.

281. Joseph F. Borzelleca, "Paracelsus: Herald of Modern Toxicology,"

Oxford Academic, Toxicological Sciences, accessed August 23, 2019, https://academic.oup.com/toxsci/article/53/1/2/1673334#targetText =Paracelsus%2C%20Philippus%20Theophrastus%20Aureolus%20 Bombastus,10%20or%2014%20November%201493.

282. James Austin Bastow, *A Biblical Dictionary*, Sagwan Press (August 22, 2015)779.

283. Redeemed Ministries. Chris Gortney, senior pastor; Brandon Gallups, associate pastor, www.redeemedmin.org.

284. Supplied and approved by Associate Pastor Brandon Gallups in email format. September 2019.

285. "Carl Jung," Wikipedia, accessed August 22, 2019, https://en.wikipedia. org/wiki/Carl_Jung.

286. Dr. Lloyd Sederer, "The Addiction Solution: Treating Our Dependence on Opioids and Other Drugs," (Scribner, 1 edition,May 8, 2018)103. Lloyd I. Sederer, MD, is chief medical officer of the New York State Office of Mental Health (OMH), the nation's largest state mental health system.

287. Ibid., 102.

288. Dr. Martti Nissinen, *Ancient Prophecy: Near Eastern, Biblical, and Greek Perspectives* (Oxford University Press, 1 edition, February 7, 2018) 338.

289. The Pythia (or Oracle of Delphi) was the priestess who held court at Pytho, the sanctuary of the Delphinians, a sanctuary dedicated to the Greek god Apollo. Pythia was highly regarded, for it was believed that she channeled prophecies from Apollo himself, while steeped in a dreamlike trance.
See Gabriel Jones, "Pythia," *Ancient History Encyclopedia*, 8-30-13, https://www.ancient.eu/Pythia/#targetText=The%20Pythia%20(or%20 Oracle%20of,steeped%20in%20a%20dreamlike%20trance.

290. Dr. Martti Nissinen, *Ancient Prophecy: Near Eastern, Biblical, and Greek Perspectives*, 199–200.

291. "Understanding the Global Problem of Drug Addiction Is a Challenge for IDARS Scientists," National Center for Biotechnology Information, March 2013, accessed September 2019, https://www.ncbi.nlm.nih.gov/ pmc/articles/PMC3137181.

292. John Fritze and Deirdre Shesgreen, "Trump Implores World Leaders at United Nations to Confront 'Scourge' of Drug Addiction," *USA*

*Today*, September 24, 2018, https://www.usatoday.com/story/news/ politics/2018/09/24/donald-trump-united-nations-must-confront-confront-scourge-drugs/1408197002.

See also: American Federation of Teacher, (AFT). "Resolution Opiods: A Global Epidemic," accessed September 22, 2019, https://www.aft.org/ resolution/opioids-global-epidemic.

293. John Binder, "Opioids Killing Young, White Suburban Americans More Than Anyone Else for 2nd Consecutive Year," Breitbart, 12-6-19, https://www.breitbart.com/politics/2019/12/06/ opioid-crisis-young-white-suburbanites.

294. "NT GK 4202, *Porneia*," *HELPS Word-studies*, Biblehub.com, https:// biblehub.com/greek/4202.htm.

295. "NT GK 4202, *Porneia*," *Strong's Exhaustive Concordance*, Biblehub.com, https://biblehub.com/greek/4202.htm.

296. National Center on Sexual Exploitation, "About Pornography: A Public Health Crisis," accessed September 11, 2019, https:// endsexualexploitation.org/publichealth.

297. S. Kühn, J. Gallinat, "Brain Structure and Functional Connectivity Associated with Pornography Consumption: The Brain on Porn," *JAMA Psychiatry*, 2014;71(7):827–834. https://doi.org/10.1001/ jamapsychiatry.2014.93.

298. "National Review: Getting Serious on Pornography," NPR, 3-3-10, https://www.npr.org/templates/story/story.php?storyId=125382361.

299. Ibid.

300. Andrew Doan, academic editor for NCBI, "Neuroscience of Internet Pornography Addiction: A Review and Update," National Center for Biotechnology Information (NCBI), September 19, 2015, https://www. ncbi.nlm.nih.gov/pmc/articles/PMC4600144.

301. Adam Withnall, "Pornography Addiction Leads to Same Brain Activity as Alcoholism or Drug Abuse, Study Shows," Independent U.K., September 22, 2013, https://www.independent.co.uk/life-style/health-and-families/ health-news/pornography-addiction-leads-to-same-brain-activity as alcoholism-or-drug-abuse-study-shows-8832708.html.

302. Sputnik News, "Binge Porn Kills Orgasm in Sex with Real-Life Partner, New Study Finds," November 29, 2019, https://sputniknews.com/

society/201911291077437427-binge-porn-kills-orgasm-in-sex-with-real-life-partner-new-study-finds/?fbclid=IwAR0j9ievYSKCid5t-xyRomHlVAmo_beaYfsupCAVHfAzatSIDTT4zVXYrcY.

303. S. Kühn S, J. Gallinat, "Brain Structure and Functional Connectivity Associated with Pornography Consumption: The Brain on Porn," *JAMA Psychiatry*, 2014;71(7):827–834. https://doi.org/10.1001/jamapsychiatry.2014.93.

304. National Center on Sexual Exploitation, "About Pornography: A Public Health Crisis," accessed September 11, 2019, https://endsexualexploitation.org/publichealth/#_edn1.

305. Andrew Doan, academic editor for NCBI, "Neuroscience of Internet Pornography Addiction: A Review and Update."

306. Luke Gibbons, "15 Mind-Blowing Statistics about Pornography and the Church," Conquer Series, accessed September 11, 2019 (Stats collected from info from the Barna Group and Covenant Eyes), https://conquerseries.com/15-mind-blowing-statistics-about-pornography-and-the-church.

307. Pornography addiction—Here are several good DVDs and other program resources that your church might want to consider using:
1) 6-DVD package designed especially for men as a five-part study-group series: https://conquerseries.com/overview-of-lessons-volume-01. Watch the trailer here: https://www.youtube.com/watch?v=--zNEGkXBwU. Conquer Series DVDs—Volume 2: https://conquerseries.com/overview-of-lessons-volume-02/. Resources for the package (bulletin inserts, posters, study guides, etc.) https://conquerseries.com/resources, phone (561) 681-9990.
2) An **EXTENSIVE Resource List of DVDS, materials, courses, etc.:** Overcoming Sexual Brokenness (Focus on the Family), http://media.focusonthefamily.com/topicinfo/overcoming_sexual_brokenness.pdf.

308. Harvard Mental Health Letter, "How Addiction Hijacks the Brain," Harvard Medical School, July 2011, https://www.health.harvard.edu/newsletter_article/how-addiction-hijacks-the-brain.

309. Fran Smith, "How Science Is Unlocking the Secrets of Addiction," *National Geographic*, Sept. 2017 magazine, https://www.nationalgeographic.com/magazine/2017/09/the-addicted-brain.

310. "OT Hebrew 5377, *Nasha*," *Hebrew*, Biblehub.com, https://biblehub.com/hebrew/5377.htm.

311. "OT Hebrew 5175, *Nachash*," *Hebrew*, Biblehub.com, https://biblehub.com/hebrew/5175.htm.

312. "OT Hebrew 5172, *Nachash*," *Hebrew*, Biblehub.com, https://biblehub.com/hebrew/5172.htm.

313. "OT Hebrew, 5172-*Nachash*," *Gesenius Hebrew and Chaldee Definition*, "to practice enchantment, *to use sorcery*," Studylight.org, https://www.studylight.org/lexicons/hebrew/5172.html.
Sorcerer—Definition
*Oxford Dictionary* (Lexico—Powered by Oxford): "wizard, witch, magician, black magician, warlock, diviner, occultist, voodooist, sorceress, enchanter, enchantress, necromancer, magus, *medicine man, medicine woman, shaman, witch doctor*," https://www.lexico.com/en/definition/sorcerer.

314. "NT Greek 3834, *Panourgia*," *Greek*, Biblehub.com, https://biblehub.com/greek/3834.htm.

315. "2 Peter 1:4," *Meyer's New Testament Commentary*, Biblehub.com, https://biblehub.com/commentaries/2_peter/1-4.htm.

316. "2 Peter 1:4," *Expositor's Greek Testament*, Biblehub.com, https://biblehub.com/commentaries/2_peter/1-4.htm.

317. Carl Gallups, *Gods of Ground Zero: The Truth of Eden's Iniquity* (Crane, MO: Defender Publishers, October 2018).

318. John W. Ritenbaugh, "Bible Verses about Demonic Principalities—From the *Forerunner Commentary*," (Matthew 12:25-26), Bibletools.org, https://www.bibletools.org/index.cfm/fuseaction/Topical.show/RTD/cgg/ID/62/Demonic-principalities.htm.

319. For an example of the prophecy of Satan's last-days attack on Israel, see Ezekiel 37–39. For Satan's onslaught aimed at the church and the Seed of the womb, see Revelation 12.

320. See Acts 3:19–21 (specifically the KJV).

321. Galatians 3:16.

322. See my book *Gods of the Final Kingdom* (Crane, MO: Defender Publishing, July 2019) for a thorough study of this biblical truth.

323. Exodus 1:15–22.

324. "Is Mary's Lineage in One of the Gospels?" Bible.org, accessed Jan. 2, 2019, https://bible.org/question/mary%E2%80%99s-lineage-one-gospels.

325. "Revelation 12:4," *Cambridge Bible for Schools and Colleges*, Biblehub.com, https://biblehub.com/commentaries/revelation/12-4.htm.

326. "Revelation 12:4," *Gill's Commentary on the Entire Bible*, Biblehub.com, https://biblehub.com/commentaries/revelation/12-4.htm.

327. Galatians 3:29.

328. "Revelation 12:1," *Cambridge Bible for Schools and Colleges*, Biblehub.com, https://biblehub.com/commentaries/revelation/12-1.htm.

329. "Revelation 12," *Jamieson-Fausset-Brown Bible Commentary*, Biblehub.com, https://biblehub.com/commentaries/jfb/revelation/12.htm.

330. Delinda Hanley, , "The Role of U.S. Churches in the BDS Movement," *Washington Report on Middle East Affairs*, May 2015 release, https://www.wrmea.org/015-may/the-role-of-u.s.-churches-in-the-bds-movement.html. Also see: BDSmovement.net, "Major Churches Divest," accessed September 12, 2019, https://bdsmovement.net/impact/major-churches-divest.

331. David Barrett, International Bulletin of Missionary Research, January 2007.
Also see Troy Lacey, "What Makes a Christian Martyr Different from Other Faiths' Martyrs?" Answers in Genesis, March 1, 2016, https://answersingenesis.org/religious-freedom/christian-martyr-different-from-other-faiths.

332. "Christian Persecution at an All Time High," Orthodox Christian Network, February 14, 2018, http://myocn.net/christian-persecution-at-an-all-time-high.

333. Lindy Lowry, "Christian Persecution by the Numbers," Open Doors, January 16, 2019, https://www.opendoorsusa.org/christian-persecution/stories/christian-persecution-by-the-numbers.

334. The World Health Organization reports that "CVDs [cardiovascular diseases] are the number 1 cause of death globally: more people die annually from CVDs than from any other cause. An estimated 17.9 million people died from CVDs in 2016, representing 31% of all global deaths." See https://www.who.int/news-room/fact-sheets/detail/cardiovascular-diseases-(cvds).

AIDs, auto accidents, smoking, alcohol, and cancer account for about nineteen million of the other leading causes of death. Added to the CVD's eighteen million, these causes of death combined still fall more than ten million short of the deaths caused by abortion each year. See https://www.washingtonexaminer.com/opinion/op-eds/abortion-is-the-worlds-leading-cause-of-death.

335. Tony Mitchell, Tony, "The Leading Causes of Death in the World—Can They Be cured?" October 5, 2017, https://www.proclinical.com/blogs/2017-5/the-leading-causes-of-death-in-the-world-can-they-be-cured.

336. Peter Cermak, "What Percent of Abortions Are Medically Necessary?" Human Life International, accessed September 17, 2019, https://www.hli.org/resources/what-percentage-of-abortions-are-medically-necessary.

337. Ronnie Floyd, "Abortion Is the World's Leading Cause of Death," *Washington Examiner*, January 22, 2019, https://www.washingtonexaminer.com/opinion/op-eds/abortion-is-the-worlds-leading-cause-of-death.

338. Ryo Yokoe, Rachel Rowe, et.al., "Unsafe Abortion and Abortion-related Death among 1.8 Million Women in India" (see introduction, first sentence), BMJ.com, 2019 report, accessed September 14, 2019.

339. Abortion Statistics, "United States Data and Trends," NRLC.org, accessed September 17, 2019, https://nrlc.org/uploads/factsheets/FS01AbortionintheUS.pdf.

340. Victor Davis Hanson, "A War Like Many Others," *National Review*, October 30, 2017, https://www.nationalreview.com/magazine/2017/10/30/war-many-others. From the article: "Some 60 million people died in World War II."

341. Abort73.com, "Worldwide Abortion Statistics," updated October 10, 2018, https://abort73.com/abortion_facts/worldwide_abortion_statistics.

342. Number of Abortions.com, "Number of Abortions—Abortion Counters," accessed September 17, 2019, http://www.numberofabortions.com.

343. Bethania Palma, "Was Abortion the 'Leading Cause of Death' in 2018?" Snopes, January 3, 2019, https://www.snopes.com/news/2019/01/03/abortion-leading-cause-of-death.

344. EPA, "Summary of the Endangered Species Act," accessed September 17, 2019, https://www.epa.gov/laws-regulations/summary-endangered-species-act.

345. Earl L. Henn, "Bible Verses about Demonic Principalities—From the *Forerunner Commentary*," (Revelation 16:13–14), Bibletools.org, https://www.bibletools.org/index.cfm/fuseaction/Topical.show/RTD/cgg/ID/62/Demonic-principalities.htm.

346. "List of Reported UFO Sightings," Wikipedia, accessed December 11, 2019, https://en.wikipedia.org/wiki/List_of_reported_UFO_sightings.

347. Dr. Michael Heiser's bio reads as follows:

    I'm a graduate of the University of Pennsylvania (MA, Ancient History) and the University of Wisconsin- Madison (MA, PhD, Hebrew Bible and Semitic Studies). I have a dozen years of classroom teaching experience on the college level and another ten in distance education. I'm currently a Scholar-in-Residence at Logos Bible Software, a company that produces ancient text databases and other digital resources for study of the ancient world and biblical studies. You can get a more detailed answer to my academic background by reading through my CV. (https://drmsh.com/wp-content/uploads/2019/01/MHeiserCV832.pdf) See https://drmsh.com/about.

348. Michael Heiser, "Book Review: Alien Intrusion: UFOs and the Evolution Connection," Gary Bates (Master Books, 2005, accessed September 21, 2019, http://www.michaelsheiser.com/Bates%20Review.htm.

349. Harry Pettit, "Team of Alien Hunters Led by Blink-182 Co-Founder Claims to Have Found UFO Material That's 'Unknown to Scientists' Fox News, September 30, 2019, https://www.foxnews.com/tech/team-of-alien-hunters-led-by-blink-182-co-founder-claims-to-have-found-ufo-material-thats-unknown-to-scientists.

350. Fox News. "UFO Sightings Hit All-Time High, Report Says," February 28, 2017, https://www.foxnews.com/science/ufo-sightings-hit-all-time-high-report-says.

351. Lydia Saad, "Americans Skeptical of UFOs, but Say Government Knows More," Gallup Poll News, September 6, 2019, https://news.gallup.com/poll/266441/americans-skeptical-ufos-say-government-knows.aspx.

352. Linda Lacina, "The First Alien-Abduction Account Described a Medical Exam with a Crude Pregnancy Test," History.com, updated June 5,

2019, original September 4, 2018, https://www.history.com/news/ first-alien-abduction-account-barney-betty-hill.

353. Kyle Mizokami, "The Navy Says Those UFO Videos Are Real," *Popular Mechanics*, September 16, 2019, https://www.popularmechanics.com/ military/a29073804/navy-ufo-videos-real.

354. Ibid.

355. Brandon Specktor, "UFOs Are Real—And You Were Never Supposed to See Them, Military Official Says," *Live Science*, 9-17-19, https://www. livescience.com/navy-ufo-videos-authentic-classified.html.

356. Helen Cooper, "'Wow, What Is That?' Navy Pilots Report Unexplained Flying Objects," *New York Times*, May 26, 2019, https://www.nytimes. com/2019/05/26/us/politics/ufo-sightings-navy-pilots.html.

357. Scoles, Sarah. "The Year UFOs Became a Little More Legit," Slate.com, December 30, 2019, https://slate.com/technology/2019/12/2019-year-in-aliens-ufos.html.

358. Anna Hopkins, "Former US Defense Official: We Know UFOs Are Real—Here's Why That's Concerning," May 29, 2019, https://www. foxnews.com/science/christopher-mellon-official-ufo-sightings-real.

359. Tim McMillan, "The Witnesses," *Popular Mechanics*, November 12, 2019, https://www.popularmechanics.com/military/research/a29771548/ navy-ufo-witnesses-tell-truth.

360. Fox News, "UFO Sightings Hit All-Time High, Report Says," February 28, 2017, https://www.foxnews.com/science/ ufo-sightings-hit-all-time-high-report-says.

361. Ibid.

362. **Project Blue Book** was one of a series of systematic studies of unidentified flying objects (UFOs) conducted by the United States Air Force. It started in 1952, the third study of its kind, following projects Sign (1947) and Grudge (1949). A termination order was given for the study in December 1969, and all activity under its auspices officially ceased in January 1970. Project Blue Book had two goals: To determine if UFOs were a threat to national security, and to scientifically analyze UFO-related data. See: https://en.wikipedia.org/wiki/Project_Blue_Book.

363. Ralph Blumenthal, "'Project Blue Book' Is Based on a True UFO Story. Here It Is," *New York Times*, January 16, 2019, https://www.nytimes.

com/2019/01/15/arts/television/project-blue-book-history-true-story.
html.

364. "Could an Alien Deception Be Part of the End Times?" GotQuestions.
org, accessed March 11, 2017, https://www.gotquestions.org/alien-
deception.html.

365. This topic is thoroughly and contextually explored in my book *Gods of the
Final Kingdom* (Crane, MO: Defender Publishing, July 2019).

366. From the website: http://reasons.org/about. RTB's mission is to spread
the Christian gospel by demonstrating that sound reason and scientific
research—including the very latest discoveries—consistently support,
rather than erode, confidence in the truth of the Bible and faith in the
personal, transcendent God revealed in both Scripture and nature.

367. Hugh Ross, Kenneth R. Samples, Mark Clark, "Lights in the Sky & Little
Green Men: A Rational Christian Look at UFOs and Extraterrestrials"
(Reasons to Believe; 1st edition [June 1, 2002]), quoted at https://www.
oneplace.com/devotionals/live-it/ufos-and-space-aliens-arent-what-they-
seem-1134948.html.

368. CBN, "Hugh Ross: Are UFOs Real?" The 700 Club, accessed Sept. 12,
2019. https://www.cbn.com/700club/guests/bios/hugh_ross_012104.
aspx?mobile=false.

369. John Keel wrote the well-known book *The Mothman Prophecies*, which
was later made into the 2002 major Hollywood movie.

370. John Keel, *Operation Trojan Horse* (Lilburn, GA: Illuminet Press,
1996) 266, accessed March 11, 2017; cited here: http://creation.com/
ufos-not-extraterrestrial.

371. Gary Bates, "UFOs Are Not Extraterrestrial!" Creation.com, July 5, 2016,
https://creation.com/ufos-not-extraterrestrial.

372. Biography: "David M. Jacobs," International Center for Abduction
Research (ICAR). Philadelphia, Pennsylvania: David M. Jacobs, accessed
December 8, 2019, https://www.ufoabduction.com/biography.htm.

373. For an example, see Pippin, Jerry, "Dr. David Jacobs" (WMA). The Jerry
Pippin Show (Podcast). Secaucus, New Jersey; Muskogee, Oklahoma:
Jerry Pippin Productions. Retrieved September 10, 2008. April 12, 2005,
interview; June 2003 interview:
Part 1, http://www.jerrypippin.com/audio/UFO%20Files%20-%20

Jacobs%20Interview-%20segment%20one.wma.

Part 2, http://www.jerrypippin.com/audio/UFO%20Files%20-%20
Jacobs%20Interview-%20segment%20two.wma.

374. "Dr. David Jacobs Presents Abductees' Hidden Lives DVD Presentation,"
International UFO Congress, 2007. Archived from the original on May
18, 2012, https://web.archive.org/web/20120518051440/http://www.
ufocongressstore.com/Dr-David-Jacobs-Presents-Abductees-Hidden-Lives-
DVD-Presentation_p_647.html. Also see https://en.wikipedia.org/wiki/
David_M._Jacobs.

375. Nick Redfern, "UFOs: Extraterrestrial? Probably Not…" Mysterious
Universe, 4-6-16, https://mysteriousuniverse.org/2016/04/
ufos-extraterrestrial-probably-not.

376. Ibid.

377. Michael Heiser, "Book Review: *Alien Intrusion: UFOs and the Evolution
Connection,* Gary Bates (Master Books, 2005) accessed September 21,
2019, http://www.michaelsheiser.com/Bates%20Review.htm.

378. Gary Bates, "UFOs Are Not Extraterrestrial!" Creation.com, July 5, 2016,
https://creation.com/ufos-not-extraterrestrial.

379. Gotquestions.org statement of identification:
"We are Christian, Protestant, evangelical, theologically
conservative, and non-denominational. We view ourselves as
a para-church ministry, coming alongside the church to help
people find answers to their spiritually related questions."
(https://www.gotquestions.org/about.html)

380. See their Statement of Faith page here: https://www.gotquestions.org/faith.
html.
Gotquestions.org, "Could an Alien Deception Be Part of the End Times?"
accessed August 23, 2019, https://www.gotquestions.org/alien-deception.
html.

381. Michael Heiser, "Book Review: *Alien Intrusion: UFOs and the Evolution
Connection.*"

382. *Thayer's Greek Lexicon* assigns a significant definition of "powers of the
heavens" as "power consisting in or resting upon armies, forces, hosts, the
hosts (angelic) of heaven." See https://biblehub.com/greek/1411.htm and
https://biblehub.com/greek/3772.htm. Also see: https://www.studylight.
org/commentaries/cgt/luke-21.html (Commentary at v. 26).

383. Some scholars even relate the prophecy's initial connection to the AD 70 destruction of the Temple in Jerusalem. Yet, most of those scholars also see its "compounded" prophetic connection to the very last days, sometime just before the return of Jesus. See https://www.studylight.org/commentaries/wbc/luke-21.html (Commentary at verse 20) for a classical example of this line of interpretation.

384. *The Expositor's Greek Testament:* "Literally, dying …Matthew 28:4. —from fear and expectation." https://www.studylight.org/commentaries/egt/luke-21.html.

385. "Luke 21:26," *Bengel's Gnomen*, Biblehub.com, https://biblehub.com/commentaries/luke/21-26.htm.

386. "Luke 21:26," *Pulpit Commentary*, Biblehub.com, https://biblehub.com/commentaries/luke/21-26.htm.

387. "Luke 21:25," *Benson Commentary*, Biblehub.com, https://biblehub.com/commentaries/luke/21-25.htm.

388. "Luke 21," *Peter Pett's Commentary on the Bible*, Studylight.org, https://www.studylight.org/commentaries/pet/luke-21.html.

389. "Luke 21," *L. M. Grant's Commentary*, Studylight.org, https://www.studylight.org/commentaries/lmg/luke-21.html.

390. "Matthew 24:24," *Matthew Henry's Concise Commentary*, Biblehub.com, https://biblehub.com/commentaries/matthew/24-24.htm.

391. "Matthew 24:24," *Ellicott's Commentary for English Readers*, Biblehub.com, https://biblehub.com/commentaries/matthew/24-24.htm.

392. "Matthew 24:24," *Expositor's Greek Testament*, Biblehub.com, https://biblehub.com/commentaries/matthew/24-24.htm.

393. "Matthew 24:24," *Vincent's Word Studies*, Biblehub.com, https://biblehub.com/commentaries/matthew/24-24.htm.

394. "Matthew 24:24," *Pulpit Commentary*, Biblehub.com, https://biblehub.com/commentaries/matthew/24-24.htm.

395. Transmogrification: to change in appearance or form, especially in a strange, unusual, or a grotesque manifestation.

396. God Sends Them a Powerful Delusion:
*Ellicott's Commentary for English Readers*:
  Here is set forth the effect upon their own selves of refusing to accept God's gift of love of truth: God takes from them (by

His natural law) their power of discerning the true from the
false, and thus (as it were) actually deceives them.

*Meyer's New Testament Commentary*:

For according to the Pauline view it is a holy ordinance of God
that the wicked by their wickedness should lose themselves
always the more in wickedness, and thus sin is punished by
sin. But what is an ordinance of God is also accomplished
by God Himself. (https://biblehub.com/commentaries/2_
thessalonians/2-11.htm)

397.  Gotquestions.org, "Could an Alien Deception Be Part of the End Times?"

398.  Deuteronomy 19:15; 2 Corinthians 13:1; Matthew 18:16.

399.  *Pulpit Commentary*:

The angels will infallibly select these from the mass of men,
either by spiritual insight or Divine direction. The elect are
not Israelites alone, but true believers of all nations (see ver.
14 and John 17:20, 21). These are first collected, and then
the reprobate are summoned, according to Matthew 25:41.
(https://biblehub.com/commentaries/matthew/24-31.htm)

*Barnes' Notes on the Bible*:

They shall gather together his elect - Elect. See the notes at
Matthew 24:22. The word means Christians— the chosen of
God…. If it refers to the last judgment, as it doubtless in a
primary or secondary sense does, then it means that he will
send his angels to gather his chosen, his elect, together from all
places, Matthew 13:39, Matthew 13:41–43. (https://biblehub.
com/commentaries/matthew/24-31.htm)

400.  PNN News and Ministry Network, "Pastor Carl Gallups Shares
Astounding Rapture Dream Account—2019 HTWC," YouTube, posted
4-18-19, https://www.youtube.com/watch?v=1JaMzdZv6b0.

401.  Jude 1:5–10.

402.  *The Bible Exposition Commentary—Old Testament* (Isaiah 14:1–23):

Like the king of Babylon, Satan will one day be humiliated
and defeated. He will be cast out of heaven (Rev 12) and
finally cast into hell (20:10). Whether God is dealing with
kings or angels, Prov 16:18 is still true: "Pride goes before

destruction, and a haughty spirit before a fall" (NKJV).
(Biblesoft PC Study Bible, copyright from 1988–2008, *Bible Exposition Commentary: Old Testament* © 2001–2004 by Warren W. Wiersbe. All rights reserved. Accessed on December 14, 2017.).

*Arno Gaebelein's Annotated Bible—Isaiah 14:*

The king of Babylon here in this chapter is not Nebuchadnezzar, nor his grandson Belshazzar, but the final great king of Babylon. It is the little horn of Daniel 7:1–28, the great political head of the restored Roman Empire. Behind this final king of the times of the Gentiles looms up Satan, who energized that wicked and false king. The description of him who was "Lucifer," the light-bearer, and his fall is of deep interest. (https://www.studylight.org/commentaries/gab/isaiah-14.html).

403.   "Isaiah 14," *Ironside's Notes on Selected Books—Isaiah 14*, Studylight.org, https://www.studylight.org/commentaries/isn/isaiah-14.html.

404.   Isaiah 43:11; 45:5.

405.   See Revelation 21 and 22.

406.   Scriptures of healing and deliverance:

Matthew 11:28–30: Come to me, all you who are weary and burdened, and I will give you rest. Take my yoke upon you and learn from me, for I am gentle and humble in heart, and you will find rest for your souls. For my yoke is easy and my burden is light.

Isaiah 41:10 So do not fear, for I am with you; do not be dismayed, for I am your God. I will strengthen you and help you; I will uphold your with my righteous right hand.

1 Corinthians 10:13–14: No temptation has overtaken you except what is common to mankind. And God is faithful; he will not let you be tempted beyond what you can bear. But when you are tempted, he will also provide a way out so that you can endure it.

Joshua 1:9: Have I not commanded you? Be strong and courageous. Do not be afraid; do not be discouraged, for the

LORD your God will be with you wherever you go.

Galatians 5:1: It is for freedom that Christ has set us free. Stand firm, then, and do not let yourselves be burdened again by a yoke of slavery.

Psalm 147:3: He heals the brokenhearted and binds up their wounds.

2 Corinthians 1:3–4: Praise be to the God and Father of our Lord Jesus Christ, the Father of compassion and the God of all comfort, who comforts us in all our troubles, so that we can comfort those in any trouble with the comfort we ourselves receive from God.

James 4:7–8: Submit yourselves, then, to God. Resist the devil, and he will flee from you. Come near to God and he will come near to you. Wash your hands, you sinners, and purify your hearts, you double-minded.

1 John 1:8–9: If we claim to be without sin, we deceive ourselves and the truth is not in us. If we confess our sins, he is faithful and just and will forgive us our sins and purify us from all unrighteousness.

Isaiah 43:2: When you pass through the waters, I will be with you; and when you pass through the rivers, they will not sweep over you. When you walk through the fire, you will not be burned; the flames will not set you ablaze.

Psalm 55:22: Cast your cares on the LORD and he will sustain you; he will never let the righteous be shaken.

Hebrews 4:15–16: For we do not have a high priest who is unable to empathize with our weaknesses, but we have one who has been tempted in every way, just as we are—yet he did not sin. Let us then approach God's throne of grace with confidence, so that we may receive mercy and find grace to help us in our time of need.

Psalm 139:11–18: If I say, "Surely the darkness will hide me and the light become night around me," even the darkness will not be dark to you; the night will shine like the day, for darkness is as light to you. For you created my inmost being;

you knit me together in my mother's womb. I praise you because I am fearfully and wonderfully made; your works are wonderful, I know that full well. My frame was not hidden from you when I was made in the secret place, when I was woven together in the depths of the earth. Your eyes saw my unformed body; all the days ordained for me were written in your book before one of them came to be. How precious to me are your thoughts, God! How vast is the sum of them! Were I to count them, they would outnumber the grains of sand – when I awake, I am still with you.

Psalm 120:1: I call on the LORD in my distress, and he answers me.

1 Peter 5:7: Cast all your anxiety on him because he cares for you.

Matthew 26:41: Watch and pray so that you will not fall into temptation. The spirit is willing, but the flesh is weak.

Psalm 23:4: Even though I walk through the valley of the shadow of death, I will fear no evil, for you are with me; your rod and your staff, they comfort me. (KJV)

Isaiah 40:30–31: Even youths grow tired and weary, and young men stumble and fall; but those who hope in the LORD will renew their strength. They will soar on wings like eagles; they will run and not grow weary, they will walk and not be faint.

Psalm 34:17–18: The righteous cry out, and the LORD hears them; he delivers them from all their troubles. The LORD is close to the brokenhearted and saves those who are crushed in spirit.

Deuteronomy 31:8: The LORD himself goes before you and will be with you; he will never leave you nor forsake you. Do not be afraid; do not be discouraged.

Psalm 46:1–3: God is our refuge and strength, an ever-present help in trouble. Therefore we will not fear, though the earth give way and the mountains fall into the heart of the sea, though its waters roar and foam and the mountains quake with their surging.

1 Peter 5:8–9: Be alert and of sober mind. Your enemy the devil prowls around like a roaring lion looking for someone to devour. Resist him, standing firm in faith, because you know the family of believers throughout the world is undergoing the same kind of sufferings.

James 1:12: Blessed is the man that endures temptation: for when he is tried, he shall receive the crown of life, which the Lord hath promised to them that love him. (KJV)

Philippians 4:8–9: Finally, brothers and sisters, whatever is true, whatever is noble, whatever is right, whatever is pure, whatever is lovely, whatever is admirable—if anything is excellent or praiseworthy – think about such things. Whatever you have learned or received or heard from me, or seen in me – put it into practice. And the God of peace will be with you.

Jeremiah 29:11–14: For I know the plans I have for you," declares the Lord, "plans to prosper you and not to harm you, plans to give you hope and a future. Then you will call on me and come and pray to me, and I will listen to you. You will seek me and find me when you seek me with all your heart. I will be found by you," declares the Lord, "and will bring you back from captivity. I will gather you from all the nations and places where I have banished you," declares the LORD, "and will bring you back to the place from where you had been carried into exile."

407. Hebrews 13:15, Colossians 3:16, Psalm 150:1–6, Ephesians 5:19.

408. "Romans 12:2," *Expositor's Greek Testament*, Biblehub.com, https://biblehub.com/commentaries/romans/12-2.htm.

409. My illustration of the "two paths" was directly inspired from a similar one found at https://www.smartrecovery.org/rewiring-your-brain.

410. Until the return of Jesus Christ and His final Kingdom, the Bible calls Satan the "prince of this world," the "prince of the power of the air," and "the god of this age." As we learned earlier, the term "mighty one" is more than likely the original meaning of the Hebrew word *cherub*.

411. See Job 38:7 and the surrounding passage.

412. Addiction recovery resources

**Pornography Addiction**
6-DVD package. Designed especially for men, as a five-part study-group series.
https://conquerseries.com/overview-of-lessons-volume-01.
Watch the Trailer HERE: https://www.youtube.com/
watch?v=--zNEGkXBwU.
Conquer Series DVDs—Volume 2
https://conquerseries.com/overview-of-lessons-volume-02/.
Resources for the package (bulletin inserts, posters, study guides, etc.)
https://conquerseries.com/resources. Phone: (561) 681-9990.
**Sexual Addiction/Brokenness**
An EXTENSIVE Resource List of DVDS, materials, courses, etc.:
Overcoming Sexual Brokenness (Focus on the Family), http://media.
focusonthefamily.com/topicinfo/overcoming_sexual_brokenness.pdf.
**Substance Abuse Addiction** – recommended contacts
a.) www.redeemedmin.com/healing-recovery-center, phone (205)
285-1688.
b.) https://americanaddictioncenters.org/rehab-guide,
A guide for renowned addiction centers across the nation, Phone: (888)
533-8802.
c.) Christian Alcohol and Drug Rehab Centers Near Me.
https://www.alltreatment.com/christian-addiction-treatment.
24/7 365 Days—CONFIDENTIAL 855-842-8862 or 855-435-1465
or 855-979-8507.